ENCOUNTERS ON THE WAY

For the earth is a living web, subtle, fragile,
Mysteriously linked
Air and water, tree and bird, are shot with the glory of God.

Frijof Capra / Alec Davison

Cover design: Mike Glover

Encounters on the Way

by

Elizabeth Wilson

Travel on, travel on, there is a river that is flowing,
The river that is flowing night and day.
Travel on, travel on, to the river that is flowing,
The river will be with you all the way.

SYDNEY CARTER

William Sessions Limited
York, England

© 1998 Elizabeth Wilson

ISBN 1 85072 209 9

Printed by
William Sessions Limited
The Ebor Press, York, England

Contents

Chapter *Page*

   Acknowledgements vi

1 Home and a Sense of Community 1

2 My First Visit to India 25

3 My Second Visit to India 52

4 Accent on the Tribal People of India 86

5 Friends World Committee for Consultation 118

6 Hong Kong Action (and further experiences of Hong Kong) 136

7 Travels in Vietnam 147

8 A Visit to Japan 153

9 Encounters on the Way 167

Acknowledgements

THE RESTRICTIONS that come with age and the pleasures of sitting in an armchair by the fire, gave me time to remember the many compassionate and loving people from many faiths I had met. I relived their companionship and their culture and can now laugh about near disasters. Writing about all this has given me enormous pleasure.

These memoirs were written for my own entertainment, at first just as separate accounts of my experiences, so the reader will find some duplication. My writings would not have had any further significance but for Brenda Vernelle who typed them out for me and coped with my hieroglyphics – rather like 'cracking the code'. I am very grateful for the generosity and efficiency with which she has undertaken this task, also to Mike Glover who drew the cover illustration to Capra's 'Fragile Web'.

ELIZABETH WILSON
March 1998

CHAPTER ONE

Home and a Sense of Community

ON MY MARRIAGE in 1936 I had to leave Richmond, Surrey with its river terrace gardens, the Old Palace where Elizabeth I died, Richmond Park and nearby Kew Gardens. This did not prepare me for living in the northern industrial town of Huddersfield. We bought a three-bedroomed house with a garage a large lounge and a balcony that overlooked a steep garden, the police sports field and hills beyond. In London coal was 2/6d a hundredweight but in Huddersfield only 1/6d, and house prices much lower in the north. I realise now how badly, very badly, our new house was insulated, but clean air and efficient use of fuel was not on the agenda. It was to come, and it cut down the awful fogs in bad weather due to smoke from chimneys.

The garden occupied a lot of time, levelling a space for a lawn, building a rock wall planted with aubretias, then another small lawn with a bank of wild thyme and daffodil to support it. Then a small level area followed by a rustic fence with climbing roses beyond the sloping vegetable garden. When we went to stay with my parents we made a point of visiting Kew Gardens and when we saw winter flowering shrubs and ericas, we made a note of the named species we could order locally for our new garden. It was a lot of pleasure and very hard work.

I had a table loom and dyed my own wool using lichens, onion skins and vegetable dyes and sold some scarves to a shop in Harrogate. It paid me about 6d an hour, but I loved doing it. With time on my hands, I bought a second-hand treadle loom with four heddles that could produce material 30" wide. It was a challenge. I wove cloth for my husband's 'plus fours'. I had the cloth finished in Scotland (a tricky process which would have entailed me jumping up and down on it in a bath of urine etc.). The local tailor made up the suit. Looking back at snapshots of this period, I have so far not found one with him wearing plus fours and I deeply regret this. However, I realise how old many of my clothes are!

When the war came, family and friends who thought anywhere north of the Wash was barbarian country, overcame the cultural barrier to get away from the bombs. Some stayed a week, some a lot longer. My husband registered as a Conscientious Objector and refused to be transferred to Manchester to do war work, but as he was already doing research on medicinals at ICI, he was allowed to continue in Huddersfield. We were very lucky and felt we were under an obligation to help those who suffered, so my husband became an ARP Warden. We also had a young Polish Jewish refugee, Joseph, to live with us. He was a furrier by trade, so in time we bought a second-hand furrier's machine and he was able to earn some pocket money repairing fur coats. He restyled my coat of Persian lamb which had been to the 1919 Peace Conference at Versailles, bought for that occasion by Arthur Henderson, the Foreign Secretary, for his wife. I do feel this coat's Peace Witness to be significant. I inherited it, wore it for some years until fur coats became unacceptable, and in any case good imitation fur fabric was available without cruelty. The coat was finally given to Oxfam for Bosnian refugees; after all the Persian lamb had died many years before and the refugees needed warm clothing now. Joseph stayed with us for about eighteen months. He was very helpful and took the baby out in its pram. My mother approved of him – she often approved of young men. He left and we never heard from him again.

Then Marlies came to stay. She was a young Jewish girl from Berlin brought over by the Quakers. She was very lively, always laughing and very artistic and helpful. I suppose she stayed about a year, then moved nearer to her job. I still hear from her and she comes to visit occasionally. She left about 1941 and now it is 1996! Her mother was Jewish and had married an Aryan who died. Having a non-Jewish surname and with considerable help from friends, her mother was able to survive. At the end of the war,

Marlies went to visit her mother in Berlin. Later she married an Englishman and now lives in the south.

Our lounge was big enough to hold Peace Pledge Union meetings. Vera Brittain stayed with us when she came to speak at a meeting in 1942 at which the formation of the Huddersfield Famine Relief Committee (Hudfam for short) was proposed. Later I became the organising secretary. It was an exciting and exhausting period of learning new skills – a challenge which I enjoyed greatly.

We were encouraged to invite black American soldiers stationed in Huddersfield home to a meal. Two visited and told us of their choir, so with their help we organised a concert for famine relief – one good thing helps another! We were interested to hear of their experiences prior to the Civil Rights movement in America and the rise of Martin Luther King.

Hugh used to visit the prison in Wakefield on Sundays but as petrol rationing became more severe and buses less frequent, it took the whole day. By this time I had three small children and was glad when he had to give up and could spend some of Sunday with us. On Saturday afternoons I organised the selling of *Peace News* in the town and was supported by one or two Quakers – a contact that developed. I had one 'night off' a week doing advanced French at the Polytechnic.

In 1936 women teachers who were married were not allowed to teach as there was so much unemployment. At that time, my social life included cooking two mornings a week at a centre for unemployed men. They got two fish cakes and a pudding for two pence. I had to give this up with a small baby to look after, but a friend of mine who had two small children suggested we started a play group at her house near Holme Bridge and invited some of the refugee children living locally. She had a sand pit and we provided a climbing frame. About 8-10 small children came, twice a week; one of us looked after the children's activities and the other prepared the modest mid-day meal. They came about 10am and left at 4pm. This greatly added to our social life and a sense of being useful. We had both been teachers. I suppose the playgroup lasted two years or so until I had another baby. It was fun and we enjoyed it.

When I had three small children and had three rolling pins helping mother make pastry, in a tiny kitchen with three doors, it was too restrictive. I wanted a larger kitchen and a large level playing area for children. In 1947 Avery Hill College which had evacuated to Huddersfield during the war was going back to London and one of the houses which they had been renting, was up for sale. It had housed about twenty people in war time. It was a semi-detached house that had a billiard room, cloak room, wash kitchen with a large range and six bedrooms. It was called 'Bournville' (Quaker connections) and was in Richmond Avenue, so I felt this was a good omen. The billiard room was a great asset as I was a country dancer. This room had a floor area greater than the floor area of our previous house. The children loved the space to make hidey holes and nests in corners. Later Johnny in his high chair could jerk it on the polished floor and impressed the others with his skill when he got hold of the corner of the tablecloth and pulled it and all our tea fell on the floor.

We let some rooms to the new Borough Engineer, his wife and boy, the same age as my youngest, until they could find a house. We got on very well and the children learnt to share Peter's tricycle – five minutes each. This must have impressed Peter for later he retired to the downstairs toilet to meditate. It was Erica's birthday a few days later. He came out smiling, "I know, I share Erica's birfday wiv her!" Don't underestimate a thoughtful child!

Having let the rooms, I called on another applicant to tell them the rooms were taken. Their house was in Paddock in the area where there is now a garage and petrol station. It had one room, a kitchen, one bedroom and the toilet was in the back yard. A family with two children lived here with some friends, a soldier and his wife who was expecting a baby in a couple of months. I was horrified. Hugh was turned out of his study and we had a basement kitchen with gas and water and a toilet. They were offered this for six months for a small rent, to give them time to get over the wife's confinement and get better accommodation. It was a mistake. I should have informed the health authority, but it was wartime and people were more self sufficient than they are now. Six months went by and I reminded them of the agreement. The husband head been moved to another area, and I received a most offensive letter from the Citizen's Advice

Bureau about my turning a mother and baby on to the street. The husband came back for a few days; I didn't know he was absent without leave (AWOL). By the strangest co-incidence my cousin who was in the army arrived in a staff car with a driver to see me and the AWOL soldier thought he was going to be arrested and gave himself up! After further enquiries, the wife and child were provided with quarters near the husband so all ended well. I was relieved as the milkman was complaining about not being paid and it was a drain on our ration of coal. It was a pleasure to clean the study and sweeten the air.

As the family grew, we only let one or two rooms at a very modest rent on condition that the occupier would stay in one night a week while Hugh and I went to a German class at Royds Hall School, where I remember learning 'Heilige nacht, stille nacht ..'. Odd how songs linger when so much else is forgotten.

Mr Korvalski had been a big landowner employing fifty workers in Poland, but when the communists invaded his country he knew it was time to leave. His escape and adventurous crossing over a war-torn Europe deserves a book of its own. As his son had been fighting in the Free Polish Army he was able to get a place at Huddersfield Polytechnic at the end of the war. His father eventually got here to join him and secured a job as a labourer doing night shifts at Robinson's chemical works. I am not sure how we met Mr Korvalski, but my husband was Chair of the Education Committee and we were often invited to student functions and chatted with the students. Mr Korvalski came to visit us once a week on his 'evening off'. He was always neatly dressed with clean and manicured hands – quite an achievement for a man now a labourer. He read the *Guardian* to us in English and we discussed the news. After coffee (as long-time customers we received 2lb of good coffee from Pumphrey and Carrick Watson of Newcastle throughout the war and for many years after) we switched to talking German. We enjoyed his company and I am sure he enjoyed visiting a family with similar interests. When his son completed his studies he got a job in Canada and his father joined him there. He gave us a book inscribed "To Dr Hugh Wilson and his 'guest-friendly' home". We heard from him for a number of years.

As a seller of *Peace News* I came to hear about Ingeborg Kuster whose husband published a German newspaper comparable to *Peace News* and was imprisoned. With enormous courage Ingeborg had tackled the top officials of the Nazi regime just before the war broke out. She had managed to get her husband sufficiently released to work on building railway lines. When the Peace Treaty was signed, he was released from this work but the Army of Occupation would not give him a permit to buy paper to start his newspaper again. We asked our MP, J.P.W.Mallalieu, to help. He took the matter up and an allocation of paper was granted, so a German variant of *Peace News* thrived again in Germany. These are such little things I write of, but I feel of great value to many people and their enterprises. After Ingeborg Kuster's husband died, she visited us and spoke at a number of meetings. I visited her in Hanover and went with her as a delegate on various women's peace conferences.

As the war came to a close the older German prisoners in a camp the other side of the Huddersfield canal on an old fairground were repatriated. We were allowed to invite two German POWs for Christmas day. As older man came, whom we never saw again, and a much younger one, Heinz Koepping. The prisoners no longer had to make bricks and rules were relaxed. Heinz was able to come over and read the *Guardian* and help me plant trees in the garden and take the children for walks. He pushed the pram and became an elder brother. He had had a spell on the Russian front and was delighted to be taken prisoner at Arnheim, His mother and father and fiance cleared bricks and rubble in a housing co-operative and when they had done 3000 hours, they were given the next house available which they could buy very cheaply on a mortgage. Thus they were rehoused much quicker than the people in the U.K. As we returned from a camping holiday in Austria, we called on Heinz and his wife a few years later. The house was small but with space to build an extension. The grownups slept indoors and all the children slept in one big tent in the garden. Margit, his wife, greeted me so warmly and thanked me for training Heinz as an English husband who will play with the children and even push a pram! German fathers seem to feel this is beneath their dignity. I hadn't realised what a valuable contribution I had made to the German family culture.

The next day we were taken to the Mohne Dam – a great tourist attraction. It is interesting that Germans have a pride and a great respect for the technical skill that went into breaching the dam. In a way I am relieved that I don't think it did as much damage as the Allies claimed at the time. It was good for Allied propaganda and not so bad as one feared. I still hear from Heinz and family. They came to stay at exactly the time when Hugh was in hospital but Robbie came home to help take them about so we managed. We had talked about arranging a visit for so long it was better to go ahead.

When the war ended Dutch children from the Arnheim area were brought over to England where they spent about two months in a group and learned a little English. They then spent two months with families. Bas, a boy of 9 or 10 came to stay with us. He went to the local school for a month and was horrified – as I was – when he told of the numbers of children lined up for the cane for the most trivial offences. (We have now gone from one extreme to another.) His father was a village schoolmaster at Opheusden. The school there was in German hands and the attached school house came under the British. No wonder the mothers and children were evacuated to a safer place, very often living in cellars. When Bas came he struggled with signs and his limited English to describe the horrors he had seen. Naturally it preyed on his mind. In the holidays we took him to the farm we so often stayed at in Sleightholmdale. It was a healing experience to be collecting eggs, helping churn the butter, making stooks stand up to help dry the barley. He learnt to swim in a pool of the small river and play cricket. When he left his conversation was more fluent and less horrifying.

A few years later we visited his family in Holland. Our car was very old, but Dutch and French garages had great creative skill developed during the scarcities of war time to keep cars moving. The eldest son, Wib, came with us as a most useful guide and interpreter, visiting the new polder being reclaimed from the Zuider Zee. We spent a night at Snaake with its network of canals. Friesian cattle did not seem to worry if they were standing on partly submerged grass. We crossed over the road bridge built over the dam that controls the water into the Zuider Zee then back to Amsterdam and Rijksmuseum. I was delighted by all the windmills, visited a cheese factory and saw village women cleaning their brick streets which they do once a year communally. Cleanliness has a high priority there. I wish it did here. Nel, Bas's older sister had had polio and was in a wheelchair. She came back with us for a holiday and was amazed at the 'mountains' she saw here – any hills in Holland are only about 300' high. She became an Advocat and had her own business in Opheusden. I hear from them still at Christmas and John visited Bas – now a sturdy Dutchman – when he went to Holland recently to buy a barge. I still have a clump of a dozen or more red tulips in the garden, sent me fifty years or so ago from Holland. Nel has recently been honoured by the Queen of Holland for her social work.

Family Service Units developed during the war and I had a friend who as a social worker was involved in the Oldham area. Overburdened families were visited once or twice a week, taking children to a clinic, giving help with housework, filling up forms, etc. As the children never had a break, families were asked to take a couple of children for a holiday. We took out insurance by buying a bottle of de-nitting lotion for ourselves and our guests. I remember a visit of two little brothers who would only eat bread and margarine, apparently their staple home diet. We took them out for a picnic in Honley woods where there is a cave and we could build a fire and cook chipolata sausages. Happily they accepted the unusual diet. They were nice kids and modest. When I bathed them before going to bed – maybe that was unusual too – they put a flannel over their private parts. We had children to stay for a week or two for a few years, but in time this scheme lapsed.

During the Hungarian rising, I was phoned up just before Christmas by a woman saying she was sure I would like to have the first two Hungarian refugees as I was the organising secretary of the Famine Relief Committee. We were pleased to have them. They spoke no English; they had a German/English dictionary and I think some Latin. Mirth and misunderstanding made Christmas merry. John had been given a puppy – a border collie. "Vat is dat?" "It's a dog." They fell about laughing, so I said to them "Vat is dat?"

"Kutchya." So Hungarian has links with Sanskrit! A 'dog' in Hungarian is a corpse! So Johnny's puppy became 'Kutchya' and Keltie, Kylin, Kerry, Kirsty and Kim followed as the years went by.

As each of my children finished their 'O' levels, I took them off school for a couple of days to go to the International Eisteddfodd at Llangollen. We camped in a field nearby in our Dormobile. The first evening in the huge marquee resplendent with locally-grown flowers, was given over to a special dance group such as the Ram Gopal dancers and one time I remember a Nigerian dance group who danced topless. I asked my Welsh neighbour in the interval if she was enjoying it. She said in a prim voice "I think it is entirely unnecessary!" All Welsh people take their dogs with them and the dog at the end of the row was an upholder of good behaviour. He growled at every dog that passed him, including ours, reminding them to be on their best behaviour.

The next day was given over to folk dancing – two dances by all the 15-20 groups who took part. The following day two folk songs and the same procedure. In the Festival grounds, along by the canal, in the market place, by the river, there was singing and dancing. The war had ended, people were free to travel – the whole valley seemed to be filled with music and friendship and a nourishing resurgence of the human spirit. We returned home before the weekend when huge choirs and the crowds of visitors would have swamped us.

As I was a keen country dancer my most blessed billiard room provided space for a country dance evening once a month. It later became an afternoon gathering as folks retired and this only ended when I was 82 – so it lasted from 1947 to 1991 – 44 years! We did mostly 'Playford dances' such as Nonesuch, named after the Palace of Nonesuch that has not survived. It was said to be Anne Boleyn's favourite dance. Greensleeves, Jack's Maggot, Step Stately, Fandango and Phoenix with its lovely syncopated rhythm, still make my toes twitch. They were done in the Assemblies during the Jane Austen period. Once or twice a year an instructor from Cecil Sharpe House, the HQ of the English Folk Dance Society in Camden Town, would come and we would have a regional gathering where one could learn sword dancing, Morris and Running Set as well as Playford dances. I value my bronze Shiva Nataraja dancing, and

Sydney Carter's 'Lord of the Dance' expresses the same rhythms of life and rebirth and the dancing sub-atomic particles of which we are composed.

At our New Year's party we also did the Eightsome Reel, the Duke of Perth and other Scottish dances. A very simple little dance for three couples, 'The Pleasures of the Town', had its difficulties for the men who had to dance round the women but looked like three different pistons hopping up and down on different beats and one of them always got left behind. The women thought this was very funny.

When my eldest son was at New College and his scout troop wanted to raise money, I organised country dances there. We made up sets each with one of my skilled dancers in and walked through it first. Naturally I chose folk dances which needed less skill than Playford dances. Shy boys were willing to get up and make up a set, and it meant they danced with many different partners without responsibility. Girls from Greenhead High School were only too pleased to come. As my optician told me a while ago, their parents were pleased when they went as a group. I know this was a valuable social opening for many boys and girls. This went on for a few years but as my son was leaving the school fashions changed, and a boy tended to take a girl to a dance; he was stuck all evening with one girl and lacked the easy freedom of group dancing.

Having six in the family, we could do some Playford dances ourselves. Rob and John were good dancers, but Peter always seemed to miss the beat. I suppose I showed my irritation, but I just felt he had no sense of rhythm. Some years later he bought a house and I went to see it when he moved in. The lounge was a large room with a long fireplace with niches in it filled with medals. I remarked on this and asked what he was collecting. He disappeared into the kitchen. I picked up a medal and turned it over. It was inscribed 'Peter Wilson, for Latin American Dancing'! There were many more! And I had thought he had no sense of rhythm. I am sure fame was not the spur – it was the satisfaction of proving me wrong. This also applied to my daughter when she went to India, where she stayed about three months and never caught a single germ until she was in the 'plane coming home and got a sore throat. I'm glad to be proved wrong in such cases.

A group of us usually went to the Mayor's Ball. During the evening a rumba was played. I had been watching and loved the rhythm. With difficulty I persuaded my husband to get up, follow what I was doing and look as if he knew what he was doing. It worked; the Mayor, that time a dancer, came over and congratulated him.

Election time came and John Drabble, a barrister from Sheffield, put up as Labour candidate and stayed with us for three weeks. When the children had gone to school in the morning we talked until someone came to pick him up to go canvassing about 10am. The last week his wife came to stay with him and she did most of the talking. I am sorry he did not get in, I liked him very much. He became a judge and his wife told me how much she liked his new status. I spent a weekend with them. They had had a refugee family living with them. Margaret and Antonia came home that weekend; it was just before exams at Cambridge. They were like their mother and I think John's steady presence was a help.

John Drabble had defended Jan Mozigemba, a Polish refugee or prisoner of war, who had been working in the mines, on a murder charge. Mining can be a dusty job and encourages the slaking of one's thirst too often, which often leads to violence. The death penalty was in force, but as there was some doubt about the part Jan had played, he got a life sentence and was in Wakefield prison. John Drabble felt that basically he was a good lad and was sorry for him. His friends who might visit him in prison did not want to become too familiar with prison authorities, and if they came under the influence of drink, might not be of any use to Jan. John asked me if I could find any Wakefield Quaker to visit, but I drew a blank. I started to go myself and often took my eldest son with me – very educational. As time went on and he got good reports, Jan was transferred to Leyhill Open Prison near Bristol.

As I was going to an Oxfam Executive Meeting one Friday, I stayed the night in Oxford and then went to visit Jan. The car was not running well but I was anxious to get there during visiting hours. On arrival I enquired about the nearest garage, but it was miles away. I was told they had an excellent motor mechanic in prison and he would do repairs while I visited Jan. The prisoners had garden plots and a lovely bunch of flowers was given to me – I'm not sure how many from Jan's plot and how much had been unknowingly contributed by others. Anyway, it was a lovely welcome and the flowers appeared at Quaker Meeting on Sunday. Jan was pleased to have a visitor and told me he would soon be returning to Wakefield to work under supervision.

The car seemed to be in good running order. It went to a garage for a check up before Hugh, Johnny, our Sheltie dog and I went to Ireland for our summer holiday. Belfast, County Mayo, camping on the Burren where unusual plants grow deep in the fissures of the rock, Dublin and its rivers and art galleries, all were a joy to visit. In Limerick we stayed in a beautiful house where the family took occasional guests and their son waited on us, which helped to fund his college fees at Dublin University. We returned home, the car appearing tired as we approached Huddersfield. We took it to the garage and they said it had a cracked distributor and that had been the case for quite a long time! To think we had done a few thousand miles dependent on a repair by a very skilled operative. What gems prisons house.

Jan Mozigemba came back to Wakefield and was billeted with the family of the man he worked with. He told them of his unhappy background and they took to him. They brought him over in their car to visit us one Saturday – a firm bond of friendship and support had been established. Later he married and settled down; we heard from him for a few years. It was an enriching encounter I value and it had such a happy ending.

I became involved with Quakers when they started a children's class at the Meeting and I was delighted to have my children taken care of for an hour. This gradually and very slowly led on to further Quaker and Inter Faith commitment and to going to Yearly Meeting at York, where I helped Margot Tennyson with her Indian and Buddhist exhibition and study groups. There I met John Drabble again who had become a Quaker and so brought him home at the end of Yearly Meeting to stay the night and talk to my husband, Hugh. We loved talking over old times and new times. We heard from him for a few years until he died. They say 'Those whom the Gods love die young'; this makes me wonder why I am still extant.

After ten years as an attender, I was urged to apply for Membership of the Society of Friends. I asked six different Quakers what they meant by God; the replies were wide ranging and I felt I was not beyond the pale. I applied and was accepted. The Society has given me the support of a seeking community and I know that if I go to a Quaker Meeting I shall find at least one or two people on the same wavelength. Having been on Quaker Peace and Service, and Sharing World Resources Committee for a number of years and through Yorkshire General Meeting and five years on the Quaker World Committee for Consultation, I have made a number of friends that have enriched my life.

After the war we met a family at a holiday camp which had been converted from an old army camp, on the coast of Cumbria. It was a new experience queuing up for meals, and the noise of four hundred families, then doing one's share of the washing up. Peter cried and wanted to come home. However we chummed up with another family. They had the day off walking in the Lake District while we looked after seven children and vice versa. The next year we all went to a Holiday Fellowship centre at Towyn. There were about sixty in residence with graded walks for climbers, walkers, pram pushers, etc. The evening meal for children was at 6.30pm and for adults at 7.30. A shared patrol of parents operated around the children's bedrooms when dancing began at about 8.30.

We went camping with this family in Austria, with all our children. At Christmas they all came to our house, with their au pair, and we spent the next Christmas with them in Loughton in Essex. Packing up Christmas presents for their children and ours, taking contributions towards Christmas fare, the drive in bad weather, seemed nothing then. It staggers me now, as does all the packing up for camping on the Franco-Spanish border, but one just took it in one's stride. When they came here, weather permitting we walked up past the reservoirs to the 'Isle of Skye' pub then down to Meltham and caught the bus home

When International Co-operation Year dawned one of the sub-committees arranged the Inter Faith services. The Council of Churches and the Quakers did not support it, but I got support from Father Baxter, Head of the Roman Catholic school. Representatives from the Muslim, Sikh, Hindu, Christian and West

Indian community came to my house and we discussed a suitable theme. Having agreed we went back to our sacred writings to find appropriate readings. We met again, discussed what we had found and built it into an acceptable pattern. The West Indians often sang. Schools that played the classical guitar sang songs such as 'When I needed a neighbour were you there?' It was an education for us all and a breakthrough.

Christmases changed and I joined an International Friendship League that offered hospitality to foreign students at Christmas or Easter. Woodbrooke Quaker college was pleased if anyone invited their foreign students for a few days. Our first Indian guest had Erica and myself cooking in the kitchen under his direction for a very long time. Cooking for an Indian housewife is a long and serious business. These contacts were invaluable and provided me with background information when I was put on the Asia Grants committee of Oxfam and gave me many contacts when I came to visit India. Later the wife of one of these contacts spent four months with us and I arranged visits to schools, family planning clinics, youth clubs, etc.. She was not always impressed with what she saw and I agreed with her in her comparison with her husband's school and youth programme. Children often seemed to lack a sense of community. My children were trained socially to help deliver leaflets when Dad was putting up for the Council, to help on flag days and house to house collections as they came of age, or to put leaflets through people's doors saying when I would be calling to collect gifts for our Famine Relief Gift Shop. My dog was trained to collect for the RSPCA. He was a gentle Sheltie, children patted him and mothers felt obliged to put something in the collecting box. The RSPCA did well out of this.

The children grew up and went away, Robbie to the University, Erica to Edinburgh to train as a blind welfare worker, Peter to Hull to train as a ship's engineer. The house seemed comparatively empty. Hugh as chairman of the Education Committee knew of the difficulty of finding suitable accommodation for students who were then known as coloured. I visited one and saw the unsatisfactory lodging he was forced to live in. Certainly these students who would have good positions on returning to their own country would not be impressed by their accommodation in the UK.

We had three unoccupied bedrooms with gas fires and wash basins. With the addition of a gas meter, cooking facilities, a fridge or cupboard with a ventilator, students would be quite comfortable in our house, I thought. They could prepare their own breakfast, eat a midday meal at the Polytechnic, and cook an evening meal of their own type of food. I had not realised that all the doors and staircases would have to be fireproofed. At considerable expense this was done with asbestos underneath the panelling which had to be removed and replaced to cover it. At least this now means that the asbestos is covered, but it was an enormous job and one which is now considered dangerous. I noted that my own family had not been thought to need such protection! The Polytechnic lodgings officer visited and approved the rooms and I said coloured students were welcome. There was no shortage of applicants. Usually I had three of a kind – all men – Rhodesians, Kenyans, Indians, Malaysians, Nigerians, Chinese from Hong Kong.

The first two students I had from Iran were from cultured families. Iraj's sister was studying in Edinburgh, and when he and his sister returned to Iran for the coronation of the Shah, they had to stop in Paris to pick up the haute couture outfits for the rest of the family. Iraj had a Lotus Europa parked outside our house facing John's three wheeled Bond he had bought for £5. John had rebuilt it, painted it red and painted his hand black and impressed it on the car. Both cars attracted the admiration of the local boys. I had another Iranian student. His wife, who was studying elsewhere came to stay for a few days – all very pleasant. When the oil boom began, Arab men could have their fares paid to go to a football match in England, they were so rich. Arab students with so much money they were unused to, came to study … mostly the permissive society. They didn't pay up; if they dropped an egg on the floor they would leave it there until my help cleaned the floor once a week. They brought in girls at night and complained to the police when I gave them notice. After great difficulty I got rid of them and then said I would take no more students from the Middle East.

I had a Chinese take-over for about three years and they were so courteous and friendly; likewise the Indians. The Africans were a more mixed bunch but they were helpful when I was organising a clean up campaign for the Thornton Lodge and Lockwood community group and they helped considerably on the community bonfire night. Sometimes we asked a student down for a meal. I remember taking some of the Chinese students to Shibden Hall, a treasure of old English/Yorkshire culture which had craft demonstrations occasionally. There is a lake too, so you can take a boat out. It is eminently suitable for foreign visitors.

When I started going to India, Cambodia, Japan, I was pleased to have responsible students in the house as Hugh had a bad heart; my domestic help came in more often, but I didn't go away until the Arab troubles were satisfactorily dealt with.

John qualified as a nurse, then did a psychiatric nursing course at The Retreat in York. He went as a Quaker volunteer to help an Indian doctor in the tribal area of South India and later he took over a clinic eighty miles away over the mountains which Dr Narasihman visited when he could. This led to more bring and buy sales for the clinic, clothes for tribal children so that they could go to school and the usual United Nations Association, Labour Party, Quaker money-raising efforts – all thanks to my billiard room.

As time went on Hugh's heart grew worse and he died. I looked for a smaller more convenient house and couldn't find one. My three Nigerian students were coming to the end of their final year and it was time to make changes. It had not been easy cleaning and redecorating three student's rooms during vacations. Rob with the skills he had acquired working voluntarily on the climbing club at Capel Curig in North Wales, now used these to divide my large house in two. This left me with a smaller billiard room as one window became the front door. A space for stairs with a bend enabled the wash kitchen to be extended under the upper stairs and become a reasonable space for my kitchen. 'Only one rolling pin now.

I still have three bedrooms, an attic and cellar, garage and greenhouse. Quite enough room for all the family when they come to stay. It caused a lot of work – steps to the cellar, stairs to the first floor and attic had to be installed. A new wall had to be put in every room and finding a plasterer capable of making the cornice to match the other three walls in each room was not easy. It was tiring having to go down into the old cellar to get into the new kitchen and to go outside in all weathers to get to the other part of the house as dividing walls were constructed. We made the final move two days before Christmas. We had a New Year's party too – a 'Steptoe' party where everyone had to wear their oldest clothes, not expect too much, but be prepared to step it out and dance. We had our usual large Christmas tree too.

So many people had helped with decorating and cleaning, almost a community support group emerged. A Quaker who came to the Polytechnic two days a week needed bed and breakfast so we supplied it. He was fascinated to see the changes each week and painted the kitchen ceiling for me. At last all the stairs and rooms were carpeted and curtains finished.

In January a year later, I went to India to visit Johnny in the Nilgiri hills. Peter, Rob and my Sheltie came to meet me on my return. The day after I left the temperature had dropped far below zero; in spite of well lagged pipes there was a burst. Peter looked in to see if everything was all right a couple of days later. My bedroom ceiling had fallen on to my bed, the water was pouring down the stairs via the newly fitted carpet, then into the billiard room with its parquet flooring, and into the kitchen and cellar. Peter turned off the water and phoned a firm of carpet cleaners, but they already had fifty or sixty homes to deal with and didn't know when they could come. Peter took two days off work to roll up the carpets and put them in the garage, where they froze while waiting to be collected. Carpets are heavy anyway but to have to deal with them single handed horrifies me. My bed, mattress and bedding, clothes and curtains had to go to be cleaned. The parquet floor had to be re-laid and a lot of redecoration had to be done. It took a month or so to get things straight again after I come home.

The next summer was very hot – very pleasant. Imagine my horror when I came down one morning to find two-thirds of the billiard room ceiling on the floor. The fallen ceiling also damaged the furniture. I thought I was having a nightmare and had better go back to bed.

I must admit I have caused – unwittingly – a lot of trouble to my children. They were always a bit critical. I remember Robbie when about four sitting beside me as I tried to start the car.

"Mummy 'top car, Daddy no 'top car". When he was six his grandmother was telling him a story. He listened intently and then said at the end "That's not what it says in my encyclopaedia!" (Arthur Mee's Children's Encyclopaedia). When we looked up 'ammonite' believing it to be a type of fossil, we found they were a tribe of people like the Israelites. It was time to change our encyclopedia.

Our community did not only include humans. Robbie when about seven had a black and white Dutch rabbit, Snowy. He had to feed her and clean out her hutch, which he did faithfully. Snowy was allowed out for a short time to roam around the garden but not in the house as she left unmistakable traces. She allowed Robbie and me to pick her up and snuggled against our necks and seemed to enjoy it. When she was taken to be mated she wore a white ribbon round her neck – a natural training in the facts of life for young children. I loved lying in the hammock with my latest baby, watching Snowy caring for her babies. As they got older and she had enough of them climbing over her, she would send them back into the bedroom area. Robbie's friends were given a baby rabbit when it was time for them to leave Snowy. I was touched when they all brought them back a week later so that the babies could see their mother. Five small boys running round the vegetable plot trying to catch their rabbits to take home, didn't do much for the vegetables, but I appreciated the children's concern for babies and mother.

Peter started off with what we caught in the canals. It was interesting to find tiny creatures like water boatmen developing that we didn't know we had caught, as well as what we knew we had caught. The interest grew with goldfish, then tropical fish that required the water to be warm and aerated. John Drabble contributed some angel fish, which meant we had to have a wormery in the cellar to feed the angels. John also gave us a copy of *The Hobbit* and we all became Tolkien addicts. Unfortunately the fish tank needed to be cleaned out regularly and that added to my duties as it was a tricky operation. We enjoyed the graceful and disgraceful movements of the fish, some of whom we discovered to be cannibals. I suppose we had them for about four years. The tank stood on a low cupboard against the wall. The children were growing bigger and more boisterous. One day, some of them banging against the cupboard, the tank smashed and fishes, pebbles, pond weed and heating apparatus flowed across the living room floor. It was a sad end, and I didn't have the heart to start again.

Johnny's puppy Kutchya grew and I hadn't realised how male dogs have an over-riding desire to find a bitch in season. Kutchya's routine was to go to bed with Johnny at 7.30pm, listen to the bedtime story, and put his paws together when we said suitable prayers. There is a place for looking back over the day and giving thanks and remembering someone who needs our love. We had two sledges and Johnny and Kutchya went out with the smaller one with some friends to a good sloping field up the road, which was a good play area before the new estate was built. We used to have deep snow and put chains on our tyres in those days. Alas the dog felt the urge to visit his lady friend the other side of Bradford Road and disappeared. About 10pm the police rang to say a doctor had run over him and had killed him. The doctor had taken the body to Flint Street, our local incinerator depot, and we could collect his collar at the police station the next day. We felt the loss keenly and I remember dreaming that Kutchya was still there sitting on the hearth rug surrounded by the children; somehow I felt he was present and cherished the thought. We sadly collected the collar next day, but as we did so the police noticed our driving licence was two days overdue. Bad luck, though at least that could be remedied.

I felt dogs were a liability, but as I was an only child and a Welsh Collie had been my cherished companion when walking on Sheen Common or Richmond Park, I wanted another but this time preferred a bitch. If you bring them up from a puppy they are easy to train, so faithful they know what you are thinking and have a deeper intuitive sense, closer than most human friends. For anyone to call me a 'bitch' I should take as an honour, but know the speaker was ignorant. Some friends minded Kutchya when we went camping for three weeks on the continent. The friends rang up when we got home very disturbed because Kutchya was lost that very day. I replied "Don't worry, he was sitting on the front doorstep to greet us when we arrived". I object to people saying animals are stupid – some may be of low ability as some people are, but animals have gifts and skills to survive and sense a situation; skills I think primitive people still have, but ours have atrophied as we become dependent on aids such as telephones. We have usually had sheep dogs that are natural carers and the family when out walking becomes a flock of sheep. They run to the children ahead and then come back for me as I cross the river slowly on stepping stones.

Hence there followed Keltie, Kylin (a mythical Japanese dog with connections to Ikebana which I was studying), then Kerry and now Kim. A friend at Quaker Meeting had two Dachshunds called Dipsophenie and Tertullian – difficult to keep up with. A wild cat used to bring her kittens into our garden to play. The dark shy one we called Ho Chi Min and the more aggressive tortoiseshell kitten we named Mao Tse Tung. There was a problem if our Sheltie was enjoying a bone when they arrived. Should she leave her bone to chase them? Wisdom usually prevailed, she turning her back on the cats so she could not see them. Johnny said she went on pussy patrol around the garden, but always went first, barking, to the side of the garden where the cat was not. If by some mistake they came face to face, each stood perfectly still then slowly, very slowly, changed their stance until they were back to back and could walk away from each other with dignity. Then the cat might climb the pear tree and enjoy looking down on the brave fierce barking dog below.

Shelties don't live long and Keltie's heart gave out. My husband had a bad heart. Kylin suffered from arthritis as I did. My present Sheltie Kim has cataracts in his eyes, a benign swelling on his back and a heart tremor – all of which I have. I feel this sympathy is going too far, especially as Kim has eczema on his tail so I am very glad not to have a tail. At eighty I felt I was too old to have another bitch; when one lives alone one is so close to one's dog that I thought it not kindly if I departed and left a lonely animal. So I got my present dog, of unknown age, from a Sheltie rescue shelter. He is a dear with a Sheltie nature, but he had not received the most basic training. Naturally his most basic urge is to look for a receptive bitch. I am sorry his considerable gifts and pleasure in sniffing have not been trained – a wasted asset and lost pleasure for the dog. He would be a champion at events for Customs sniffer dogs.

A few years ago an old cat with torn ears came and sat beside me in the garden; later he sat with blood dripping from his mouth. My youngest son, a nurse, said I should take him to the vet immediately. I did as I was told. The vet said the cat had cancer of the mouth and an ulcer, gave me some antibiotics and said the cat would only live about three weeks as he wouldn't be able to eat. I decided to make it a comfortable end. There were two old armchairs in something like a summer house in the garden and he slept there. Then a wild kitten came to sleep in the other chair. As the nights grew colder. they shacked up together, so I made a pussy house out of a large box with bedding inside and carpet over the top. Kim was fed in the kitchen, the old cat at the top of the cellar stairs. The wild cat was fed outside and had a very loud voice when he knew it was feeding time. Oddly enough all of them took part in a ceremonial licking of each other's dishes at the end of the meal. The old cat that should have died in three weeks, lived happily for three years.

    The wild kitten, now a cat, would feed just inside the kitchen door and would take a titbit from my hand. He came in, walked upstairs, explored and sat in front of the fire. One day, forgetting he was a wild cat, I picked him up and put him on my knee. Claws came out swiftly and blood flowed, so I didn't do that again. As time went by he stopped taking titbits from my hand and ate less and less. I didn't worry much as he still slept outside and would have his hunting ground and his own methods of finding food. A few weeks later Kim would not come upstairs to sleep on the cushion outside my room as usual. I realised that the cat, who often came in to snuggle up to him, was with him in the kitchen. I left them together but in the morning I saw the cat was wet and Kim had been licking him. I pretended to lick him and gently stroked his back and then realised he was just a bag of bones in a fur coat. I phoned the RSPCA and they told me which vet was open on a Saturday and made an appointment for me. Happily a friend arrived with a car and solved my transport problem – one of those strange and happy experiences which seems in right ordering! The cat had a liver complaint and had to be put down immediately. Kim and I missed him very much. The care of the old cat and of Kim for the wild kitten, touched my heart. On David Attenborough's films we can see what we call a 'wild beast' like a crocodile caring for her young, taking them gently in her mouth with their legs and tails dangling as she carries them to a safer place,. Such scenes confirm my belief in creation spirituality. When I hear on the news about the horrors people inflict on each other, I begin to question human spirituality.

Another stray cat has decided to take up residence with us and Kim and I are very pleased. The cat always goes up to Kim and greets him first in the morning if he has slept out. He is a very clever cat who closely inspects the handles of doors that he wants opening. If he is hungry and it is not yet feeding time, he walks over my papers and the books I am trying to read until I give in. Kim and cat gang up on me.

The children each had their own small plot in the garden. Planting seeds and bulbs, watching them grow, is such a joy and links one into the rhythms of nature, of life and decay and compost and regeneration. The failure of one year can be the success story of the next. There is no sandpit, swings and climbing frame in the garden now. There is a greenhouse where I grow tomatoes and chrysanthemums, rhubarb, strawberry beds, raspberries, black currants, pears, apples and plums. There is enough for me and I give a good deal to friends. Runner beans, sprouting broccoli, spinach, beet and sprouts are all the vegetables I now grow, and all the plants are nourished by the produce of the three compost heaps. I spend an hour in the garden doing a quarter of an hour's work, then have a rest. If it is warm, I can sit in the garden, happy to be in the company of trees and all the plants working on my behalf, listening to birds, reading and often having a doze.

Of the home helps I have had, two have been memorable. Mrs Booth came from Emley twice a week. Her husband was a miner and chairman of the District Council. When he died she said she might as well come and work for me as my husband was a Labour Councillor – it would be better than going to the local psychiatric hospital at Storth's Hall! She was not the most efficient cleaner, but she was good with the four children and was very dependable and if I wanted to go to the Ladies' Luncheon Club she would stay longer. She had a nephew who was a physicist at Harwell, during the war her daughter taught maths at the boys' grammar school and her son became one of the top HMIs at that time. At her funeral he thanked me for giving his mother something she valued to do and said that seeing my children twice a week she was closer to them than to her grandchildren who lived in the south of England and whom she only saw occasionally.

I cannot understand why my Sheltie did not like her, though the dog always accepted a bit of her morning snack. If Keltie growled and I looked out of our projecting porch, I would see Mrs Booth just starting to walk up the road. Very odd.

The help I have now has been with me for twenty-six years. She used to clean my student rooms once a week as well as the rest of the house and took over extra responsibility when I went travelling. Her husband died when quite young, leaving her with a small child who needed special care. She helped voluntarily at the school her daughter attended and takes an active part in the local community. She brushes my dog and has him to stay if I am away and does most of my shopping. When my husband died and we divided the house, I continued to ask for her help as an insurance and I'm glad I did. It was a rewarding decision.

So many people I meet remind me they have been to some function at my house. A few months ago, a woman came up and reminded me how she had helped at an election in Almondbury when my husband won a very Conservative seat for Labour for the first time. That must have occurred at least forty years ago, if not more.

I am proud of my children – all caring people who do some voluntary work. Rob worked voluntarily for the London Climbing Club at Capel Curig and later when his job in finance (which involved making out redundancy payments) ended with his being made redundant himself, used his money to help Johnny who was building a house and clinic for tribal people in the Nilgiri hills in south India.

Erica, my daughter, who was not expected to live or walk, and spent most of her early years in hospitals, went walking in Nepal! She is qualified as a social worker for the blind. She has a BA Hons from the Open University, taken during the period when she was working voluntarily at the Citizen's Advice Centre three days a week. She now has an MA and hopes to do some paid and some voluntary work counselling. I am very proud of her, she has had so many difficulties to face. Peter lives in Huddersfield, has a full time job, yet finds time to do voluntary work and keeps an eye on me during my numerous sojourns in hospital and comes to my rescue at short notice, as do most of my friends.

Mine has been a house and family that has reached out to the community, creating a loving web of relationships. As the Dalai Lama says, "Be kind and generous to yourself in the joy of helping others in need." It works!

Chapter Two

My First Visit to India January-April 1966

ONE OF THE MOST valuable steps that Oxfam took to improve its fieldwork was the appointment of Field Directors in the areas where Oxfam was helping. We did not usually set up our own projects but worked through agencies already in the field, at that time most likely to be Missions. If the application was written by one who had gifts in this direction and an idea of what the donors were looking for, it naturally appeared in the applications. However sometimes the application was written by one who was dedicated to the work he was doing but hadn't the time or gift for such reports, but on visiting the project it was found to be an extremely worthwhile enterprise. With this in mind, field committees with a secretary were set up for Asia, Africa and South America. Each included two members of the Executive, together with others who had experience of working in those countries. To begin with there were only one or two Field Directors in each continent, but as it as found valuable to have reports when making decisions on grants by these sub-committees, which met about four times a year, the number of Field Directors gradually increased.

By this time I was on the Council of Management that met three times a year and the Executive, which met monthly. The Executive members were given a choice of which committee they would like to serve on and, as many countries in Africa were becoming independent, this was a popular choice. As I had no experience to offer I said I was open to suggestions. I was asked to serve on the Asia grants committee and I was overjoyed. As some overseas students had stayed with us for Christmas and a friend of mine was working in the Khasi hills in Assam, and a number of Quakers I knew had worked with Gandhi, I could see some shafts of light. Most of the members of the Asia committee were drawn from the British Raj. Some had considerable expertise, such as Dr W.R.Ackroyd, who had been Director of the Nutrition Research Laboratories in Delhi and had published a most valuable book on the *Nutritive Value of Indian Foods* and planning satisfactory diets. It included not only the names of the foodstuffs in eleven Indian languages, but the nutritive detail about the foods. I have his book, which is why I remember his name, but there were many others, including an ex-governor of Hong Kong, in whom I found a sympathetic listener to my modest contributions. Of course what they did not have was any contact with young India, the followers of Gandhi, the dedicated people who tried to serve their own community. Naturally I then began to follow up the contacts I had with Gandhian Quakers, Asian students and my friend in Assam, who gave me further contacts with the Ramakrishna Mission in Calcutta, and a whole web of glistening threads came to light connecting me with those who served their fellow men and women.

At this time too many discussions about Family Planning had taken place on the Executive. We had a charming Catholic priest on the Executive, so were moving cautiously, but I felt it was something that should be considered in India. There was a lot of heart searching on my part first as there had been before I went to Morocco. Was I really just going because I wanted to travel? I am sure that was part of it. A member of the Executive going back to Manchester gave me a lift and we talked as we had never talked before, or since; odd how these things just seem to happen. My mother had died a few years before and left me a little money. My youngest son was at a school that was much too academic for him; he had given up trying and was not the merry child he had been. A dream came to guide me. After talking things over with my husband, John went to Ackworth, a Quaker boarding school, and I made plans to go to India. It was 1966 and I was frightened at the thought of wandering round India on my own, being already in my mid-fifties. My anxiety was not without cause when travel there was quite unlike anything I had experienced in England, and telegrams telling of my arrival turned up two days after I had, with some difficulty, arrived. But somehow it didn't really matter, as I felt what I was doing was worth while. I suppose I was sustained by something deeper, which I had experienced before in times of stress.

The Bird Flies

Flying by Air India to Bombay at that time was gracious and elegant – the Maharaja lounge at Heathrow impressive in its splendour and beautiful air hostesses in lovely silk saris in muted colours. I was so overjoyed and could hardly believe it was not just a dream. I found that having a typewriter with me was very useful, as the editor of the local newspaper, *The Examiner*, who gave a lot of publicity to the work of the Huddersfield Famine Relief Committee, had offered to print my reports and gave me £2 for each one. This was extremely valuable publicity. As I sat, doubtless glowing with joy, one of the young stewards came up and started to chat about India and its culture. He said that I would find that people had not the same feeling of envy and accepted their poverty as they felt it was their Karma, and the result of the way they had behaved in previous lives. In some ways this belief seems to release people from an unpleasant and useless attitude and encourages them to make the best use of their situation and behave better in this life.

I was grateful that Diwarkar Agashe, brother of Shikrant, who had spent Christmas with us a year or so before, met me at Bombay airport. We took a taxi into the city and travelled through an area of swamps in which groups of people were actually living – I felt like turning around and fleeing in horror. I am glad to say much of the area has now been drained and provides a better first impression of India. I spent the night with friends of Diwarkar. The next day we visited the Parsi headquarters and, more important to me, the impressive Mrs Avabai Wadia, who was the head of the International Planned Parenthood Association in India. She provided me with contacts in the areas I was intending to visit. We took the night train north to an Oxfam-aided milk co-operative in Anand. It was so hot; when we stopped at a station I saw bottles of refrigerated milk from Anand on sale. I eagerly bought a bottle to find it was sweetened and scented – a dreadful disappointment! The co-operative was run by a very young and lively group of highly skilled young men. Village people brought their pots of milk into the village centres very early in the morning where it was tested for fat content and the villagers were paid. Then the milk went to the central dairy. After treatment some was sent by refrigerated train to Bombay where it was sold for less than that supplied by cows reared in the cellars of Bombay. Some milk was used to make Amul cheese, which later I was able to buy tinned in south India.

The fact that people were paid promptly for the milk encouraged them to find out more about the care and feeding of their animals, about artificial insemination and a clean water supply, which started an upward spiral of confidence and self-help. For instance, when there was a glut of limes in the area, which could not be sold, with the expert help available they started processing their own limes and tinning the juice. It was a wonderfully encouraging start to visiting Indian projects.

We returned to Bombay, Diwarkar to go back to his school while I went to visit a Gandhian ashram in the hills north of Bombay. The Gandhian contact had been given me by Donald Groome, a Quaker who had worked with Gandhi and was very sensitive to Indians and their culture. This provided me with a wonderful opportunity to see village India. I was met by Bhau at Dadghaon and taken by jeep into the hills where the little group of Gandhians was helping the tribal people to dam streams for irrigation, to produce more food for people and animals, run a small clinic and balwadi – a nursery group for children. Here I saw small children singing and dancing with small pots on their heads singing praises to Krishna and the milkmaids – the Gopis. They loved having a visitor to appreciate their dancing.

I was escorted to my room in a pleasant wooden hut by some dozen people, then there was a kerfuffle at the door, everybody had to make way for the 'Thunder Box'. They knew English women liked privacy – a strange idea to them – so a chair with a hole in the seat and a box underneath was provided and they waited for my approval and thanks ceremoniously given. For Indian villagers it is a social occasion to defecate while chatting by the riverside in the early morning.

I had taken some saplings, cypresses I think, with me so we had a ceremonial planting with Hindu rites. I doubt whether they survived but I know others did without the aid of a puja at Rasulia Quaker centre.

The next morning, after looking at the activities being carried on in the village, we set off in the jeep towards more hills. We then left the jeep and started walking. It is customary to welcome guests with garlands and I remember once in Bombay airport I had three wet garlands hung around my neck. However in the hills when people come to meet you, singing seems to be the preferred way of greeting, and in this case it was the whole school in a wandering, singing procession that escorted us back to the school. Here we were given food and this was followed by the children dancing and acting short plays. The one I remember vividly was about a young woman working quietly with dedication at her sweeping, spinning, food preparation, etc. Neighbours saw this and marvelled, they knelt before her as they saw the God in her and Vishnu appeared to bless them all. Of course the greeting with hands together and a bow to another person is basically recognition of that of God within; a Hindu bathing in the morning singing his bajans – Holy songs – pours water on his head anointing the God within; a dancer will perform a short dance offering her gifts to God before she dances in public. As a Quaker I accept and cherish this attitude to people and to work as an offering to something beyond the immediate end. I am reminded of Jan Vermeer's painting of a servant girl pouring milk, referred to in one Swarthmoor lecture. About sixty tribal children attended this school which was residential as the children came from many scattered villages. In some Gandhian schools the children were near enough to go home at weekends. I visited a number of others. The older ones would get agricultural training as well as crafts such as spinning, woodwork and very simple metalwork that would be useful to them in a village. There was always emphasis on cultural training, dance and song, infused with moral training and a sense of community. Often the children had to wash their own clothes and help prepare the food, which creates a family atmosphere. It is good training. I remember my grandmother teaching me to make a beefsteak pudding and the four little rolling pins that waved about in my kitchen when my children were 'helping' mummy.

Going down to the lowlands and the railway by jeep unnerved me somewhat as we had to get out of the jeep on a very steep hairpin bend in order to reverse before it could get round, the men pushing and trying to get the wheels into a tighter turn. I was glad to have an inner confidence that in some way all would be well, but heights were always a trouble to me and I was glad when we were safely down. A very busy and important railway links Bombay, Nagpur and Calcutta and I now travelled on this line hopping off at different stations to make visits to Diwarkar's school, a Nagpur Women's Hospital and the Quaker schools and centre at Rasulia.

From the train I had to travel about forty miles by bus to the school at Buldana. I chatted to a man who was a very well placed official for the whole state of Maharasthra, to do with buses I think. I laughingly said when he told me this "You must be a wealthy man." He gave me a long look. He said he had two brothers who worked the family land. With their families and his aunts, uncles and grandparents, there were forty-two people in his extended family. There is no social security in India and anyone with a good job attracts all the needy of the extended family. The system has had its strengths and weaknesses in discouraging enterprise and service beyond the extended family. In quite a number of families I visited, the house-holder had a main job but also another smaller enterprise in case the main one should fold up. I am sure it is this careful attitude backed by a close-knit, hard-working family that has enabled so many Asians to come to Britain and make a success of their businesses, particularly their shops.

Indians often carry a little box of tasty seeds – jeerah, dhanya, betel nut, cardamon, that they share with you when travelling. It's a friendly gesture, so I nibbled my seeds and reflected on the demands of having forty-two in the family. My husband and I were both only children.

Diwarkar Agashe, whom I was now about to visit, was a young teacher who believed that book learning was not enough and that children should learn by doing, and by doing useful voluntary work in the community. He encouraged them to visit elderly people who needed help, took them on expeditions at weekends and established a small park with shady trees where young children could play. The headmaster and other teachers looked askance, said it was detracting from the children's school work and I think feared that they might be expected to do likewise. The parents of the children noticed how much more lively and alert their children were and supported Diwarkar.

Finally a piece of land was bought, a well dug, parents, children and Diwarkar put up some simple wooden buildings with a veranda and work and learning went on hand in hand. With water to irrigate, the children learnt to garden; they kept chickens, each kept under a basket until it had laid an egg and then released for its free range scratching for food. Gradually more simple bungalows with verandas were built so that boarders came to this progressive school – a lot more progressive than the Quaker schools I visited later. As news of this school spread and examination results showed that practical work did not detract from school work, more pupils and young staff came offering their services. They and their families had small mud brick houses on the compound.

One hostel was constructed for outcaste boys. The problems of finance were there but had never been allowed to dominate the situation. These new pupils could bring some rice or meal with them, but never enough to last the term. Diwarkar arranged for them to work for a local farmer instead of helping on the school garden. All the boys had to promise to urinate in a bucket and the valuable contents were sold as fertiliser. The outcaste boys ate separately as is Hindu custom, but they were fed and got an education, something they would be unlikely to get in their villages.

When I arrived I suppose there must have been about two hundred in the school and on my next visit a junior school for day pupils had been added. These children brought their mid-day meal – tiffin – of rice and lentils with them so it did not add to the work of the cooks.

A useful visit was made to some of the villages from which the outcaste boys came. It was an opportunity to look at some of the problems, and consider if any help could be given. In one case the well was situated down a very steep track. The boys camped there during their holidays and constructed a road that could be used by a bullock cart, which carried the water up the hill instead of the women doing so.

As I sat under the tree in the compound a much older student came up to me. He was lame and lived at the school as it was near the college he was attending. "Please could you give an account of the life and times of Thomas Hardy? I have an exam soon." I replied that although I had read some of the books some time ago I really could not produce a summary. "But you are an educated lady, you must know." I asked to look at the books he had with him. I can't remember whether it was *Tess* or *Jude the Obscure*. He also had a book of questions with answers which he was learning by heart. We talked a bit about passages from the book, but poor lad, how could he understand the background of Hardy when all he knew about was the customs of village India? This explained a lot when I was talking to many Indians – when I asked them a question they never said they did not know the answer; they called up out of the stock of learning they had by heart something with a slight connection and produced that. I can see why Diwarkar felt the education system needed an overhaul. There was no training in facing a situation and finding for oneself a practical solution, because one had never been encouraged to think.

After school Diwarkar often took me out travelling by a slow moving unsprung ox cart to see jaggery (coarse sugar) being made by a travelling team that crushed the sugar cane, added some oil from a plant growing nearby then poured the mixture into huge shallow vats with fires of wood beneath. They stirred the mixture until it thickened and then poured it into pails until it set. A thick rich dark sugar resulted called jaggery. It was made at night and the fires and the busy workers had a feeling of magic about them.

Another time we went to see some of the school boys tending a crop that would produce food for the school. Nearby there was a small shrine and a Muslim came up, said a few prayers and then passed on. Presently a Hindu came to the shrine and paid his respects. I said "I thought you told me this was a shrine to a Pir, a Muslim holy man, but a Hindu visits it?" Diwarkar looked surprised at my question. "Yes, but he was a holy man." The Moslem Pir had left land to the village and the crops from that land were to be given to any in need, whether Muslim or Hindu. It was an eye opener to me as we had heard so much about Hindus and Muslims hating each other, not about their living in amity, nor had I heard at that time about states in southern India where the ruler was a Muslim whose subjects were Hindus and they seemed to have a good working relationship. It is when politicians use religion as a cloak for their activities that trouble and fanaticism rise to the surface.

I have forgotten much of the detail of the ritual of a village wedding, but I can see the bride and groom now, magnificently attired, garlanded and sitting on cushions. At the end of the ceremony the bride was expected to make some poetic utterances to grace the ceremony. I remember it was evening and long lines of people sat on mats and were served by many gaily dressed women. The weddings of my Sikh and Hindu neighbours used to be community affairs when they first came to live in Huddersfield, but times have changed. In India it was part of village entertainment like the wandering singer, dancers and jugglers.

A very special visit was to the cave temples of Ajanta and Ellora, which is described in Chapter Nine. After seeing the caves at Ajanta, I went down by the stream while Diwarkar went back to meditate in one of the cave temples. As I sat watching, some girls in brightly coloured saris were collecting mud from the stream and carrying it up the hillside. They looked so pretty and their voices were happy and musical. They came and looked at me and saw I had no gold ear rings or a ring in my nose – not even glass bangles. They felt sorry for me and offered me a bangle. I am ashamed to say now that I refused. They seemed so poor that I felt I couldn't take from them. Thinking it over I was sorry I felt like that – if I had accepted they would have felt so rich and generous. I regretted I was not able to look at it from their point of view and I tried to be more sensitive as I went on my way.

We spent the night with a cousin of Diwarkar's – I had the only bed and the family slept on the floor – not uncommon in India. I have slept on the floor many times since then. The next day we visited the caves at Ellora. These were not so extensive as at Ajanta. Some were partly open to the sky and the very fine sculptures which were both Hindu and Buddhist could be seen more clearly. But it did not touch my heart as much as Ajanta did with its beautiful setting and varied caves.

I feel I ought to pay a small tribute to Diwarkar Agashe here. He was the younger brother of one of two engineers in charge of one of the big power stations in India who had spent Christmas with us some years before. Later Diwarkar came over to Leeds on a Commonwealth scholarship at a time when he had already established his school. He did not find the lectures at Leeds much help and felt he was more usefully employed running his school in India, so he gave up his scholarship and returned.

The boys from his school have in many cases got good qualifications and are now teachers themselves using his methods. He is able to go and visit them to help and advise and has become a highly respected educationalist known in the whole of Maharasthra. I certainly owe him much for the trouble he took to educate me in Indian culture and the face of modern India.

I was invited to tea by missionaries living in Buidana. They suggested I stayed with them as I should be so much more comfortable. Diwarkar looked a bit sideways. I thanked them but said I was happy staying with my friends. It is true there would have been mod cons and privacy, which is lacking in an Indian household, but the loss would have been much greater if I had accepted what was meant as a kind offer. Certainly my 'room' was far from private. The bathroom consisted of a raised area with a place for the feet and one had to squat – a thing I now find difficult, at least the getting up is difficult. One was provided with a bucket of hot water and one of cold and a little brass pot. One poured the water over one's head and it ran away down a drain. I sometimes used to wash my smalls in the remaining water in the bucket, but alas one time I emptied the water down the waste pipe with some of my smalls in the bucket. I learned to be more careful. All this was experiencing life as lived by the majority of people in India. I see no point in visiting foreign parts to live as if in England.

From Buidana I went to the Quaker Rural Centre at Rasulia near Hoshangabad. Here there was a large Meeting House that was used as a balwadi for young children, a junior school, a hostel for students, a clinic, a well-digging programme and provision for making cement well-rings and a cement water-seal latrine fitment. There was also a farm that grew oranges. Nagpur oranges are the best in India. Quaker workers went into the surrounding villages to encourage farmers to improve their methods and stock. There were four English people there and two Canadian doctors at that time. Earlier Quakers had gone to the area in time of famine and had set up orphanages but their evangelical missionary attitudes were not in harmony with London Yearly Meeting. Years later some of the Indian converts left to join more missionary-based groups. Schools had been established, one for boys and a few miles away a boarding school for girls. The headmaster took me round and remembered with nostalgia the old Quaker Raj when so much land and people belonged to the Quakers. Both the schools were friendly but their attitude was one of begging, showing me the wall they needed, the buildings that required renovating. The boys' playground was littered with paper. I asked why. The answer was that the sweepers had not come that morning. In Diwarkar's school the boys did it themselves and learned not to throw paper down. I know this would do the sweepers out of a job, but this attitude of leaving unpleasant jobs to lower castes has a canker in it which spreads throughout society. Some of Diwarkar's boys were of low caste and were being educated to take their place in a more egalitarian society. Middle class Indian boys just do not know how to mend a motor bike or car or electric pump, or change a tyre.

The buildings at Rasulia were bungalow type, with wide verandas and high rooms with fans slowly circulating the hot air, old and gracious. The Canadians and English thought it a bit shabby but that it would not put Indians off. Then a new Director (an Indian) was appointed with a different attitude. The old buildings were replaced with modern cement structures – nowhere near so cool and shady. Perhaps Indians were drawn to it, but it certainly put this English woman off.

From Itarsi I went by train to Nagpur. Alas the riots against Hindi as a national language were on; southern India wanted to keep English as the second language and not Hindi which was the language of the north. So trains were disrupted, and as I was not on a main line train we were shunted into a siding for hours and I missed a Hindu wedding I was going to ... this sort of thing is accepted as natural in India. At Nagpur I was visiting a contact given me by the International Planned Parenthood Association in Bombay.

Some forty or fifty years ago, a well-off Hindu daughter wanted to become a nurse. This was unthinkable in a well-to-do Indian family. However the daughter and a friend hired a house in a slum area of Nagpur in order to care for mothers in childbirth. The news got round. Indians often have a very tender centre. The family became proud of their daughter – perhaps they saw the Goddess in her. They relented and she was allowed to train as a nurse. This started a trend – hardly a fashion – but other daughters began to feel the call and a number trained and trained others in their turn. When I visited, the original founder, Mrs Kamalbai Hospet, was still alive. She and some of her old nurses were living outside Nagpur in bungalows and looking after some twenty or thirty orphan children in their retirement. In the meantime about twenty women's hospitals had been established in and around Nagpur. Prime Minister Nehru had given Mrs Hospet a special award for her work. The doctor now in charge of the Matru Seva Sangh in Nagpur was Dr Kusum Wankar. Her husband, also a doctor, lectured at the big civil hospital in the town. They had a very small flat at the Matru Seva Sangh where Dr Kusum did all the operations, ran a family planning clinic, established a home for handicapped children born at the hospital and helped run a welfare programme training health visitors. For this she received an honorarium of £200 per annum. Now both she and her husband have retired, live on a microscopic pension and still give their services to small women's organisations and balwadis. It was such a pleasure to meet such dedicated people and go back to the Famine Relief Committee in Huddersfield and be able to send a grant. Dr Kusum was invited to go to America to see work being done to help the mentally handicapped. She stayed with me for a few days and was able to meet members of the Hudfam committee. She was invited to give a talk at All Saints Catholic School in Huddersfield where she was given a donation towards her work. I was impressed that a Catholic school recognised the work of a Hindu doctor. The school looked behind the labels.

From Nagpur I was taken to Wardha and shown the simple room where Gandhi lived, with a big peepul tree outside where he held meetings. The cleanliness of the room and the basic simplicity is dear to my heart. I expect it was comparatively easy to live like this in a village but simplicity carried out in a town in other people's homes which are not geared to it, is a very different matter. For example, the goats were lined up so that the right one could be chosen to produce milk for the Mahatma and certain foods had to be ready in case they were asked for. Nearby is the village of Sevagram which is a training centre for Gandhian rural workers.

If one visits missionaries one gets into the missionary network, which is easy as they are likely to have a car and a telephone, but I was in the Hindu network. This led me to visit Baba Amte. He was at the University at the time when Gandhi was urging his followers to leave their book learning and get out and learn about the life of the down-trodden masses of India. Many young men did just that and Baba Amte went to work with the sweepers who collect the night soil and carry it to a dump on the outskirts of the town. This was a tremendous challenge. At first, strong and well fed and filled with the Holy Zeal all went well, but one day taking the refuse to the local midden he found a leper lying in the filth. There is a deep seated horror of leprosy in India and this was too much. Amte went home, bathed and sat facing his fears and horror for a long time, realising he was facing a challenge that he had to meet. Finally he went back to the midden; the leper was still there and he carried him to a place where he could wash him and then took him to a leprosarium where he could be treated. He then went to college to take a course in leprosy treatment using the modern drugs that are now available to arrest the disease. Leprosy is very contagious in its early stages. It has been the custom for those who have the disease to leave home hoping not to spread it further in the family, and the sufferer becomes a homeless wanderer, a beggar shunned by all. I can well understand the horror that Indians have of the disease and can admire Baba Amte's courage in facing the situation.

On completion of his training Amte opened a clinic and many came to him for treatment. He asked the government for land and, as usual in India, there was much delay. So he just took over some barren land realising that with the support he got from the Gandhians the government was unlikely to turn him off. I suppose I met him ten to fifteen years later. I arrived in the afternoon when it was too hot to go looking round the settlement, so I sat cross legged at the feet of the master listening for an hour or so, until my knees told me it was time to be walking around. The trouble was that by 4 pm when it was more comfortable to be walking around the light is not so good for photographs. Some patients had the use of one hand or one foot and by working together they could make lamps out of old tin cans. Some were mixing cement or carrying stones to build an agricultural college that was nearly finished. Some ordinary labour was used for the more difficult or skilled jobs, but the college was about to open and applications were coming from able-bodied people as well as the leprosy patients. Little wooden houses had been built where husband and wife could live together. These people looked after cows and the milk was sold in the open market. Having established a village for homeless leprosy patients, Baba Amte then started a travelling clinic visiting the villages and giving treatment so that the patient need not leave home. This also provided a watchful eye on the rest of the family, in case of further infection.

ICI was most helpful and enabled me to get some recently developed leprosy drugs to send to India. The last I heard of Baba Amte was that he had started another settlement and his leprosy patients were able to help some tribal people in the hills. I remember thinking that was typical of Baba Amte's work – to get one deprived group to help another and feel the proper pride that this engendered. Needless to say I put Oxfam in touch with both him and Dr Kusum in Nagpur.

It was a long train journey to Calcutta, upper bunks were let down at night and the jogging of the train sent me to sleep. In the morning waiters came round so that you could book a meal. This would be phoned through to the next station, and when the train arrived waiters would board the train with half a dozen trays one on top of the other, collect money and jump off just as the train was pulling out of the station. They were acrobats at the job and the food was good and very reasonable.

I was delighted to be met by Swami Lokeswarananda, a friend of a friend of mine (Margaret Barr in the Khasi hills in Assam). We soon struck up a friendship as he had first taken an active part in famine relief during the Bengal famine, in aid of which I organised my first flag day in January 1942. I stayed at the Ramakrishna headquarters in Gol Park. This was a very pleasant building, constructed round a garden that was watered every day and had a balcony looking down into it from the rooms. I was shown some appalling slums in Calcutta, tiny one-room shacks with no windows, a drain outside and a standpipe some distance away.

The RKM ran workshops and training centres and a maternity home. About ten miles away at Naredrapur they were left a large estate by a Muslim who left for East Pakistan at the time of Partition. There was a lovely bungalow with a small lake, gay with a hedge of bougainvillaea. In the grounds a large boys' school had been built and a school for the blind where they were taught to play music for village festivals. No village could celebrate without musicians, so this was a very useful skill for them. I had visited a school for blind children run by the Salvation Army in Calcutta and suggested the SA should be invited to bring some of its students to meet and share their experience with those at Narendrapur. This the Swami did and some of the SA officials came to discuss the visit. So often project holders are so busy with their own affairs and simply have no time and do not know what others nearby are doing, and of course there is always an uneasy feeling amongst most missionaries that you must be careful with the heathen! It is notable that the RKM made the first move. The RKM also ran an advisory service for farmers and once a year held a mela – an agricultural show giving farmers new insights into farming and agriculture.

The Ramakrishna Mission is the modern face of Hinduism with well educated swamis. I paid my respects at the temple where Ramakrishna had a great spiritual experience contemplating Kali, the black Goddess with her tongue protruding, a garland of skulls, hands holding weapons and severed heads and standing on the prostrate form of her consort Shiva. I suppose if one accepts reincarnation one accepts the endless cycle of birth and death, and death and disease is close to people in India. I have a statue of Shiva dancing in his ring of fire which appeals to me because he is dancing. Kali triggered off something in Ramakrishna which seems as strange to me as contemplating a tortured man on a cross seemed to the Swami. Vivekananda, a follower and chosen pupil of Ramakrishna, took the teachings to Chicago where a big Congress of Faiths was being held in 1893 and made a great impression by giving the teaching of modern Hinduism.

The RKM established clinics, student hostels and libraries in remote areas. I visited one near Shillong with a Khasi tribal girl. The two young swamis had closed the clinic and been lent a car for the afternoon, so they took Maida and me for a ride. Somehow I didn't expect to meet a merry swami and was surprised again when some years later I met him when he was in charge of the RKM centre in London.

I visited a number of other projects in Calcutta, notably Mother Theresa's hospice for the dying near the Kali temple and her orphanage. Of course all the children were brought up as Catholics and the swami did not approve of divorcing children from their culture. Then there was a Major who when he left the army stayed on in Calcutta and organised a food distribution in the poorest areas of the city – he ran it out of his pension. I was extremely lucky when staying in Calcutta. A huge basket of fruit was left for me at Gol Park and a car put at my disposal every morning at 7am if I wanted it. This was a most valuable gift in a huge place like Calcutta.

One of my Indian students in Huddersfield had a friend who wanted to ring his father, a judge in Calcutta, but often there was a wait of a few hours before he could get through, so he spent the afternoon with his friend in one of my bedsits, which was much more pleasant than hanging around a public phone box. It was the father of this lad who provided me with the car – blessings on him. I had had some delightful Arab students staying in my home before the oil boom. My husband had helped one of these students with some application, so I was invited to spend one night with his family in Teheran on the way home from India.

With the help of the RKM I obtained a pass to visit Assam – there had been trouble with China on the borders and strict controls were in force. One can waste such a lot of time in Government Offices so the RKM help was invaluable. I had to fly to Gauhati as partition had upset the railway system. From there I took a bus to Shillong – about thirty miles and dozens of severe hairpin bends. I stayed overnight with friends of Margaret Barr and they put me on another country bus next day to a village where the priestess was said to rule, but to do this through her son. Stupidly I asked for a toilet and was shown a very small bush up the hillside. Four girls came to meet me and carry my luggage on the baskets they carried on their backs. They were barefooted and sped easily over the ten miles of rocky footpaths. Spring was lovely in the hills and the air fresh but the sudden change in altitude made it difficult for me and I was exhausted when I arrived.

Margaret Barr had taken a degree and then come to Cambridge to take a teaching qualification when I met her at the Unitarian Church. For me the Unitarian Church was like coming home. People of all faiths were invited to preach at the evening service. Gandhi had spoken there just before I arrived but I was lucky to hear the President of India, Dr Radakrishnan, speak amongst many others. Margaret qualified as an Unitarian Minister and went to India to work with the Brahmo Samaj with whom Unitarians had links. She started a school in Shillong which flourished greatly until Partition, when she handed it over to the Indian authorities and chose to go into a remote area amongst tribal people where schools and clinics were desperately needed.

In this area Margaret had established a clinic run by a 'compounder', a 'somewhat' qualified male assistant who also cut my hair. There was a balwadi for the children – I knew the nursery rhymes they sang by the tunes and their actions as they sang in Khasi. They looked a lovely little group as they sang 'Sing a Song of Sixpence' and 'Hickory Dickory Dock'. There was also a school where girls were taught the three Rs, weaving and English country dancing. Margaret had got one or two tribal girls to the standard where they could go to Shillong to take nursing and midwifery, and Maida aforementioned was one of these, who had come back to work among her own people. A stream had been dammed so we hoped for fish on the menu sometime, and it provided a lovely swimming pool for an early morning dip. The house was small – my room had been added and there was only room for the ladder to climb up in to it and the bed. I'm glad I didn't fall out of bed as I should have descended the ladder promptly.

On Sunday I was taken to a little Meeting House where, as happens to all rare strangers, I was asked to speak. Luckily I had noticed a patch of beautiful little flowers struggling to survive in the cracks between two stones, what better opening to talk about beauty, endurance and care in walking that we do not harm the world we live in. Margaret translated briefly, unlike Diwarkar who took an awful long time to translate when I was asked to speak at village gatherings in his area. I often wondered how he embroidered my simple remarks with his ideas.

Food was very simple – rice, greens and a little meat. We sat over a small smoky fire in the evenings and talked. There was so much to share. She still had the recorder that I remembered her playing in our garden when she came to visit us in Huddersfield. Needless to say, Margaret appreciated a chance to talk as there were so few visitors in this remote area and we had so much in common. I was glad to hand over to Margaret the typewriter as it lightened my luggage. She was very pleased to have it and I realised how much I would miss it, but it was too heavy to carry any further.

It was courageous of Margaret to start this project in such a remote area. I don't think people realise the effort involved – when a person is turned forty they do not usually have the same driving energy they had when younger, though they may have more skills. It must get increasingly difficult to live in a home ten miles from the nearest bus and many more from any town, with no local resources for illness and no luxuries at all. She did a great deal to help the Khasi people.

After a week it was time to leave and I looked at the little house remembering all the tiles on the roof and so much of the equipment had come from Shillong and been carried by the sturdy girls. The journey back was easier as I was used to the altitude.

As I was staying with Margaret's friends in Shillong I could give their address and qualify as a resident which enabled me to get a three day pass for Darjeeling. Then I went down the twenty-seven hairpin bends to Gauhati where I stayed in a Kasturba ashram. Kasturba was Gandhi's wife and the women's ashrams are called after her. This one was clean, simple, beautiful and surrounded by trees. Up at 4 am for prayers, songs and meditation and the joy of seeing the increasing light of sunrise. The sunsets in India are also glorious with orange and gold, it makes one feel worshipful. It is the natural time for prayer. I had a room to myself with the usual Indian washing facilities which I find quite adequate. The room had a new surface of cow dung and mud every day; it was clean, odourless and pleasant to walk on. We sat on mats with a tray in front of us for meals and servers would go round and put food on the sections of your grooved tray. I never really acquired the skill of throwing balls of rice and lentils into my mouth. At the end of the meal we were given water to drink, wash our hands and wipe over the cow dung floor in front of us. It dried quickly. I was told that part of the pleasure of a meal was kneading balls of food in the hand first – I suppose it got the saliva moving; they thought putting metal in one's mouth was too horrible to contemplate.

The Kasturba women go out into the villages in ones and twos to help village women. There was a great air of excitement in the ashram as the following day we were all going by train to North Lakimpur which is a long way up the Brahmaputra valley, to visit the Gandhian International Peace Centre. From this centre a number of Gandhians go out to work with the tribal people, then, about every three months, they return to base to report on what they have done, discuss problems and share experiences. So this is what we were going to attend. I had a problem as they had booked me a first class sleeper and I usually travel third, as they were doing, but looking at it from their point of view they would feel constrained by my presence and not enjoy the outing half so much, so I let things be.

Again the Peace Centre was a series of bungalows with verandas, the meeting hall long and narrow, men sitting cross legged on one side spinning on their ambar charkers. The women did the cooking, so when they sat, they were allowed just to sit. I was glad I could sit and rest my back against the wall. There was a photo of Gandhi and, to my surprise, one of John Kennedy, the U.S. President at that time. There was a shrine but I have forgotten what it contained. It is customary in India when there are celebrations to make beautiful patterns in chalk before the shrine or house entrance. There was a wonderful one in front of this shrine. I had also seen them in Calcutta where a side street was blocked off and a shrine to Saraswati, Goddess of learning and music was erected. The patterns are called rangoli and of course are blown away by the next day.

On this occasion whoever came, of whatever religion, was asked to sing or say a prayer from their own tradition. I fell back on 'God be in my head and in my understanding.' It was a short and simple song and something I thought the Indians would appreciate. (I plan to have it played at my cremation.) Then various workers present, both men and women, gave their reports. So many Indians speak English I was never short of an interpreter. If I ever hear English spoken extremely well, it is usually by wealthy Indians who have been educated at the older British Universities or schools such as Roedean and Cheltenham Ladies' College.

I was also taken round some nearby villages where a Gandhian woman had established a balwadi and a grain store. Villagers contributed to the grain store at harvest so that those in need later could receive some grain from the village store rather than borrow at exorbitant rates of interest from money lenders.

I broke my train journey on my return to visit a well planned 200 bed mission hospital where the verandah was screened by fine gauze wire to keep out the mosquitoes. It was a relief to be able to sit on a chair and eat English style. This was a project that Oxfam was supporting. The next day I was picked up in a jeep by another missionary. Alas, by the time we reached the Brahmaputra river the last ferry that night had left. We found the Government Rest House full, so we went to a coach park and installed ourselves there for the night. The missionary put on his dhoti and was asleep in five minutes. It is a pity we happened to choose a coach to sleep in that was leaving very early, so we still had a long wait for the ferry.

Upon arriving at the missionary's own village, we were welcomed by his wife who had breakfast ready. After breakfast and a wash I was taken to see the village work. A number of people from East Pakistan were infiltrating into Assam to escape the poverty in their own country. The areas of work were divided up among a number of Christian groups who were helping the refugees to establish themselves, contributing tools, seeds and community development. What I did not like was being shown the different Christian churches which create further divisions in these scattered communities. The next day I left, armed with my pass for Darjeeling, but even at the station they did not know the time of the train. As the station was not far away, the station master agreed to let us know when it arrived somewhat later in the evening. When I arrived in Siligiri, the little mountain train that goes up to Darjeeling had left so l went up by jeep. It was a magnificent drive with extensive views and I saw the little train which I had missed, crossing and re-crossing the road as it gained height. I was booked into a pleasant hotel with marvellous views and English food if required. The next day there was a steep walk up through the tea gardens to where, on some levelled ground, Mrs Gylo Thondup had homes for elderly Tibetans and workshops making rugs, weaving cloth, carving etc. The compound was gaily decorated with prayer flags and a busy happiness prevailed. Hudfam sent her a grant and I managed to get some dyes to take the place of those she could not now get from Tibet.

Mrs Thondup was one of the top category of women organisers I met in India. These women were sensitive to people's needs, showed tremendous initiative in finding out the needs of a community and investing small amounts of money they were given to make the community self-supporting. In this category I think especially of Mrs Hema of Bangalore and her training for the physically handicapped, and Mrs Krishna Rao of Madras who gives training to destitute women who can then get married without a dowry because they are self-supporting and of value in their own right.

Many Tibetans are employed in India to work on the roads, but as this was not a suitable environment for children the Dalai Lama had established a number of boarding schools where the children could be taught and kept aware of their own culture. The Indian Army had vacated a large house and handed it over to the Tibetans. It was in very poor condition as one would expect. Many floors had holes in them and the roof had partly blown off the children's sleeping shed. The first job was to install some decent latrines, not usually very high on an Indian agenda. The children ate their meals sitting in lines on little straw mats in the compound and gave thanks for what they had before each meal. Classes were being held in all sorts of places. In this decrepit place there was an air of happy confidence – they were all working hard and enjoying the challenge.

There was one smallish room to remind them of home. An old Raj wash stand had been painted with Tibetan designs and on it were put the treasures that they had carried all those miles across rocky tracks, fearing they would be caught by the Chinese. There was a Buddha that must have been very heavy, little butter lamps, some lovely tankas – wall hangings on sacred themes – a reminder of home and it touched my heart. I visited other Tibetan groups in Mussorie where there was a big school and in south India where the climate and lack of immunity to Indian diseases took a heavy toll, but I suppose they had been bred in austere conditions in Tibet and they carried this gaiety and will to endure adversity wherever they went. I admire them tremendously.

I got a first class sleeper on a small train. Before nightfall I was the only occupant of the carriage. "You must not travel alone – dacoits come in and knife you on these little trains – you must lock yourself in," I was told. This woman's advice may have been good but as she showed me the lock it came off in her hand. Typical of India. I have been mugged once just near home and once in Spain but never in India. However I made a point of travelling third class after that.

My visit to Dehra Dun was to see a Cheshire Home. I arrived very early in the morning while the head of the home was at her meditations. She said she arranged flowers as part of the ritual. I felt a common bond. There was a good-sized hospital and a school for the children of leprosy patients who had houses nearby. It meant the children could be protected at a vulnerable age and the parents could see the children and talk to them by the fence of the playground. A master from the Dun school came to lunch and took me off to talk to his sixth form. This Public School had been established during the British Raj for the sons of the higher ranks of the Raj and wealthy upper caste Indians. English meals were served alternately with Indian meals, so that all had a training in good table manners, wherever they dined. I could have done with a course in this. There was also a light aircraft the boys learned to fly and service and a Daimler for the same purpose. This British influence in practical education had been carried on. The boys were intelligent, not having learned blocks of answers by heart, and quite a pleasure to talk to. Of course they wanted to know why I was wandering around India and they had the opportunity of hearing colloquial English spoken. A lot of Indians use phrases that were in vogue sixty or seventy years ago. It also seems that any word can be made into an adjective or adverb. Words are used differently: I was having tea with an Indian lady who showed me her front garden and then said 'You must come and see my backside where I have flowers growing.'

I went higher up the mountain by jeep to Mussorie where it was snowing. There I stayed the night with a nurse whose bungalow was perched on such a steep hill that the balcony frightened me. In the morning we went to a long hall where monks were sitting on the floor with their narrow Tibetan books propped up before them. They were all reading aloud from different scriptures; they could concentrate as they heard only themselves read – it was like the hum of a beehive. There were a number of young monks who were receiving special training so that they could get medical qualifications in India. Their power of concentration allowed them to pick up English very quickly as I found out when a number came to the Buddhist Society summer school in England.

Down from the cool of the hills to visit the Gandhian headquarters at Benares, now Varanasi. They wanted to know why I had come and it gave me a chance to talk about the way Oxfam helped indigenous agencies. Later, during the Bihar famine, this co-operation worked well and made a valuable contribution to cross-cultural understanding. Of course I also talked about family planning but that was not so acceptable; they were all men. We went by boat to the burning ghats where people came to die, knowing their ashes would be scattered in the sacred Ganga. Indians don't want you to see only their poverty, they like you to enjoy their culture and treasures. I was taken by a swami by rickshaw to Sarnath where Buddha preached his first sermon after his enlightenment at Bodh Gaya under the Bo tree. My account of this visit is in Chapter Nine.

The next day I was to be taken to the local prison where so many Gandhians had been guests of Her Imperial Majesty. I was very disappointed when this visit was cancelled as it was the feast of Holi when people squirt each other with dye. As this is a time of great excitement it's best to lie low. The Gandhians put on their oldest clothes and had a merry time on the compound showering each other with colours.

My journey by train to Delhi was in the company of a Gandhian, with two soldiers in the compartment. The train had a dining car and the soldiers asked us to mind their guns while they went for a meal. It seemed a bit droll as we were pacifists. In Delhi I stayed at the Quaker Centre but did not feel at home there. This Quaker Embassy was in the charge of an American Quaker and his wife, who made little effort to meet Gandhians and tended to give the impression that Indians were not people they liked. We were served at dinner in a very formal way that I had not met in India before. I spent the next couple of days looking at a hospital and its family planning programme, and visiting the Red Fort and Qutub Minar and some of the very fine government buildings built during the British Raj.

I was leaving the next day, so I took the last opportunity to visit the Taj Mahal and see it by moonlight. I got the train to Agra then a rickshaw to take me to the Taj. When I arrived they were closing the gates as it was only open in the evenings three days before and three after the full moon. My rickshaw driver, bless him, told how I had travelled thousands of miles just to see the Taj; he touched the doorkeeper's heart – not with money, just his pleading, and I was allowed in. There were still some visitors looking round. I was enchanted by it, more than I had ever expected, but soon we were all ushered out by a side door. In the meantime many more car-loads of people had arrived and found the gates shut, they were making such a noise that finally the gates were opened to prevent a riot, so I had another look round. It was only on a later visit that I saw the beautiful intricate details of the inlaid marble of the tombs of Shah Jahan and his wife. The love of Shah Jahan for his wife and the skill of the architect have produced a jewel of delicate white towers like minarets, surrounding a dome which glows in the moonlight and casts a fragile beauty behind the lake bordered by cypresses. I must have been nearly the last to leave, and then I began to wonder how I was to get back to the station – all the cars and visitors had gone. I looked round desperately, then from the shadow emerged my friend the rickshaw driver. I greeted him enthusiastically. Luckily in the excitement of getting into the Taj I had forgotten to pay him. Back at the station the train was not due for an hour or so, with the result that I joined all the other Indians lying asleep on the platform. Even that becomes comfortable when you are very tired. The cultural divide was growing thinner.

The next day I took my luggage and went to have a meal with a friend before going to the airport. The plane, a Quantas, came from Australia and was delayed by 18 hours. so I went back to my friend's and slept on her floor. It was dark when I returned to the airport so my friend got me a reliable taxi driver whom she used, so I was grateful.

I broke my homeward journey in Teheran. It was a pleasure to be met by an Oxfam organiser who had booked me into a hotel where the dining room on the top floor gave a panoramic view of snow-capped mountains. After all my wandering on my own it was such a welcome change for someone to look after me, so that I did not have to be making all the transport arrangements – someone to lean on. David Mitchnick was a lively young man who took me to the area in the north of the country where there had recently been a bad earthquake. Rebuilding was taking place but without consideration of the needs and customs of the people. A Muslim family needs separate quarters for the women and a fenced area round the house so the goats, sheep and any other animals can be brought in at night and none of this was provided, so there were problems – not caused by Oxfam.

We went to a village where David had discussions: the room was small and the large table allowed us to sit around it on the floor with our backs resting against the wall. A large rug was thrown over the table which was big enough to tuck round our waists so that the brazier under the table kept us warm. A good idea which I used when I came home, without sitting on the floor. The talks were long and we drank several cups of hot coffee and after some time I needed to go to the toilet. I went outside to see the women, who were of course not present at the discussions, but forgot to ask David for the word for 'toilet' before I went. I found this difficult to mime but at last they understood and I was taken to a semi-underground place. In fact much of their dwellings seemed to be underground which I suppose is warmer in a cold mountainous area. The communal bath was down a tunnel and at the end was a very large bath of steaming water enough for three or four people to get in at once. The water was kept hot, by which means I do not know, and had a cover over it to keep in the heat when not in use. Probably a smouldering wood fire was underneath. They bake the thin, flat bread in a large hole with smooth sides, the hole had a fire in it until the correct heat was obtained and then the flat bread was slowly pressed round the sides once by which time it was cooked.

The melting snow from the snow-covered mountains is fed into underground canals called quanats. Pits are dug at intervals which connect with underground tunnels between villages whose responsibility it is to dig and maintain the tunnels. The pit is also used as a well, where fresh cool clear water can be obtained and where there is little loss by evaporation during the long hot summer. The skill of a 'primitive' people in meeting their basic needs in a simple way, but one requiring much heavy labour, without the use of modern machinery, excites my admiration – and humility. I am the primitive one. It is I who am dependent upon machines and knobs for my basic needs, and my skill is nil if any of them go wrong.

A farm we used to stay at during the war had a large oven which was heated by burning wood, the wood was cleared out when the right amount of heat was sensed by the farmer's wife and wonderful bread and sponge cakes cooked in the retained heat. I could never make such lovely light sponges with all my modern equipment.

As I mentioned before, I spent one night with an Iranian family whose son was at the Polytechnic. This gave me the chance to see how the 'natives' lived. On one occasion four representatives of the main newspapers of India who were visiting Leeds were brought by the British Consul to visit my house to see the 'natives'. I wished Johnny hadn't chosen that day to spread sewage from the local sewage works over the front gardens. I expect they felt they were enjoying 'native culture'.

As it was my last day before returning home I would have liked a trip to Shiraz. David advised Isfahan as it was much nearer and had more than just the ruins of Persepolis to visit. I agreed and we flew there: it exceeded all my expectations. The domes and portals with designs in jade and blue, purple, cobalt and white – a range of colours that are close to my heart. There were madrassa and mosques, all had cool courtyards and pools so that the Faithful could perform the ritual washing before entering. The old bridge across the wide river had a little sitting-out area where the local citizens could cool themselves in the spray and fresh air from the river. It was all so beautiful and practical. Besides this there were so many crafts to be seen – the making of rugs, the fine paintings and inlay work, the pottery – a feast of craft work. I know of no more beautiful place, but it is seldom mentioned as a holiday venue, for which I suppose one should be thankful. Tourism tends to devalue rather than enhance and one of the results of the harsh regime in Iran has been to keep foreigners away, so perhaps this place is still unspoiled.

There was a large caravanserai at Isfahan where animals were bedded down on the ground floor while the camel drivers slept in the cubicles on the balconies above. This building was being converted into a hotel using all the skills that express local culture. I would like to have stayed there when it was completed – I can't believe it would have been nothing more than another Hilton. Isfahan was rich in experience of things I love and I enjoyed having a companion who also appreciated them.

Flying home, the plane arrived much earlier than expected so there was a pile of washing up waiting at home to start on. Hugh was at a council meeting and had expected to be home in time to have a clear up before I arrived. Washing up is a pleasant, homely and useful job to start on. He had not really liked my going, but people had taken pity on him, invited him out to meals and been so helpful that he overcame some of his shyness and gained more confidence.

The people of compassion that I had met, their dedication and integrity, the beauty of India as well as its appalling poverty and richness, the information that I brought back for the Huddersfield Famine Relief Committee and to put before the Oxfam Asia grants committee made the trip valuable. Curiously enough I had not caught any Asian germs that besiege one – that was to come on a later visit. The three months was a great enrichment and a treasure house to remember in old age.

Chapter Three

My Second Visit to India
October 1971 to February 1972
The Years Between

WHEN I FIRST went to India in 1966 it required me to hand over many of my responsibilities on the Huddersfield Famine Relief Committee. As organising secretary I ran the flag day and house to house collections, which meant handling five hundred collecting tins, permits, flags, etc., organising the Christmas Appeal, which I usually wrote and the Mayor signed. I had started a gift shop, rent free, in the Market Place, so the rota of helpers had to be arranged, gift appeals and house to house collections of gifts organised, and of course the usual secretarial work, writing to agencies and so on. It was a full time job. It was a relief for me, and better for the committee, when five members took over these jobs.

When I returned from India after my first visit my time was taken up with family affairs, Famine Relief and Oxfam committees, speaking at meetings and showing slides of the projects I had visited. There were also useful visits to be arranged for an Indian woman staying with us – a teacher and social worker – so that she could profit from her time in Huddersfield. She stayed an extra month teaching Asian children, which was useful experience of working in an English infants' school and earned some money to take presents back for her family. The upshot of this was that there was nobody to take over her class when she left. So I agreed to teach three days a week and an Indian teacher did two and a half days. This was a challenging experience which I enjoyed very much, and it financed my next trip to India. You wouldn't think I had 'free time' but it was freer than it had been. The children were growing up and leaving home.

In 1965 the Mayor called an inaugural meeting for International Co-operation Year (ICY) which naturally I attended. At the end he asked if someone would call the next meeting to arrange officers, discuss activities and set up sub-committees, saying the Town Hall would send out notices. No one seemed anxious to take it on so I said I would call the first meeting as a goodwill gesture. As a result I became the vice-chairman – the Mayor was chairman, but was usually too busy to attend. We appointed a secretary – a poor choice – but most of the work was done by the three sub-committees: education, social events and inter-faith, so it wasn't the disaster it might have been. I began to learn about the many problems that rural people from poor villages in India and Pakistan have to face in a sophisticated alien culture. Somehow it seemed inadequate to care for Asians in Asia and not be concerned about people on your own doorstep.

Representatives from different faiths, Hindus, Muslims, Buddhists, Sikhs, West Indians and a few open minded Christians, met at our house and discussed a suitable theme for an inter-faith gathering. One suggestion was the theme of 'Seeking the Light' but the West Indians said they already had the Light, so we called it simply 'The Light' after a Sikh moved in to ease feeling amongst the diverse Christian groups. At the next meeting we came with suitable readings from our Holy Books and planned the best way of presenting them. Often the West Indians sang and the Sikhs brought their musicians from the Gudwara and gave interpretations of their song.

As an active member of the Inter Faith group I organised some events and one year I invited school children who played the classical guitar to come and play and help with the singing of such songs as 'When I needed a neighbour were you there?' It was a period of popular youth songs which carried a caring social message suitable for an inter-faith occasion. I found a 'sermon' difficult when so many did not speak English easily. On one occasion I solved this beautifully. The theme was 'Unity in Diversity'. A nearby senior school taught creative dance and the teacher in charge was delighted to be asked to interpret the theme. There was an older group and a younger one, all wearing skirts over their leotards, so as not to offend an Asian sense of decorum. They all came in dancing to 'A Pavane for a Dead Infanta'. Gradually the music became more strident, anger and aggression took over and caused devastation. Then in ones and twos the children from each group emerged and started to play with each other. The pavane music returned and the adults slowly joined in with their offspring in a dance of joyful reunion. It was most moving.

When our International Women's Society presented the story of Rama and Sita at the Town Hall for Diwali, this very gifted teacher also arranged the dances for the animals – mostly monkeys – and villagers. A classical Indian dancer coached the principal dancers. It was not easy arranging rehearsals but the results were enjoyed by a large audience who at that time knew little about Indian festivals.

It is interesting that I received very little support from my Quaker Meeting for inter-faith activities. At the last service I organised I asked the Quaker Meeting if members would make tea at the end of the gathering. This they did, and stayed in the kitchen the whole time. It was good of them to make tea, but they missed so much. The change in attitude now, some thirty years later, towards 'seeking the light where ever it may be found' is heart warming. My interest in living a long time is seeing change, sometimes for what one believes to be better and alas, sometimes not.

The education sub-committee of ICY was supported by the Polytechnic and the schools. We organised a Sixth Form conference towards the end of the summer term and a Youth Forum during the Christmas holidays for Senior Schools. These continued for a number of years. During ICY we invited Frank Judd MP, later to become Director General of Oxfam, to speak about his experiences of community development in Sheffield. We also invited some immigrants and the Community Relations Officer to attend. Out of this forum the Home Tutor scheme was established, where girls and a few boys, supported by their schools, visited an Asian family once a week to help with spoken English and be helpful friends to the family. The Sixth Form colleges took it up as part of their Community Service at a time when this was popular. After a few years the schools gradually withdrew but older women came and offered their services. A very dedicated woman, Miss Walton, took over. She was retired and had lived in India. She organised groups in different parts of the town and started meetings for tutors in teaching English as a second language. The Christmas parties for Asian ladies were very popular. They loved doing the Hokey Kokey and always beat us at musical chairs as they ran bare-footed.

We had about one hundred and twenty girls and women acting as home tutors visiting weekly for about five years, and all this was done voluntarily. Finally we handed over to the local authority who made it part of their further education programme. I am sure that so much visiting of Asian families and the friendships formed helped to break down the barriers between the newcomers and the host community and built up a feeling of mutual respect.

Many of these activities started in ICY opened up new opportunities and needs. The government, becoming aware of the great influx of people of a different culture, offered financial help to towns to set up a Liaison Committee. The Huddersfield Council was luke warm about this, but, with the support of our MP, J.P.W. Mallalieu, and financial help, a Community Relations Committee was set up, consisting of representatives of ethnic groups, churches and other town organisations. Mrs Kulvietus was appointed Community Relations Officer and did an outstanding job. I wish I could say the same for those who followed. The Home Tutor scheme and the International Women's Society came under this umbrella. For non-English speaking people, and particularly for Asian women, the advice centre became very valuable.

In 1968 there was deep feeling against the American War in Vietnam and protests were held, which I joined, outside the American Embassy in London. A peace group planned to go to Cambodia and Hanoi to show solidarity and offer help. I thought about this but turned it down as impractical. However as time drew near the group was short in numbers so I offered to go and, as a seasoned Polaris protester with some prison experience I was accepted. We were to leave in three weeks' time, just after Christmas, with a training weekend to fit in. Christmas is busy at an infants' school, with a Nativity play, each child to make a party hat and present and card to take home. It's lovely but hectic. At home there was much to prepare with four 'children' coming home. I also have a bad habit of buying presents for Christmas, putting them away 'safely' and then not being able to find them. I handed in my notice at school and did my best.

The extraordinary thing was that I suppose somehow I had got my priorities right and things went off more smoothly than any Christmas before or since. I wish I could recapture whatever the ingredient was that smoothed the way! The teacher who took over my job did not want to continue, so I took it up again when I returned. My visit to Cambodia is described in the chapters on 'Encounters on the Way' and 'Vietnam'. I returned home and to school, enriched by the experience.

The second visit to India was interwoven with Oxfam and Famine Relief visits and Community Relations contacts here. A Sikh friend arranged for me to stay in Amritsar with the cricketer Bisham Bedi Singh, and to stay in Chandigarh. The secretary of our International Women's Society invited me to stay with her sister in Ludhiana. I visited the Sikh Gudwara in Huddersfield one Sunday morning to ask for their help in the Bihar famine, where Oxfam was working with Gandhians. I was amazed by their generosity and I became friendly with a number of them. When the new Gudwara was built some years later I was asked to speak at the opening ceremony ... they meant to show their tolerant attitude to women, but they would have found it difficult to invite one of their own women to speak. A number of Pakistani immigrants in Huddersfield come from Lyallpur near Lahore, which I arranged to visit. If I flew to Karachi I could get a BOAC ticket that lasted four months, allowing me three months in India and one month in East and West Pakistan. My plans were delayed as there was a postal strike in India. The amount of planning and writing was tremendous. It involved finding out exactly where projects were, often in the country miles from a railway station ... so delay seemed best. However war between India and Pakistan broke out while I was on my delayed visit so I missed Lahore, Mohenjodaro and the remains of the Indus civilisation.

Hugh found Christmas rather exhausting and the family were beginning to want to do their own thing, so when I was invited as part of my next visit to India to spend Christmas with a friend in the Nilgiri hills in South India, I accepted. Oddly enough all the family came home for Christmas as they thought Dad would be lonely, and they have all come home for Christmas ever since, then go off for New Year.

I flew to Karachi and had to spend the night there at a delightful guest house near the airport; it was reserved for flight personnel and had a lovely swimming pool. I phoned a contact in Karachi and he took me to visit his clinic and then to a beautiful garden restaurant for refreshments with his family.

The next morning I flew to Delhi and went to Quaker House where the Lintons were in charge. They were appreciative of Indians and their culture. They took me to a large park where the Ramillilla – the story of Rama and Sita – was being performed. There was a great stage; the colour, dancing, music and warm scented evening made it a magical occasion. From Delhi I visited a number of village clinics and crèches enabling mothers to go out to work in the fields. I saw young volunteers working during holidays in villages and sleeping in huge coloured tents called chaminades.

There is a simple beauty about many of the village homes that I visited with an Indian social worker. There is often a courtyard where animals are brought in at night and a pump. The family live above with a balcony looking over the courtyard. The air is kept cool by hanging rattan mats from apertures and splashing water over them; the air cools as the water evaporates. So many old systems are cheap and effective.

From Delhi I took the train to Chandigarh to stay with the mother of a Sikh friend. This modern town was designed by Le Corbusier and looks like concrete blocks with lace work concrete verandahs. It has five subsidiary towns, situated around magnificent public buildings which keep a dusty distance from their satellites. Each small town has its shops and facilities, and each is designed for different income groups. However, as the rich need servants this is a problem, and if the rich find expenses too heavy, they rent out their garages as living accommodation. I disliked the place, it seemed to have no heart.

From here we went to see the huge Gudwara of Amulpursahib with its wonderful backdrop of the Himalayas. The quiet beauty of its white walls, balconies and turrets, gave one a feeling of awe and reverence. Many Sikhs came to listen to the chanting of Guru Granth Sahib which was placed under a canopy in the centre of the Gudwara. As Sikhs have broken with the caste system of the Hindus, everyone was expected to share a simple meal communally. It was a lovely day.

The bus to Ludhiana was crowded, hot and dusty, so at a stop where I saw fresh oranges being crushed I stopped for a drink. It was delicious but I should have known better and used my own mug.

At Ludhiana I stayed in a pleasant, cool house with a courtyard. The next day I went to visit the Rajan Memorial eye hospital. The newly qualified doctor, son of the chief of the general hospital, had died, and so his father had started this eye hospital in his memory. Eye camps were held in the villages and a number of doctors gave one day a week. Dr Om Parkash came from Amritsar two days a week to do the operations. I was tremendously impressed with the enormous crowd being dealt with and the amount of voluntary work being done. I spent the day in the hospital and was taken to a restaurant for a meal. Naturally I offered to pay, but this was refused as the proprietor felt he was making a contribution to the hospital by this service.

On my return to England the Famine Relief Committee bought ophthalmic equipment that was not available in India and sent it out. This sounds easy but there are so many restrictions – the receiving charity must be registered for receiving foreign equipment, the customs rate is very high and the rules are always changing. For example we were asked to send ten wheelchairs of different sizes for children to the Association for the Physically Handicapped in Bangalore. I got them at a very reasonable price from the Joint Hospitals Mission Board which acquires redundant equipment from hospitals. As there are now very few direct sailings from England to Madras we were delayed for six months or more. Though the Indian charity was registered to receive gifts the rules were changed – each individual child had to register. This was impossible and in any case, the chairs were to belong to the Association so the chairs could be changed as the children grew. The customs demand was exorbitant and our attempts to deal with the matter delayed it by more than another six months. I know Indians have a tender heart if one gets to the top people. Our secretary wrote a letter to Mrs Gandhi telling her of the problem, and of how the children here had helped to collect money ... at a magic word the chairs were released without paying customs, and I saw them in action a year or so later. It had been an exhausting business for everybody. You can see why after two or three dispatches of equipment to the eye hospital, we suggested that they apply to Oxfam for their needs.

One afternoon five Indian ladies came to the house where I was staying. We sat on the floor and they sang bajans – holy songs – and read from their scriptures. It was a holy day, which one I cannot remember. It was restful and enjoyable after all my travel. My tummy was giving me trouble and the toilet – cleaned out by a daily sweeper – was on the roof. To get there one had to climb two flights of uneven stone steps built into the side of the inner courtyard with a frail looking handrail. I dragged myself to the top, reached the toilet and fainted, twisting my ankle. It was really awful as my tummy troubles grew worse. Luckily Dr Om Parkash had asked me to visit him when I went to Amritsar. I asked someone to send him a telegram to say I was coming, got a rickshaw and went to the station. I travelled first class where the air conditioning was freezing. When I reached Amritsar there was no one to meet me and I collapsed on the nearest bench in misery for what seemed like hours. At last I heard a voice I knew – I had forgotten to put the time of the train in the telegram. Knowing what I did later I ought to have been more thankful that the telegram reached Amritsar so quickly – sometimes telegrams got to my destination as much as two days after I arrived. To be taken home and put to bed with towels around me and an adjacent toilet was bliss ... and a doctor to look after me too. I was a stranger and they took me in and I bow to that of God in this family. Hindus too have the same attitude to strangers. As my troubles improved I was taken to the hospital to check that my ankle was not badly damaged and the next evening taken out in a car to see the great sight of Amritsar when the Golden Temple was lit up for Diwali. The illuminations all over the town were magnificent, but closer to my heart are the small clay lamps people put along their verandahs in all the little villages – they are more moving than all the electric wonders.

It was agreed that I should stay with the doctor rather than move to the Bisham Singh household, but I went there for lunch and met the family. Then I was taken on the back of the cricketer's motor bike to the Golden Temple and he showed me round. Guru Nanak, the first Sikh guru, was reverenced as a Holy man by the Muslims and Hindus. He travelled through India as far as Assam, Ceylon, Tibet and Mecca, travelling with Mardana (a Muslim) singing hymns and preaching or perhaps it should be teaching. The land on which the Gudwara was built was given by one of the Moghul rulers of Northern India. Shoes are left at the entrance as one walks on to a tiled pavement, kept spotlessly clean by voluntary work of the faithful. The large blue lake is the setting for the inner shrine, the Golden Temple itself, where under a rich canopy, the Guru Granth Sahib lies. There reading and chanting of the Holy Scriptures takes place, attended by a reverent crowd. It is customary to wash in the lake before entering the Holy Place – the women have a private area for their ablutions. There are some enormous kitchens where Sikh women show their devotion by cooking meals, so that all comers partake of food in a casteless community.

Unfortunately hippies found they could make a prolonged stay, so now it is restricted to three days maximum. One feels ashamed that this should be necessary. It is also sad that the Sikhs, who started out as a pacifist society, were decimated and had to take to arms to preserve themselves. The Khalsa formed by Guru Gobind Singh used the Gudwara as an arsenal during the struggle to establish a Sikh state. This meant that Mrs Gandhi had a difficult choice to make – storm the temple or lay siege and starve the defenders out. Would the latter have been any better?

From Amritsar I went by bus to Batala where a Quaker was teaching linguistics at the University. Joan Humby had been the principal at a women's college in Australia, but was urged by another Quaker, Ranjit Chetsingh, to come and help establish Baring College. Feeling she was ready for a change, she took up the challenge. It was fun talking to her students and a good opportunity for them to hear English spoken and practise their own English. The college buildings were magnificent, especially the library, it just lacked books. I found it a remarkable achievement for Joan to have put on two plays, *A Midsummer Night's Dream* and *The Prodigal Son*, involving not only the students but other workers on the campus including gardeners, builders, etc. In a caste-ridden society it is wonderful to involve a community in this way.

The journey back to Ludhiana was very slow as the roads were clogged up with army vehicles going west. I wondered why. I had been invited to spend a night in what turned out to be a newly developed area with only a few partly-made roads and higgledy-piggledy buildings, so we wandered about in the dark and I felt sorry for the driver from the hospital who had offered to take me. I was relieved at last to be given a bare room with just a bed in it. It was a very primitive setup and I couldn't imagine why they were so pressing for me to come. I was glad to return to Ludhiana town the next day where a brother of the family was anxious to take me visiting. After all, I wanted to see life as lived by Indians, and know something of their culture. I was taken on the back of his motor bike to what, by my standards, was a very slummy area and introduced to the family. As they could not speak any English and after a time sign language began to pall, I asked for the man who had brought me, but he was not to be found. Local people came crowding into the room and filled up the doorway so I supposed they had come to look at me, as I had come to see them. It was fair enough, but I felt like a non-performing monkey at a zoo, very disappointing. It was getting late and I was tired and wanted to go back to base. At last my 'guide' returned and I was told we were staying there for the night. I felt this was too much and said I should start out walking straight away. I had the address but I know I should have had a very difficult job to return as there was a black out. My bluff worked I am thankful to say. I wondered why I had been taken and dumped and decided that having a white person visiting your house was a status symbol – one role I would have preferred not to play. I now have a particularly tender spot for monkeys at the zoo.

I was glad to get on a train – it actually travelled nearly two thousand miles to Calcutta, but I got off at Patna. Bunks were let down at night and could be booked in advance. Meals were good and inexpensive and it gave my ankle a good rest. At Patna I visited another of the great Sikh Gudwaras and then flew to Kathmandu in Nepal, where I spent a few nights at the Garden Hotel. There is so much to see in Kathmandu and the neighbouring towns of Patan and Badghaon besides the hospitals and clinics. There were so many temples, Buddhist and Hindu; the temple of Swyanbu had its resident monkeys, ancient royal palaces with magnificent carving, burning ghats by the rivers, acrobats and the Living Goddess (a young girl who is chosen for cloistered seclusion except for feast day processions).

The old palaces did not have glass in the windows, but light filtered through finely carved lattice. Alas the wood of the lattices is rotting away; UNESCO has tried to help but the fine craft work is very expensive when such an enormous amount needs to be done.

A Quaker nurse, Ilfra Loveday, working for WHO, invited me to go out visiting the clinics and small hospitals which filled a great need in the land. She had been working at establishing clinics in the villages, setting standards for hygiene and training nurses in modern skills. The rice harvest was spread out to dry on the flat surfaces available, that is, the roads. Cars and carts passed over it pushing and wafting it here and there. The terracing of the hills was beautiful. Each terrace must have been about three feet wide, climbing up the steep hillsides. The amount of work to construct these terraces must have been enormous, but imperative as there is so little flat land.

One morning before it was light, I got a taxi up to a vantage point to see the sun rise; it was impressive, but not so much as I had expected. The sunrise I struggled up a holy mountain to see in China was more colourful, but having breakfast on the roof of Ilfra's flat with the white peaks of the Himalayas looking down on us I found a wonderful experience.

I flew from Kathmandu to Britnagar where a British and Nepalese team were running a hospital and a few outlying clinics. As we flew the sun shone directly on range after range of snowy peaks. It was breathtaking, an experience to be treasured. I have no urge to get more familiar with the mountain tops as I am not a climber and dislike heights.

I stayed with the British team of medical workers; having seen the hospital it was decided to take me to stay at one of their distant clinics. I was taken by jeep to the beginning of a steep and rocky path and wondered if my ankle would stand it – it was worth trying. It was a very busy path with little, very primitive, tea houses every mile or so. Goods were being carried into the interior and sturdy young men were carrying ill people to hospital. Apparently this is a well paid job but the strain on the heart of the porters means they have to retire very early. The views and the trees were impressive in their variety. I struggled but walked slower and slower and when we came to the first summit I could see the clinic – a little white dot about a thousand feet down and the five hundred feet up again – there was no way I could get there before nightfall, and back next day. It was disappointing. We enjoyed the view and then started walking back down; coming down from the ridge was worse than going up and it jerks the feet, so stopping between each step I very thankfully got down to the jeep. It was bliss to be able to sit down and relax. I am sure I would have done the trek quite comfortably if I hadn't twisted my ankle. At least I had the satisfaction of trying and seeing some wonderful scenery and people passing on the track.

I returned to Kathmandu but this time the sun was not shining on the peaks. My last expedition was by car up the road the Chinese were constructing to the frontier with Tibet. One was not even allowed to take a picture of the ceremonial gate at the border. The road the Chinese were making often ran up a very steep ravine where frequent landslides blocked the road and gangs of workmen were employed continuously in clearing these away. The Chinese finance the road by sending cargoes of bicycles, sewing machines and other manufactured goods into Nepal. This not only helps their export trade but also provides a news link about conditions in border areas at a time when Indo-Chinese relations were strained. It was a well thought out plan. In the primitive villages we passed through, many children were playing with kites and at a number of places nearer the border there were hot springs where people enjoyed the hot baths.

From Kathmandu I flew back to Patna, travelled to the area of Bihar where there had been a famine the year before and stayed at a Gandhian ashram at Sokodora. In this area Vinobe Bhave, a follower of Gandhi, had travelled widely, asking the landed farmers to give land to landless peasants and to establish self-help Gandhian communities. He was supported by the ashram where I was staying. Bhave met with a good response but naturally, it was the poorest land that was given. After emergency feeding and 'food for work' programmes, Oxfam worked with the Gandhians providing agriculturists and water engineers and equipment. It is not easy to get two different cultures to work together smoothly but this had been a great success. By the time I visited the Oxfam workers had left, having constructed the wells and pumps. They had 'bunded' the land, that is, made shallow terraces so that water flowing from the highest bund would naturally flow, irrigating the lower bunds. The peasants were very proud of the 'food for work' efforts which now resulted in a good grain harvest. It was a joy to see their pride ... there was no civil war in this area as there is in Somalia and the Sudan to obliterate all progress. We went to visit some tribal people in the area. I admired the skill with which they made roof tiles and pots using a bicycle wheel as a potter's wheel, giving it a turn with a stick to keep up the momentum – all so skilfully done. I think people in this country have forgotten so many skills as everything is bought ready made. We shall soon be a people of a few machine-makers and the rest will learn only to press knobs and play computer games. There is a loss of pride as each individual has had no creative joy in simple tasks such as making a cake or designing a dress for a child out of a remnant.

As fate would have it, the area of drought had had very heavy rain while I was there, so the jeep we were travelling in got stuck in the mud. A great deal of manpower was needed to extricate it. The tribal people show their hospitality by dancing to drums and pipes – it was a most enjoyable occasion as we realised, once the jeep was free of mud.

From Sokodora I went to stay at another ashram at Bodh Gaya. Here the breakfast was cooked by using the methane gas from a biogas plant that was fed with sewage and manure from the farm, which was the first time I had seen a biogas plant working efficiently. We visited a boarding school where young people were trained in agriculture. The children helped with the running of the school, did their own washing and put on a very good display of what might be called sword dancing in England, using sticks. There was also a dance of a snake charmer and circle dances as we see in many village communities the world over.

Bodh Gaya is a major pilgrimage centre for Buddhists as Buddha became 'enlightened' after some forty days of contemplation under a Bo tree here, which is still alive. He had practised much fasting and austerities before this. There is a main temple by the Bo tree where worshipers measure their length on the ground for some distance before they enter the shrine where a golden Buddha is displayed. There is also a Tibetan and a Thai temple and many other Buddhist temples, each with a guest house. There were also a number of young white men and women, wearing Indian dress and identifying with the reverent atmosphere of the place. I always found it easier to wear a sari, it was cooler and one could sit cross legged without any indecent exposure and was no hindrance as one never runs in India. I did not only see 'projects' and poverty; there was such a rich culture which Indians were anxious to share with me, and ordinary people were so kind and helpful to an elderly woman travelling on her own. If I had had a companion they would probably have been too shy to make contact.

During these travels war had broken out between East and West Pakistan, and thousands of Bengalis who were Hindu had moved across the border into India. Oxfam had set up an office in Calcutta and was not only supplying food to the many huge camps on the border but also was responsible for transporting doctors and nurses who volunteered to go out from Calcutta for short periods to help in the camps. Oxfam workers took me with them to visit some of the camps. A woman arrived at one camp, a walking cadaver with a small child, but it was full and she was told she must go on to the next camp ... shattering news to one in her condition. However, other camp people had heard of this, so they went to the camp authorities and begged that she be allowed to stay, saying they would share their rations with her and the child. She stayed. People who have suffered so much can appreciate the plight of others. There is a great generosity in many Indians and in the Indian government that fed two million refugees for nearly two years. The rest of the world helped, especially in additional medical facilities, but the total of that help would not have kept the refugees for more than a couple of months.

Oxfam booked me into an old Raj hotel in Calcutta. It provided me with a very large room with a European bath, something I had not experienced before in India. I don't think there was any hot water in the tap, and cold water did not run freely. As usual there was no plug, as Indians only bathe in running water, pouring it over their heads as they sing praises to their particular aspect of God. I moved to the guest house of the Ramakrishna Mission where Indian sanitary arrangements were more satisfactory and I met friends made on my previous visit.

The Ramakrishna Mission was active in another of those huge camps and some of their workers offered to take me out with them. A German woman doctor staying at their rural centre ten miles away heard about this and asked to come too. We were delayed by going out to fetch her and then she moaned all the way to the camp that she had not had time for breakfast, so she was taken and given a good meal on arrival. I was furious, and when invited to join the meal said I had come to see the camp. not to eat. The conditions were indescribable as the water level was so high that channels for dirty water had overflowed. There were some latrines made of poles and canvas, but the excrement spread for twenty or thirty yards round the latrines. Long queues were waiting for rations which the refugees took back to their small family space in long five foot high shelters covered with thick tarpaulin, the ground space little above mud level. As the German doctor was leaving that day, we had to cut short our visit at both ends which did not endear her to me. In retrospect, I saw that my anger was a blessing in disguise.

I visited Mother Theresa's home for the dying near the Kali temple, and a number of projects where Oxfam was helping. A hurricane had recently swept the coast of Orissa. With the Oxfam representative I was able to fly over the mounds of mud that had been villages – a huge area of devastation. We then took the jeep inland to see the temporary shelter for the villagers. The Indian government was sending in food, but shortage of transport slowed up the distribution. I can see now the rows of children sitting on the ground with a large leaf in front of them on which was placed some rice or chappatti and dahl. They ate with the right hand only, the left being reserved for toilet purposes. At the end of the meal there is no washing up, as the leaves are collected and given as fodder to the cattle ... basic simplicity and economy that appeals to me.

The Coromandel express took me overnight and with a bit more time to Madras. I was met by one of the lecturers from Holly Bank College in Huddersfield who were helping with the development of the Technical College on the outskirts of Madras. At that time my husband was chairman of the Huddersfield Education Committee and we went often to Holly Bank functions. A number of foreign students went there for Technical College training, hence the connection. The Principal of Holly Bank at that time, named Mr McKenna, was a very forceful character, an extremely able man with a deep sense of international responsibility and a commanding voice. Imagine my amazement when I met the Principal of the Indian college who spoke using the same phrases and dynamism as the one we called 'Mack'. There were placards up in the college proclaiming ' NOTHING IS IMPOSSIBLE; IT ONLY TAKES LONGER'. This man became an authority on technical colleges in India and went far. The college had pleasant buildings of clean white cement recently whitewashed and grassy courtyards, but after the monsoon algae begins to cover the cement walls, so they need a lot of maintenance. I stayed at a very pleasant private home in an upmarket part of the city. The rains had just ended and pools abounded, filled to capacity with very noisy frogs or toads – I couldn't believe they could make such a din. It amazed me that some of the lecturers in the college met once a week to do Scottish dancing. I enjoy Scottish reels but I thought the idea behind the dance was to keep warm and work off surplus energy. That was hardly necessary in the steamy heat of Madras, but I suppose one aches for one's culture when in foreign parts.

The Raj still lingers in Madras with its fine shopping centres and its churches and government buildings left from when it was the first trading port, before the British moved to Calcutta and later to Delhi. I visited a number of crèches and small schools in the slums where the children were given a midday meal. There were many very unstable houses made of wood, thatch and old tins built along the side of the sea road to the north of the city. There was no sanitation or fresh water for these fragile beach homes. One project I visited was training young men to become fabric printers. The skill already existed, using intricately designed wooden blocks which are carefully stamped on the cloth by hand, but to supply the tourist market, dyes need to be stable, and the garments suited to Western taste. This became a well run, self-supporting project with a high standard of workmanship. The government emporia in Madras, Mysore, Bangalore and Delhi sold fine quality regional artefacts – wood carvings, mirror embroidery, hand-printed bedspreads and wall hangings. I bought two bedspreads just to hang on the walls at home. Alas the colours faded. The carved elephants made you want to handle them. They must now be mass produced, but in spite of the howdah on their backs they are rough, splintery and unfinished, untouched by craftsman's hands. The handprinted bedspreads have now disappeared – later I found in the Mysore emporium that the bedspreads were made in nylon with an edging of roses! This loss of a craftsman's pride in his skill grieves me.

The most impressive project I visited in Madras was the Sarva Seva Sangh. Mrs Krishna Rao and her husband had sold their house, rented a smaller one and some buildings vacated by the Ramakrishna Mission. Here they welcomed destitute women and their children, gave them simple work, a mat to sleep on, a sari a year and food for the mother and children. Gradually the more able were trained in such things as tie-dyeing, toy making and the production of educational toys. They could also learn to print letter heads which led on to other printing. Oddly enough the women could not read, but they could copy a script by picking out the appropriate letters from the compositor's bench and fitting them into the printing frame – a method that was used not so long ago in this country. A crèche was started for the children which provided a testing ground for the educational toys. Another fee paying school developed from this which helped to finance other work. When I first visited, a piece of ground on the outskirts of Madras had been bought, a hostel built with the help of Oxfam, and two lathes established. Light engineering requires manual skills but it is not heavy work. Some girls were taught electronics, others book-keeping – the range grows every year. I have visited here over a number of years, seen girls grow up, become skilled and get married without a dowry – they are people of value in their own right. There are too many cases of brides who fall in the fire because the husband's family demand an additional dowry which cannot be produced by the bride's family – and her own family is never there to see what really happens. Even though the dowry system has been outlawed, it still continues.

I think the most imaginative idea was when the husband of Mrs Krishna Rao set up about forty simple scientific experiments for children. The hostel girls were taught to make the equipment and schools were invited send a class for a morning to be shown how to use the apparatus. One hostel girl would look after five children doing an experiment, then when finished the children would move on to another. At the end of the term another group of experiments were made and set up. This was called a 'Rent a Lab scheme' and the schools paid for the service. On Saturday the staff from the school could go and learn how to make the equipment themselves. To look around the community, find an urgent need and then to develop the skill to meet it, training local unskilled girls to the new skill, without any input of government funding, is an achievement of high order.

I think the best organisers I knew were women. They are comparatively few, but those who have the gift and sensitivity to people's needs are outstanding. A training centre has now been set up in one village, training women in village crafts and agriculture and helping with the marketing. Quite a lot of flowers were being grown, some for market and some because, as Mrs Krishna Rao explained, "Our girls love wearing flowers in their hair." I doubt if a man would have thought of that, but it makes such a difference to girls who have so little.

On Sunday another kindness was shown to me when I was offered the use of the car, the driver and one of the girls to take me and a couple of friends to visit the shore temples and Mahabalipuram and other South Indian gopurams with their intricate carving and huge tanks where the worshippers can bathe before going into the temple. I took a number of photos but was not allowed to photograph an elephant that was giving blessings to the devotees. Perhaps that was extra sacred.

The secretary of the Huddersfield Famine Relief committee at that time was married to an HMI (inspector of schools) who knew another HMI in Leeds who had taken early retirement. This was Victoria Armstrong who had gone to India to become secretary to a Hindu doctor working in the Nilgiri hills in South India. The committee had sent a number of grants to help with the tribal work. I was invited to visit Victoria for Christmas. I took the overnight train from Madras to Coimbatore. There is a little rack railway that provides fantastic views and stops at tiny stations. It goes to Coonoor and then one gets a bus to Kotagiri.

Dr Narasihman ran his own clinic to support his wife and three children and in his free time took an interest in the flora and fauna of the surrounding forest. He found so many little groups of people living in caves and primitive shelters with no health care that he set up three tiny hospitals in very remote places and would try and visit them, taking supplies once a week. The tracks were narrow and often very steep or impassable because of land slips. As it is dark by 6 pm, coming back at night was dangerous and it was often 10 or 11 pm when he returned. The doctor would be up by 6 am the next morning to visit his other patients. Alas he died too young. He also had a Paniyar Farm and clinic eighty miles away over the mountains where later my son John worked for eight years. John and Dr Narasihman got on very well – they had the same quality of dedication and caring.

Victoria had a lovely bungalow with a view across a well wooded valley – and I had a toilet adjoining my bedroom. My ankle had stood up pretty well as I was not doing a lot of walking, my other troubles became active as I moved from one state to another with varying food and water. One needed to take care and have a supply of sulphur quinadines available in case of need. The change from sea level to 6,000 feet needs adjustment too.

We brought in a little evergreen tree and tried to make some decorations. Dr and Mrs Narasihman were invited round but I cannot remember anything else Christmassy. I think it was an effort for the doctor to drag himself away from his many other duties. Five Quakers attended Meeting for Worship outside Marjorie Sykes' bungalow, which was not far from Victoria's house. The silence and the wonderful view of nearby steep wooded slopes and distant mountains was inspiring.

There were still a few old people from the British Raj living in wonderfully situated bungalows on the hillsides; they could afford servants and so were looked after in their declining years. They had lived in India too long to be able to pick up life in England. England had changed so much since they lived there. They could not have afforded servants, nor coped with the weather and the different pace of life.

I left Kotagiri by bus to get the train at Coimbatore. The drop of thousands of feet involves fine views but so many hairpin bends that I did not like to sit near a window. The bus stopped at a little shrine for the driver to get out and pray for guidance before we attempted the steepest section. I hoped that the brakes had been checked over too. Quite often a Holy Man will get on the bus when it stops; each passenger will be given a blessing and a red tikka on the forehead and one puts a donation in his tray. Sometimes the bus also has a garland of marigolds on a hook near the driver's seat, which makes it into a shrine and shows appreciation of the bus. This is an extension of the worship that is also shown to animals that give you service, so that the horns of cows and buffaloes often are painted red and have garlands of marigolds. Christians are shocked that Indians worship cows. 'Worship' has such a weight of holiness about it, but to give worth and respect to people, animals, trees, water and air seems a very proper thing. It is our lack of reverence for all LIFE that leads to the pollution and destruction of the planet.

I had to change trains in Madurai and had an hour and a half to wait, so I took a rickshaw to the famous Meekanashi temple. It is huge. It was about 7 am, cool and fresh and luckily for me, a festival. An avenue of small shops selling children's toys, statues, pictures of the local deities that are manifestations of the One, garlands to adorn the many different shrines one is visiting and coloured powders for making rangoli patterns on the threshold of a house. Sumptuously caparisoned elephants stood watching the crowd. At first I thought they were sculptures, they stood so still. Worshippers stood in lines outside the little shrines, so that when the priest emerged they could pass their hands over the sacred fire and receive its blessing. There was a courtyard with a shrine where marriages took place. I have visited the temple a number of times since and marvelled at it, but I have never again felt that ' first fine careless rapture' of the early morning and joyous devotion.

The train from Madurai took me to Trivandrum on the coast of Kerala, which used to be the kingdom of Travancore. Kerala is said to have a Communist government, but it is a different communism from that of Russia or China. It has the highest literacy rate of all the states in India, 80%, and many of its literate inhabitants find work in other states. Land is very expensive along the coastal strip as it makes excellent rice-paddy, so houses for the less affluent must be small and use odd corners. I went to Trivandrum to visit a Quaker, Laurie Baker, and his wife Kuni. Laurie had been working in Northern India in some kind of relief work and there he met Kuni, a doctor from Kerala. They married and returned to Kuni's state and set up a clinic in a remote hilly region. As the children grew up it became necessary to move into a town for their education. Kuni continued her medical work and Laurie reverted to his original occupation of architect. When I visited them Laurie had built a church, a library on a university campus, a training college, a number of specially designed houses to fit into odd corners of land not wanted for paddy fields and some very small houses on land released by the Church of South India for its adherents.

Laurie had taken much care in studying the indigenous architecture. The modern buildings of cement are like ovens in the sun and often lack courtyards and verandahs which prevents the air from circulating freely. They need white-washing every year after the monsoon as mould forms, making them unsightly. By using brick he could make open work walls to rooms and courtyards, which gave privacy and allowed the hot, humid air to circulate. By using a double layer of tiles for the roof he provided insulation from the mid-day sun. Indian builders said the buildings would fall down, but the design and the skill with which they were constructed proved otherwise. Government, churches and ordinary households sought him out. I remember one not very big church which had half a roof – the roofed part was for use during the monsoon, or when shade was needed. It didn't look odd, just a very pleasant.

practical design and built much more cheaply than a conventional building. Laurie was always talking about his discussions with 'Grace'. His liaison was with HIS Grace, one of the hierarchy of the church. The whole experience of being in this church was so stimulating – its practicality, imagination and beauty – plus the company of a humorous guide. Laurie was the first Englishman that I know to be given Indian nationality since Indian independence. He had an illness soon after and had to be given a blood transfusion, so he says he really is an Indian now.

I was taken to see a lovely little palace of the Raja of Travancore where Laurie got ideas when designing. There was an intimacy about it – a smallish hall where 'audiences' and entertainments took place, and where ladies of the court sat behind a fine screen. As I remember the palace was made of wood but had many little tiled roofs. Carved wood allowed light and air to filter through.

We went as far south as possible to Cape Kumari. There are flat stone platforms looking out to sea. A roof is built over the platform, upheld by great stone pillars – so you can sit there in the shade and look out to sea where so many tides meet. It is dangerous to swim, but I could not resist a dip close inshore. It was so unspoilt. The next time I went I did not enjoy it so much – it had been 'developed'. I am afraid this is what happens to so many unspoilt areas.

A good road runs along the coast that is fringed with coconut palms. As I walked along the road a man kept accosting me with a large sack. I heard Laurie laugh and I looked round. "He's trying to sell you a bag of snakes." I fled. It had been a fascinating time staying with the Bakers, particularly visiting Kuni's leprosy clinic. Laurie introduced me to simple, basic architecture based on the demands of the climate, careful use of expensive land and with a strong link to local traditional ways of building.

You used to be able to travel from Cochin to Trivandrum by canal. It had been my dream to do so. A few years later John and I started from Cochin by boat, but the boat only took us a few miles. We tried in vain to find other boats but there was only one that did the journey by night. If there had been a full moon it might have been worthwhile.

I needed to get some money. It takes ages in a bank, but often you can buy a flight using a traveller's cheque. I booked a flight to Bangalore the next day and offered a traveller's cheque. Yes, they accepted traveller's cheques but not today – a typical answer. Then they said they would book the flight for me as there was a foreign exchange desk at the airport and I could pay there. All seemed well until we found no ticket had been booked and the exchange desk was closed. Laurie, a man of some importance in Trivandrum, asked to see the manager. A crowd gathered hoping to see some fun. At last the manager appeared, saw the crowd and heard Laurie's loud voice and well chosen words. Graciously, as Indians respond when in a tight corner, he delayed the plane and came with us in an airport bus to the nearest bank, where the transaction was done at high speed. Could such a thing have happened in England? I remember having to go into three large banks in Calcutta to change traveller's cheques – the first two said they were too busy, though as I saw it many clerks were sitting at their desks chatting to each other.

The plane was being met at Bangalore by an Oxfam representative who fixed me up at the Woodlands Hotel. The room was spacious, clean and had its own simple Indian bathroom. I think it cost £2 a night and I paid extra for the food I ate in the restaurant.

In Bangalore I visited a school for the mentally handicapped, another for the blind, and a secondary school where a young Quaker volunteer was working. The Indian government was encouraging family planning and giving inducements in money or 'gifts' to encourage people to accept. The Christian Medical hospitals were doing their share and giving good, careful treatment, but that was not always the case in government hospitals and the money given to the patient usually nearly all vanished paying the nurse or ward boy, so family planning got a very bad name in India. The government doctors had a quota of vasectomies to meet and so many young men got caught in the system.

Oxfam was now recruiting Field Directors who were better equipped to deal with and be more sensitive to Indian culture. Dr Staley, based in Bangalore, was one of these and this made a great difference to the quality of work and the relationships formed within the project holders that Oxfam supported. He valued Indian culture and Indians responded to this. He took me to visit the Association for the Physically Handicapped. A young Indian girl, Hema Ienggar, contracted polio when she was about eleven. Her father worked for ICI, so they were not poor but the proper treatment was not available at the time, so she stayed in her wheel chair. Had she been in England it would have been very different. She wanted to do something useful, so a lathe was fitted up in the garage and she had lessons. Then she started teaching other handicapped people. When I first met her she had a training centre in the town. Some crawled to work there with pieces of wood tied to their knees and arms. Simple work obtained from factories was divided up, so that those with a hand or a foot could be integrated into the scheme. The workers were given a mid-day meal and some cash, and where possible some treatment. There was an air of hopefulness and good companionship about the place that was heartwarming. A few years later Hema started a school, teaching in English. Paying pupils helped to pay for those unable to pay. Hema felt that if she could get treatment for the children at an early age, and give them a good education based on small classes, they would later be able to take their place in an English medium school. She now has a social worker who knows the children and visits the schools which these handicapped children attend, so it has been a worthwhile development. These imaginative, capable women always see another goal ahead; they are such a joy to help as you know whatever you give it will be used wisely and give joy to others. Recently Hema, with help, has bought some barren land, sunk a well, and built a small house with a classroom adjoining. A fence had to be built around the land to keep the stray cows and others out. Here some disabled boys are growing vegetables and pot plants and flowers for sale in the local market. They have to learn about the soil, the plant's needs, rotation of crops and keeping accounts. They are now self-supporting and because of this training some boys have got jobs elsewhere. The next time I went to visit Hema she was running a flag day to raise money and I had to take the collecting boxes out for her – something I have done many times in England.

Mysore, thirty or forty miles south of Bangalore, is a smaller town with a palace, lit up on special days, and has many other gracious Indian and Raj buildings of pre-concrete period. In part of a house owned by, but not near the Holdsworth Memorial Hospital, lived Mrs Webb. She had been a planter's wife and ran a clinic for the workers. When her husband died she stayed helping, with money she raised or at her own expense, the Tibetans who were pouring into India. As they became settled she turned her attention to the Indian villagers. She went out in her jeep for three or four days a week visiting the social workers who followed up the work in her weekly clinic in nearby villages. During the clinic one worker would talk to mothers on child care, another organised the making and fitting of boots for leprosy cases, another followed up on the prescribed treatment and handed out the pills. We stayed one night with a tiny Christian community. In the evening people brought in the embroidery they had done, designed by Mrs Webb. I remember a lovely white table cloth with a procession of people and elephants around the edge, guest towels with a girl fetching water from the well. I imported many of these to sell at our gift shop in Huddersfield.

The village was extremely poor. There had been no rain, so the mulberry bushes had no leaves, so there was no food for the silkworms therefore no work or food in the village. The embroidery helped in a desperate situation. One man had sold his son to a farmer thinking he would get fed there. A few weeks later he brought the miserable unfed child to the clinic while I was there. Bond slavery is against the law in India but what can a parent do when a whole village is desperate and there is no one able to help? Mrs Webb bought the boy back, but she thinks the father took him to Mysore to beg. One grieves and feels so helpless.

Mrs Webb was another of the dynamic people I met at Oxfam conferences. She was practical, hardworking, a good organiser and typical of the Raj period, in that she spoke her mind in no uncertain terms to villagers who had not carried out her instructions. The only time I was called 'Memsahib' in India was when I stuck up for an Indian who was being unfairly treated. The official said "Yes, Memsahib" in a most docile way and did what was required. Some officials can be exasperating.

About forty or fifty miles away land had been given for a Tibetan settlement that I was going to visit. I got to the nearest village but the settlement was still some miles away and there was no transport. I sat with my luggage and pondered. I often thought how much easier it would be just to be equipped with a begging bowl. But then of course I needed my passport, my air ticket, a map, a change of clothes, a note book and pen, soap and towel, a present for particular friends – in fact, there was soon a good deal of luggage – which included various tablets to cope with the tummy troubles. Being white is noticeable in these villages and people are very helpful if one is elderly and alone. Presently a lorry driver came up and said he could go that way – blessings on him.

I am tremendously impressed with the courage and humour in the most difficult circumstances of two hundred monks on a barren land, digging wells, building small houses for the elderly in a climate they were not accustomed to and with diseases against which they had no natural immunity – and yet remaining cheerful. I salute them. The Indian government was generous, as apart from giving the Tibetans land, a monthly grant was made for each refugee and services such as the supplying of two Indian doctors and a clinic. However Indian doctors can do very well in private practice if they are good at their work; often those who take government employment want an easy job. There was great feeling in the camp as a day before a woman had gone to the clinic after a snake bite. I suppose the doctor hadn't any serum as he told her she would be alright. She died the next day. The Tibetan administrator of the camp, Mr Tethong, had married an Australian VSO who was an excellent 'mother' to the young Tibetans; she was helping them with English and hoped to get some of them into medical school at Madras in the near future. As at Darjeeling there was one room set aside, a small wooden hall where all their Tibetan treasures were gathered; the tankas, butter lamps, gongs and any Buddha rupas they had managed to bring with them. There was a large raised chair where the Dalai Lama sat when he came to talk to his countrymen. Tibetans speak of him in very reverent tones; he seems able to make a loving place in his heart for all and they feel his deep supporting presence.

During my visit to South India, Mrs Gandhi had given support in their struggle for independence to what we now know as Bangladesh and India was therefore at war with Pakistan, which meant that I could not get my flight home from Karachi. Lesley Kirkley, Director of Oxfam, who knew I had booked a flight to

Dacca, urged me to go if at all possible as the war was coming to an end in Bangladesh. With this in mind I went to Bombay, to the British Airways office, and asked if I could go home via Bombay, instead of Karachi, which was agreed. I then took a return ticket to Calcutta. There, with the help of the Ramakrishna Mission I managed to get a pass allowing me into the new Bangladesh, but all the planes were booked up for a week or so ahead. The only way was to travel back with thousands of refugees, starting off by train from a suburban station. Needless to say the returning refugees carried bedding, cooking pots, food and their bundles into the carriages, blocking up the windows with the bodies and baggage. I began to feel what the black hole of Calcutta must have been like as we were in darkness. The train chugged along slowly and was stifling in the heat. At last we came to the border station of Bongaon and were deposited on a platform already covered with refugees and their packages. I picked my way carefully out of the station and got a rickshaw to the Block Development Officer's office. He was having a siesta and did not want to be disturbed. I wrote a message saying the Swami Lokeswarananda had told me to contact him. When the Swami suggested it I asked him to write me a note to take, but he said "If you pronounce my name properly he will know you come from me". At last the gentleman arose unwillingly from his siesta and, naturally, was not in a pleasant mood. He told me I had no right to leave India without permission – which I knew was unnecessary – and that there were no boats from Khulna to Dacca. I said I had heard there were one or two still sailing. The lorries and coaches taking refugees were overloaded – I knew that was true, I had seen so many perched dangerously on the roof. He was rude and aggressive and I had nearly given up hope when suddenly he said he had a jeep going down to the Ramakrishna transit camp at Jessore and I could go in that. What a relief! At last luck was on my side, as the young swami who had taken me to the RKM camp outside Calcutta was in charge at Jessore and remembered me. He was welcoming and said "You were so angry, weren't you?" Perhaps he would not have remembered if I hadn't been so angry, so it was a blessing in disguise. This also made it clear to the jeep driver, who could report to his chief, that I was genuinely from the RKM. Having seen the food and care that was being provided at the camp, I was put on a train going to Khulna, a river port. The young swami told me to go to the government Rest House there or, if full, to the Catholic Brothers if I needed a bed.

I was put on the train in a tiny first class compartment on my own. The only seat had a broken leg and, of course, by this time it was dark and there was no light. The train went slowly, soldiers guarding the train firing into the darkness. At long last we reached Khulna with its masses of people camping on the platform. I got a rickshaw to the Rest House, but there was no room there, it was overflowing. We had some way to go back into town, and driving through the sporadic shots that were being fired from all quarters made me feel like vowing I would not do this again; but of course these things happen, one does not plan them. My faithful rickshaw driver took me to the Catholic Brothers, but they would not even open their gate and told me the sisters were some way away. At last we reached them and banged on their gate for some time. Finally the sisters came, opened the gate a crack and let me in; then I had to throw the money for the rickshaw man over the gate as they would not open it again. I hope he found the money.

The two remaining Bengali nuns had tried to look after what had been a school. They were so pleased to see me and showed the damage to the buildings and all the problems they had had during the war. Another sister had managed to return that day so there was quite a festive air, a pleasant simple meal and a comfortable bed. I have found many Catholic nunneries to be simple, clean and basic and so welcoming. In the morning after this heart-warming interlude, I took some food and went down to the steamer wharf. Many little boats were taking people back to the nearby islands, and thousands of people were waiting for the paddle steamer to Dacca. I waited all day but it did not come by nightfall so I went back and had another comfortable night with the sisters.

By six o'clock next morning I was back and on the wharf to hear the steamer had come in, but it had gone upstream for fuel. I had waited, it seemed for hours, before it arrived and when it finally did so it was full to overflowing. I found out later there were 3,000 on board instead of the permitted 1200. No gangway was put out, but a friendly hand helped me to climb aboard over the paddles.

Trying to avoid treading on people I carefully made my way to the first class saloon where at least there was space to sit on the floor. As the steamer used to go every day but now went only twice a week, I was glad to be on board. Many government officials, business men and college lecturers were returning as well as a group of university students, and they were all pleased to talk to me. The students had been 'Mukhti Bahini', freedom fighters, and were pleased to show me where they had blown up Pakistani boats or outposts. There were eight of them and they had a cabin for two; they generously let me share their rota for having two hours' sleep in the bunks. We delivered a number of returnees at river ports along the route – the boat still seemed as full as ever. The low lying islands were barely above water level. When the islanders dig soil to make a platform for their houses the hole becomes a pond. This unstable platform is washed away so easily and so often, especially at monsoon time. We passed the sunderbunds, a low lying area of forest and the home of the Bengal tiger. At the time of prayer the Muslims went up on deck, spread out a cloth and performed their ritual devotions. They were Muslims as well as Bengalis – as Muslims they had much in common with Pakistan, as Bengalis they were enemies. I was very surprised when I was asked if I wished to order dinner. Apparently these boats had a name for good food. I was pleased to give the food I had brought with me to the non-first class passengers, and have the good meal provided.

We arrived at Dacca where gaily ornamented rickshaws abounded. Getting about in a rickshaw is easier than a bus, the driver takes you to the actual place and not just a bus stop, and although he may not know the place he asks and asks and you get there in the end. Alas the first two hotels we visited were full, but someone had told me sometime, if I was in difficulty, to go to the Holy Cross College, near the airport. Again I was welcomed most warmly, and two people whom I had been asked to contact, Father Timm and Father Labbe, were there for the evening meal. They had themselves just arrived as it was weeks since they had been able to reach the College due to the troubled situation. This gave me a chance to hear about what had been happening and the meetings that were going to take place with the new minister for rehabilitation. The overseas aid organisations (CORR, CARE, Oxfam, Save the Children and many others) were there or sending representatives now that the war was over. I attended some of these meetings as an Oxfam representative until the Oxfam Field Director arrived, a Quaker, Jim Howard, a water engineer who had been with Oxfam for many years. I was glad to be relieved of these very technical meetings as I could then spend more time visiting various projects and also be shown where so many horrors had taken place during the war. As the Holy Cross College was some way out of Dacca I was invited to stay with Henry Selz who is a Quaker and was working for CARE, a Canadian agency. One of the most interesting groups I met was part of the Service Civil International – SCI. Its 350 members in Dacca look out for trouble and report it to the police quickly so that action can be taken. They run a school and a clinic in an area affected by the cyclones and have been distributing seeds to the farmers there. The group in Dacca meet every day after work and were making a survey of a selected area to enable help to be given to war casualties, orphans and the chronically ill. They were a most lively group of young men and I enjoyed talking to them. This group has gone on from strength to strength, working in a number of areas, setting up schools and training centres, and building up a network of inter-related self-help projects. It is now called Gono Unan Prochester. The Huddersfield Relief Committee helped them for a number of years and one of the founder members came to speak at an AGM when he was in England. Quaker Peace and Service has also given them generous support.

Sewage has always been a great problem, especially in refugee camps where often the water level is high and the ground flat. Jim Howard, Oxfam's water engineer, with help, worked out a system where effluent from a hospital was piped into thick plastic bags, which, when full were sealed for two weeks or so. By the end of that time the many germs, deprived of air, had died and the effluent could be released into nearby streams, where it had previously been discharged untreated. I visited one of the discharge points. It was a simple and effective breakthrough.

It was difficult to get out of Dacca as so many people were on the move, but I heard of a little train going up country to a Catholic centre I wanted to visit. It meant getting up very early and somehow getting on a train with as many people on the roof and hanging on the sides as in the carriages. The train chugged along slowly; bridges had been damaged and were to be treated with respect. Many people were working in the roads and were being paid in food by the relief agencies. Again the local nuns were delighted to have a visitor to share all their experiences of the fight for independence. The nuns were, after all, Bengalis who pride themselves on their culture, their poets and singers especially. After showing me round we heard some singing across the paddy fields and went to investigate. It was the Hindu festival of Shri Panchami, celebrating the goddess of music and learning, Saraswati. Some young men had fixed up banners and garlands and a number of children were singing her praises – Bengali songs and hymns I suppose. The nuns had never been encouraged to go to a Hindu celebration before, and now they were welcomed with prasad, a sweet mixture of sugar, dried milk and flour which has been blessed. As we left one of the sisters said "You know, they were Muslim boys who arranged this for the children!" It seemed to me that this was a tender plant of Inter-Faith growing, Muslims, Hindus and Catholics, that I hoped and prayed might flourish.

It was easy to get a flight to Calcutta. I met the head of RKM at the airport arrivals. I told him his name worked wonders at Bongaon. I admire RKM very much. It is the modern, educated face of Hinduism, and I have been grateful for their help on many occasions. I collected all the luggage I had left in Calcutta and set off for Bombay and the flight home. I must admit I was feeling pretty exhausted; the tension and nervous strain, meeting so many people and so many new experiences, and the internal disorders which flared up as one moved frequently to different food and water took its toll.

It was a great relief to arrive at Bombay airport in time for my flight home and I joyfully went to the counter to hand over my luggage, hoping then to go to the toilet without lugging it with me. Alas, alack, there was no booking for me on the flight and I was told to go to the office in Bombay as no instructions had come through. My luggage was not accepted as there was a bomb scare. The office is about twenty miles from the airport and by the time I arrived it was closed, and the next day was a Sunday. There seemed nothing to do but go back to the airport and plead with the officials. After further enquiries they found out the office would be open on Sunday afternoon for an hour, so I must go into Bombay again then. At last the officials took pity on me and took my baggage. There was a BOAC flight the next evening so I hoped to catch that. As my family expected me by the earlier flight I asked if they would send a signal to the London office to phone my home. I settled myself down on a bit of floor space not too far from the toilet, my faithful woollen coat around me – at least I was lying down near what I needed. (See *A Coat Tale* at the end of the chapter.)

I was at the office in Bombay when it opened; I think they had just forgotten to send my permission to travel to the airport, or thought I would be collecting a note to that effect before it closed on the Saturday. They phoned through to the airport while I was there and all was well. I felt so exhausted that the relief in getting on the plane and knowing I was going home was bliss – for the time being, until I wondered how I would cope with getting off the plane, dealing with my luggage and getting to King's Cross. Well, I had a good rest on the plane and was struggling with my baggage and wondering how to cope when I saw Rob in the crowd. Never have I been so pleased to be welcomed by a good, strong capable lad. He was living in Teddington and worked for United Glass; he had happened to call in at home when visiting some factories in the north just when BOAC phoned about my delayed flight. It gave him just time to get from Huddersfield to Heathrow to meet me. I felt the Lord was looking after me in my need.

I spent the next few days very gently. When the local paper came to interview me about Bangladesh, it was an awful effort to communicate. Naturally I felt better with rest and English food, but flare-ups of tummy trouble every week or so which were not responding to treatment resulted in my sojourn at the London School of Tropical Medicine – 'Hotel Tropicana' as some of the patients called it. There were endless tests but we could get up and go out for a walk as we got better. I went to a session of Yearly Meeting as the hospital was not far from Friends House. The hospital was a very friendly place with a number of wealthy Africans who were paying guests and needed treatment. I went into the lounge and one called out to me "Come on, you'd like to play (I've forgotten which game) with us black bastards, wouldn't you." I said I would and we had a very merry time. The symptoms had eased and as I was awaiting the results of the tests I was allowed to go home to go to the Mayor's dinner – my husband was a councillor. As the time was short a nurse offered to help me wash and set my hair. It was amazingly kind of her. It was a pleasure to be able to walk about without feeling dizzy and sick. I didn't have another attack until I went to Japan, when I fainted on the stairs of the underground. Four Japanese ambulance men smiled down on me, lifted me onto a stretcher and got me to hospital in no time. They spotted what was wrong in an hour and provided me with the medicines I needed.

This visit to India was the longest I undertook and the most exhausting. Oddly enough when I am far away from home I don't worry about the family as, being so far away, there is nothing I can do. My attention is all taken up with my travel; after all I wasn't on a package tour and had to make all my own arrangements. The projects I visited, and I went to many more than I have spoken about in this narrative, were of great interest to Hudfam and the Oxfam Asia grants committee, and of course a pleasure and a stimulus to me.

My travelling was not just a 'look see', it was a tapestry of interwoven threads of 'Famine Relief', of community relations, of visiting isolated Quakers and personal seeking – a pilgrimage and of course a deep joy in seeing the glory of the Himalayas, the tropical forests, the Flame of the Forest, the jacaranda tree and the many unusual flowers. Some of the most delicious meals I have ever had were vegetarian, their delicate flavours prepared by the housewife over a little stove who may well have spent hours cooking. I would not spend such a long time over a smoky tula, but a lot of people spend an awful lot of time on less productive skills. I prefer to spend time working in a garden, but I recognise that Indian cooking can be a fine art.

Not every experience is the peak of enjoyment. It is not a pleasure to visit appalling refugee camps, or to hear of the atrocities committed in Bangladesh, or travel at night in a rickshaw with firing around you while looking for a bed for the night – but it is a joy when you find a welcoming nun. At one time I stayed with a strict Hindu family with its visiting priest and cultural taboos based on the caste system, which gave me insight into the culture and the problems if India. It encourages one to learn more of the ancient writings of the Vedas and the Upanishads when meeting so many selfless Hindus who cared for the destitute and gave them skills to help themselves. I saw 'that of God' in action in many followers of other faiths, and felt humble, enriched.

Was my journey worthwhile? I suppose one then asks if life is worthwhile and that depends on the liver, in all senses. The many dedicated and selfless people I met, the beauty, the challenge of problems overcome, as one knows in retrospect, is a treasure house I draw on in old age, and remember the many who gave me a helping hand, some who had nothing else to give, and it touches my heart.

A Coat Tail

The first time I went to India I took a nylon coat – easy to wash, I thought. That was a mistake. It always wanted washing and was no use at night as a warm blanket. The next time I bought a light fawn woollen coat for fifteen shillings (75p) at our local Famine Relief shop. I enlarged the pockets. It didn't show the dirt and it was useful as a blanket travelling at night. I brought it home, had it cleaned and wore it all summer. Then I took it to Japan where the climate was hot and humid, so I asked my Japanese friends if I could give it to someone in need. "Japanese do not wear other people's clothes," was the answer. I took the coat, unwillingly, to Hong Kong where the children where I was staying were organising a sale to raise money for a clinic. The coat was immediately bought by their amah who was working in the kitchen. She took it that weekend when she went to visit her mother in Canton. So that coat has raised money for Oxfam, helped me for two years, helped a clinic in Hong Kong and a woman in Canton. Blessings on it – it brought blessings to so many.

CHAPTER FOUR

Accent on the Tribal People of India - with Digressions

BEFORE GOING TO INDIA for the first time in 1965 I had been encouraged to read books by V.S.Naipul and a book by Verrier Elwyn on his experiences living with tribal people in central India and Assam. He lived during the period of the British Raj when little interest was shown in Indian culture and even less interest in the tribal people. He married a tribal girl, became an authority on many tribal cultures and, alas, died a few months before I got to Shillong where he lived in Assam. I would have greatly valued meeting him.

My first encounter with tribal people was in the Vindhya hills north of Bombay, where the Gandhians had a centre. There are people called dacoits – robbers – not necessarily tribals but they live in the hills. One village was said to contain some of these brigands, so three or four Gandhian workers went to the village to discuss their problems. Fearing punishment, the dacoits left the village, so the Gandhians said they would wait until they returned. One by one the dacoits returned and talked over their problems with the Gandhians. They found more satisfactory ways of making a living and became useful members of the Gandhian community – practical conciliation work.

There was a Kasturba ashram at Gauhati in Assam where I stayed. They took me to a special celebration at the Peace centre at North Lakimpur, where the Bramaputra river does a U turn. The Gandhian Peace Centre sent its workers out to work amongst the tribal people, helping with agriculture and hygiene. They established a grain bank for a village where surplus grain is stored at harvest time, so that those whose rice was insufficient could be given rice from the grain bank, saving them going to moneylenders and paying exorbitant interest. The Nagas were in revolt against the Indian government; they thought that, when India was free, they would regain their independent status, and this did not happen. Marjorie Sykes, a Quaker Gandhian, with others, spent some time in this area negotiating with them.

   My next tribal encounter was some years later, visiting Victoria Armstrong, an ex-education HMI from Leeds who was acting as secretary to a Hindu doctor who helped tribal people in the Nilgiri hills in South India. The Huddersfield Famine Relief Committee had helped with his work for tribal health care. Dr Narasihman had a thriving practice at Kotagiri which, like Ootacamund, had been a hill station during the British Raj. In his spare time, the doctor walked in the forest collecting herbal medicines and became aware of the many shy tribal people who lacked any medical care. They were hunter/gatherers for whom, as the forest was felled and the monsoon leached the soil, the food chain was broken. He started a food kitchen, showing them how to cook nourishing meals of available foods and plants, and gradually won their confidence. By the time I visited he had three very small clinics with a few beds in remote places difficult of access. His day would begin in his own clinic and visiting his paying patients, then, late afternoon, he would visit his three more remote clinics in turn, taking supplies and medicines and giving help and advice to the two or three partially trained nurses in each clinic. He often arrived home about 2am. It was a gruelling programme, and Victoria Armstrong had taken over the secretarial work and money raising with Marjorie Sykes who lived not far away.

   Kotagiri is the home of the Kota tribe and there are a number of other tribes. The Todas were especially interesting; fine, tall, well-built people with a band of red and black embroidery in their garments. They lived in beautifully constructed beehive-shaped dwellings and had what might be called a small prayer house, with a small opening so that a young boy could attend to the religious duties inside whilst the older men looked after their cattle. The lad must have been pleased to hand over his duties as he grew larger.

Victoria had started a tourist shop in Kotagiri and the Todas brought her their thick, rich embroidery to sell in her craft shop. Paid for their work, they went back to celebrate and continued until their funds ran out, then they started work again. They were not idle tipplers living on the dole.

The Quakers had been planning to send a medical team to East Pakistan, and my youngest son John applied to go. He had trained as a nurse, then did his psychiatric training at the Retreat in York. However the idea of that project was dropped. At a group meeting at Friends House I met Esther Muirhead, who had Indian connections. She had 'second sight' and told me in a most authoritative way that John would go to help a Hindu doctor in the Nilgiri hills in South India. I was surprised but knew the hills had Quaker connections as Marjorie Sykes, whom I knew quite well, co-worked with Rabindrath Tagore and Gandhi and had a home near Kotagiri.

After some delay, John went to work for Dr Narasihman as a Quaker volunteer for two years. He spent a few weeks at Kotagiri under the doctor's guidance. The doctor had been given land for a clinic and settlement for Paniyar tribal people to help them adjust from being hunter/gatherers to agriculturists. As this was situated 80 miles over the mountains, at Kayunni, he needed John to take over the clinic. There was a tiny house; the doctor had asked that it be cleaned, but on arrival with John he found nothing had been done and prepared to take John back with him. John felt this was no solution and stayed to do the cleaning himself rather than wait for other people. He cleaned and decorated and got a bed long enough for him, a few chairs and a table, cleaned the clinic and stocked up with some basic medicines. All this he did with no local language, strange food and only a tiny local shop. Life was hard. Then Amah came to cook for him and her son helped him in the clinic. John had a tiny bedroom and Amah and her son slept on the floor of the living room. There was a very small kitchen.

I sent some money for John to get shelves put up in the clinic. If one needed to buy a stamp – local ones only – one had to shoo the chickens off a ladder and climb up to the post office, manned by a teacher in his spare time. If Amah heard that an animal was being killed in a village a few miles away, Reggie, her son, went out to buy some meat. Tribals, unlike Hindus, eat cows, wild pigs etc. Owing to the heat, the meat could not be 'hung' for a few days to tenderise it, but had to be cooked straight away. Stewing with papaya was 'said' to make it more tender. The gravy was tasty.

Dr Narasihman came over when he could, or when sent for by John, if there was an emergency. Happily they got on very well and valued each other. John sent for him once, and the patient was so ill that the doctor wondered how he had got to the clinic. Apparently John had found him collapsed in the forest when he was returning from a distant village and the patient's family had carried him all the way back to the clinic – there were too many hungry animals there to leave him. One of John's dogs was eaten. John did not tell me of this, another young doctor who worked for Dr Narasihman did. This young man believed that John had carried the patient himself, but this was a mistake. The fact that this was attributed to John did indicate that he had won the love and respect of the tribal people who came to his clinic in increasing numbers.

Later when I visited John I went with him to some of the villages, and I have a snap of him nursing a baby while the parents lit a fire to boil some water. John was pondering which one of the baby's medical problems he should deal with first.

There was also a balwadi – nursery school – in the compound, where local helpers gave the children a wash at the well – much yelling ensued. The children were taught songs and games and given a mid-day meal. A Quaker volunteer, Allison, came from time to time to introduce new activities. Some children wore clothes. I remember two little naked children with plates of food on their heads, about to run home with it. Then they saw me with my white face and they were so frightened that they ran back into the balwadi.

Once we had a special celebration. Americans had sent some possibly useful clothes for the children and some shoes. Most people walk barefoot. Dr Narasihman and Victoria Armstrong came and, I think, so did Michael Rowntree and his wife. The tribal people sang and danced what I should call the 'shuffle' in lines. Food was prepared in the balwadi kitchen and gifts distributed. A busy cheerful day. I slept in a small room in the balwadi which had en-suite facilities, that is, a back door leading to the outside. I was woken in the night by shovings and pushings and rattling of the door in the adjoining room. As dacoits were increasing in the area, I became more and more uneasy. At last I crawled to the door to the outside, hoping not to be seen. I also feared snakes. I made my way cautiously to the window of John's room and knocked. John sat up in bed, then, thinking he was having a nightmare, sank back into the bedclothes. At last I convinced him of my reality and we had a conference. A dacoit could easily stab us in the dark and we couldn't recognise him. John went and fetched some tribal men to surround the balwadi, then opened the main door. A dog came leaping out; he had had a good time finishing up the left-overs from the celebration in the kitchen. It all gave rise to much hilarity!

They were nearly all tribal people who came to the clinic; most noticeable were the Paniyars with their fuzzy hair and a white garment wrapped round them. All the women looked pregnant as they tied their garment round their waist and made a pouch in front to carry their worldly goods. There were also Kurumbas, Irulas, Mullakurumbar and others. The women walked with beauty and dignity as they carried waterpots on their heads safely over ruts and tracks in the forest.

About once a week a man came up overnight from Cochin on the coast with a basket of small fish on his head and a layer of ice on top of the basket. The tiny fish were topped and tailed and fried with all the bones as a useful addition of calcium, vitamins and added taste to the restricted menu.

John was looked down on by Dr Narasihman's useful secretary because he was 'only a nurse' and 'all clinics must be staffed by doctors'. As a result a doctor was duly appointed. He visited for a few hours each day so he did not have to deal with the results of his treatments. He was doing so many things that John knew to be wrong and it is difficult for a nurse to tell a doctor this. To avoid doing what John was told to do as the doctor's assistant, he made a point of taking his basic medical kit and going out to visit more distant villages before the doctor arrived, making contact with people who had no health care. It is amazing how news spreads 80 miles over the mountains though tribals don't write letters. Dr Narasihman found out that the doctor was not giving satisfaction and to John's relief, he was removed.

As the Mudamali game forest was not far away, John decided to take me there. When Victoria Armstrong heard this, she decided we should book a night at the rest house in the park, and she, Dr Narasihman and the other two Quaker volunteers at Kotagiri should also go. When we arrived the rest house staff had to be encouraged to get us a simple meal; they were just sitting chatting in the kitchen. The next morning two elephants arrived carrying their howdahs; we climbed up some steps on to a platform and ensconced ourselves on benches, facing sideways. Then the mahouts gave the signal to proceed. The grass was long and the jungle well wooded and we proceeded in a stately manner swishing through the undergrowth. The elephant I was on suddenly got frisky; we felt better when he settled down again. Apart from seeing one small deer, that frisky episode was the liveliest event. It was interesting to go to the elephant compound to see them being fed and trained to put their trunks on people's heads and give a blessing to devotees in the temples and allow themselves to be photographed in the act, a suitable offer of money being given. After half-hearted service and some of us sleeping on the floor, we left the next morning. All this was explained when we heard that a party of government officers had just spent a few days there; the wild animals had the sense to make themselves scarce and the domestic staff were just recovering and needed their rest!

We missed seeing the elephant in muste that came thrashing around the guest house while we were out. The bus route that goes near the game park has an alternative route near danger spots so that elephants in muste can be avoided. They can tip over a car, so an escape route is necessary.

At the end of his first two-year period John returned to England and took a year's training in intensive care in Sheffield. However, as the Paniyal Farm clinic where he worked was so remote, it was impossible to find any suitable replacements, so he returned for another two years. After morning clinic at 7am and lunch, he went into the forest to visit the scattered communities. No Indian doctor, except Narasihman, ever did this. Sundays were busy as the patients were not working at the tea and coffee plantations. So village people came in groups to help each other on the way.

Amah who cooked for John was getting old and had no home, so as part of her wages, John bought a house so that she could live in it when he left, to give her some security. However, when she died some time later, her eldest son, who habitually drank to drown his sorrows, took over the house. John undertook all the funeral arrangements and of course the costs that the sale of the home would have covered. It is interesting that the extended family extends beyond the family if the responsibility can be shifted. (This seems to apply also in Africa when white planters became co-opted members of the family. I suppose this is akin to Rowntree and Cadbury 'paternalism' that is, care for their workers.)

As John's second period came to an end and his wanderings in the forest had shown him more remote areas with no health care he talked things over with Dr Narasihman. Land allocated for tribal welfare could be obtained by a registered society to build a clinic, a house and for cultivation. The land given had been deforested and leached by many monsoons; it needed time and considerable skill to bring it back into cultivation – maybe seven to ten years. Quaker Peace and Service combed John's estimates and supported his initiative. I don't think Oxfam would have done this, as it looks for projects that are set up by local initiatives or work that can be done through local organisations, and in this case, there were none.

In 1973 John began to set up an Indian organisation in the region where he hoped to get land at Ambalamoola. This included the local headmaster and the Pujari (the priest) and local farmers. It all sounded so easy – but it meant going to Coimbatore, 500 miles away down the steep winding ghat roads where the driver goes into a wayside shrine to pray for help before the hazardous descent. Of course John arrived after dark and the office was closed, so next morning he went to the office and was told to come again in a week's time. When he returned the appropriate clerk was away 'out of station' as they say. When John was told this on his third visit and the final date by which the land application had to be handed in in Ootacumund was two days later, needing the newly-created society's registration certificate, John said he was remaining in the office until they gave him the necessary form. So he sat there all day until about 6pm when they were going home – they gave him at last what he had asked for. They had been waiting for a bribe. It had already cost John a lot of time and money for fares and overnight accommodation, but once you give a bribe you are caught in a steel trap and become known as a soft touch.

John managed to get the overnight bus to Ootacamund where he handed in his documents on the last day. Then another two or three buses back to Paniyam Farm clinic – exhausted but relieved.

Part Two and a Diversion

After innumerable delays and red tape the land was allocated to the Nilgiri Wynaad Tribal Welfare Society that John had set up. The land had to be measured and a hedge/barrier constructed to discourage wandering animals (elephants are not discouraged by a hedge if there is anything worth eating, but on barren ground, there wasn't). John rented a small house nearby. With the help of Laurie Baker, a Quaker architect in Kerala, estimates were made of the number of bricks to be manufactured – mud bricks baked in the sun – plus estimates for the amount of wood needed for floors, window frames and doors. All these needed a permit and the wood had to be paid for in advance. When at last it arrived it was not all that had been ordered and paid for. Another permit had to be obtained and the wood paid for again in advance.

The land was levelled for the clinic and simple non-cavity walls were put up. The result was a verandah, clinic, large cupboard and an additional room for overnight patients. A few trees were planted nearby to provide shade for waiting patients and nearby bushes provided toilet facilities. Another piece of ground was levelled further up the hillside for a house and a drying ground where coffee beans and pepper could be spread out to dry in the sun. To nourish the leached soil, holes were dug and filled with tea waste from adjoining plantations and cow manure when available. Cows are reared mainly for their manure, which is used as fuel, made into flat cakes and slapped on to house walls to dry in the sun or can be mixed with mud to form a clean and pleasant floor covering in houses or a drying ground surface for coffee beans. The tribal people find milk is a useful extra but cows only give a small yield. Silver oaks were planted to provide shade and support for the climbing pepper plants.

All these activities gave paid work to tribal people. It was a hive of activity interspersed with periods of waiting for permits and supplies. My eldest son Rob had become redundant so he spent his redundancy money going to help John and I went with him. The house and clinic should have been finished but ...

Digression

In January 1981, Rob and I arranged to meet John in Sri Lanka and I arranged, through an agent, a tour by car with a driver, visiting Gandhian projects, staying in Government Rest Houses and visiting Willpattu Game Park at great expense and seeing no animals. Admittedly we climbed into a tree house and were shown what appeared to be lengths of rope in a lake which we were told were crocodiles (Kenya is the place if you want to see wild life). We saw the ancient sites of Anaradhapura (built in approximately 350 BC and fifty miles in circumference) and Pollonarua with their civic buildings and Buddhist temples. We saw a Bodhi tree whose 'parent' was the Bodhi tree at Bodhgaya in India where Buddha became enlightened. The many Buddha rupas (statues) were richly rewarding. The most effective irrigation system based on 'tanks' – small reservoirs, built in the 12th Century and still working – are a fine tribute to the skill of the water engineers. At the lovely Government Rest House at Pallonarua our huge room had a patio with steps leading down into a large tank and I was able to have a swim by moonlight in warm but refreshing water.

The northern half of Sri Lanka was governed by an Indian/Tamil dynasty and was independent until Britain took over the whole country and its administration. The British considered the Tamils much better workers than the Singhalese, so they imported Tamils from Southern India to work in the tea plantations they were establishing in Southern Ceylon. After Ceylon gained independence and reverted to the old name of Sri Lanka, trouble broke out between the Singhalese and the imported Tamil workers. The

Indian government agreed to the gradual repatriation of the Tamils and gave them grants to help them resettle in India. When I first visited resettlement areas I found that although the Indian Government had given a great many grants to help, I grieved to see how the general ignorance of real conditions had been exploited – land had been purchased where the wells were saline and barren, or would need a great deal of skill to develop. I knew a Mr Appavoo, a Tamil from Sri Lanka with managerial abilities who, with the help of Oxfam, set up training workshops, which when running efficiently he handed to the operatives; but alas the standards fell. It is not easy for a tea picker to become an artisan – the time it takes to change a life style is not appreciated and is insufficient – like the time needed to turn hunter/gatherers to agriculturalists.

We continued our travels in Sri Lanka by visiting Sirigea. A Tamil king in the North had a guilty conscience and built his capital for security on top of a hill, which to reach , any visitor would have to climb a very steep footpath up precipitous rocks. I went part of the way up but the last couple of hundred feet on a bare rock face was not for me. My sons went up, but I rested half way up and enjoyed the view and watching the activities of others.

We were taken to see where *The Bridge Over the River Kwai* was filmed and saw the tree houses where people perch and make a noise to frighten marauding elephants. We were taken round a spice garden – unlawful stripping of the bark of a cinnamon tree was a capital offence under the British. Wall hangings of pockets of a dozen or so different spices made interesting and useful small presents to bring home for friends. Then we went on to Kandy in the hills with its lovely lake, the famous Peradenyia Botanic gardens, the huge lake and temple of the tooth (Buddha's). Beautifully arranged flower posies could be bought outside the temple to be presented to the Buddha by pilgrims. There were such masses of offerings that too quickly they had to be swept away to make room for others. It grieved me. Buddha did not believe in taking life and this seemed such a wanton waste of life and beauty although the scent of the flowers and many musicians made it a powerful, heady, worshipful experience. It was not a very large temple but of great beauty and overlooked the lake.

There many cobras danced on the nearby pavement to the reed pipes of their masters; I'm told they enjoy the vibrations though I am not sure they hear the music. It was an added pleasure to stay in the home of a college lecturer and his family for two days. One can talk and get some local colour and colour was everywhere, especially in the orchids and unusual trees in the botanic garden. We saw the elephants having a bath in the river. We then went on to stay at a tea plantation with a guest house in Nurya Elia, where the broad sweep of the hills was dominated by neatly ordered rows of tea bushes and groups of tea pickers. We were shown over a tea factory and all its processes. There are 12 grades of tea. The 11th grade was used for making Earl Grey and it had many additives. The Earl Grey of the time of my visit was also the proprietor of the many sex shops that were mushrooming at that time. My appreciation of Earl Grey tea dropped to nil.

From the guest house in Nuwara Eliya we left about 6am for a long drive then a climb to the top of Adams Peak to see the sunrise. Leaving the car in a huge car park, we started to climb. I realised after an exhausting stint that it would be too far for me, so I saw a stone veranda-type entrance to a small temple and settled down to sleep there – the boys would pick me up as they came down. Hundreds of pilgrims swarmed past me shuffling but not talking as they concentrated on the climb. A party of young schoolgirls came up with gay bird-like voices that twinkled in the air – they seemed beautifully light-heated. I hope they reached the top. Time passed and I snoozed and then the great descent began. I waited and waited; nobody came to pick me up. The crowd became a trickle, so I decided to go down on my own. John had thought he had seen me in the crowd, so had gone down earlier. At last I got back to the car and John, but Rob was missing, so John went back to look for him looking for me. At last we were all re-assembled but the worse for wear.

The driver who was a Christian did not approve of taking me to active Buddhist projects, only ancient prehistoric sites. It was always too late ... or too far ... we were always in convenient places to visit Christian welfare projects. When a Christian woman dies in Sri Lanka, she often leaves money to buy a special memorial celebration meal for an old women's home. As a very dear and generous member of the Famine Relief Committee had died recently and left Hudfam her considerable estate, when I came home we agreed to send a memorial donation to the Christian Home on behalf of Miss Daisy Mellor.

Our journey in Sri Lanka was ending. We went in a glass-bottomed boat to see the coral reef and the varieties of coloured fish amongst the coral, had a bathe and ate some pineapple for 2/- each, prepared and cut in slices as you watched – delicious. We caught the night train that runs North to the ferry crossing – the train and the boat laden with returning repatriates. It is a fairly short, therefore cheap, crossing and a lighter took us off the ferry boat to the harbour at Rameswaram. There we had some hours to wait but it gave me time to explore one of the largest temple complexes in the Indian sub-continent. Pilgrims flock to visit its many shrines. So many shrines need so many priests to attend to the pujas. Perhaps it was a temple that included all Brahma's many aspects and avatars.

At long last the train for Madurai arrived and we settled down thankfully. After 20 miles the train stopped as it had run out of coal. A long wait before another train brought us some and we did another 20 miles or so. We had run out of coal again – more waiting. It was a long and tiring journey and we were hungry as the train never managed to stop at a station where food would have been available. At last we reached Madurai where I stayed the night as I wanted to visit the aforementioned Mr Appavoo and his Tamil repatriates, and then to stay at Father Bede's ashram near Tiruchchirappalli for a week. Rob and John continued another day and a half travelling back, anxious to see how the building of the clinic and house was progressing. When I left Madurai I spent the night at a Hansenorium (a hospital for leprosy patients) I had visited before, as one of the Catholic sisters said she would come with me to visit Father Bede. (This visit is described in Chapter Nine.) The week there went too quickly but the thought of returning to Johnny's new clinic called me.

End of Sri Lankan digression.

I was glad to get up into the hills where it was cooler. I took the little rack railway that climbs up into the Nilgiri Hills from

Coimbatore. It is definitely a slow train with magnificent views. It stopped at lots of tiny stations where passengers get out to look from viewpoints and eat tasty morsels or drink coffee at 2p a cup. For the next stage of the journey I had to clamber on three different buses. This is a challenging experience. The buses are few and far between and crowded. Those anxious to board the bus do not wait for passengers to alight – the ensuing mayhem is better imagined than experienced.

On meeting John I found that the owner of the house John had been renting for the time being had let it to a longer staying tenant. Rob, John, Reggie the young helper, slept on the floor in the clinic and I had a bed in the store cupboard. They had palliasses on the floor but as there was no glass in the windows and there was an unexpected storm, the bedding was soaked. We had a hurricane lamp for lighting. Wood on an open fire outside allowed one to boil and fry. Water was obtainable by going down a very steep track to a stream in the paddy field. It seemed a lot steeper carrying a heavy bucket of water up the hill. The shelter of a bush provided toilet facilities. As I think I was the first white woman they had seen in this area, everything I did was of absorbing interest. When it was put to him, John realised the problem and had a hole dug higher up the hill, put poles around it and attached a screen of sacking. Depending on the angle of the sun, a fine shadow display was produced.

Down in the paddy a well had been dug using a series of cement rings, one on top of the other as the well was deepened. A pump house was also built on the hill just above the well. Subsidence had caused the downfall of the pump house, dumping it into the well and pushing the cement rings out of the vertical. The first job was to clear the debris out of the well and get the rings vertical again. The tribal people are not well fed and could not stand working in the cold water at the bottom of the well and hadn't the muscles to lever the well rings into position. Luckily Rob, a climber, was deemed to have the necessary muscles for a well digger. QPS had a blue printed tea towel (taken from a photograph) of John and some tribals looking down a well at Rob, unseen in the picture. Gradually with levers the rings were put back in place and the well started to fill up with water. Rob then built a new pump house in a safer position and fixed a pump to send water to the house and clinic high above the paddy. Diesel oil had to be bought in the nearest town, Sultan's Battery (15 miles away) and carried on the bus. John applied to have his house and clinic connected to an electricity supply, a long and expensive business. This took two years but when it was done, a month later it was discontinued as the employee who did it had no business to be doing it! The trials of faith and patience in India are unbelievable. I suppose it may be spiritual training?

Rob complained that he was not being adequately fed for the work he was doing. It was true. He ate a lot of sugar which at that time was more expensive in India than in England. He made me an oven of a tin box supported on stones and I lit a fire underneath. I tried my hand at baking bread but the bottom was burnt and the top was uncooked. Rice was rationed; there were a few vegetables at the local store that sold everything, but little was available in a tribal area. Rob is now a vegan. The most delicious meals I have ever had have been vegetarian prepared by an Indian housewife who may spend all day cooking. Her tula (a small stove made of mud and cow dung) allows two or three pots to simmer over a wood fire in her kitchen. Later Rob constructed a cooking bench for John who had obtained an iron range to cook and heat water.

Visits to Ootacamund, 60 miles and two buses away, allowed me to buy Amul tinned cheese made at a big milk co-operative I had visited north of Bombay. A variety of fruit and vegetables were available in the market as they grew locally. Ooty had been a hill station for the British during the hot season. It had some shops with glass windows and a door rather than a shutter that came down at night. Many shops were built like garages and the family would sleep there at night. Ooty still had its rather dusty and faded memories of its club for 'members of the British Raj only' at that time. Its botanical gardens were modest but expressive of its sense of culture. A dog show used to be held once a year. Maybe it still is. This is certainly a relic of the Raj. An English-bred dog would come up to me and be friendly in a house that I might visit, but Indian dogs are not treated as pets of the family. They are given little care and are often driven away as thieves and potential carriers of rabies. I used to take my Sheltie to school when I taught

Asian infants – their fear of dogs receded and their reward for good behaviour was to give her a little drop of their morning milk. I do not encourage children to accost stray dogs, but fear is destructive to child and animal.

I was only spending six weeks away from England this time, and the week before I left John was to move into the new house. A front door had been made, but it had warped and had to be propped up against the entrance. As John had set up an Indian organisation it was necessary to have a puja before moving in. The local pujari was consulted and the date and time of John's birth had to be considered. The pujari said that 3am on a certain night would be propitious. All the committee were invited and all except me, who had a bucket of water brought to me, had to go down to the well and bathe immediately before the ceremony. This was a challenge in the dark and with the steep path. We all had to sit cross-legged around a hearth made of stones in the middle of the room. Rice on the stalk was placed first on the hearth, then polished rice, followed by fruit honey, then a coconut with the top cut off so the white interior could be seen. Into this was inserted three fine sticks representing Shiva, Vishnu and Krishna which were bound together at the top symbolising Brahma, the universal spirit. Ghee, a form of butter, was poured over this and was set alight. As the flames rose the pujari intoned the appropriate prayers. Prasad, a mixture of dried milk and sugar, was passed round as a symbolic sharing, and some of this wrapped in leaves and later taken to those invited but unable to be present. Another shorter puja took place in the kitchen in which I as the (unsatisfactory) housewife asked for and, I hope received, a blessing.

At a Quaker Meeting in England John was talking about his work and describing the puja when one of those present objected to his lapse into Hinduism. John maintained that asking for help and a blessing on the work of the clinic was just as much Quaker as Hindu. When John told me this I felt I had brought my children up in the right spirit.

I invited the young pujari to lunch the next day – a curry made of a half ripe pineapple and rice. He explained the symbolism of the offerings at the puja, the seeking and refining of the human spirit, the opening up of the inner light in the whiteness of the inner flesh of the coconut and the enlightenment and oneness of Brahma. He was a young man I liked and respected very much; I was sorry when I heard he had left the village.

I took the overnight bus on a 24-hour journey down the ghat road to Cochin, then along the coast road with coconut palms, rice paddy and vistas of islands forming what appeared to be a wide canal down to Trivandrum. Happily, there I had a chat and a laugh with Laurie and Kuni Baker, to whom bringers of news are always welcome. Then I took a short flight to Colombo and thence home.

Rob stayed on another three months. He fitted out the kitchen with a work bench. He managed to buy a very large metal bowl in Sultan's Battery. He made a hole in it, fitted a plug and a pipe, so that the dirty water could run away outside. All the water had to be carried up the steep track from the paddy, so dirty water was used for watering. The toilet needed careful construction. On a high platform there was a hole and a place for each foot as one squatted. At a lower level was a shallow concrete area where one stood to take a bath, pouring water over one's head, taken from a nearby bucket with a brass pot, preferably singing bajans (praises to the gods) as one anointed the god within. Cement was extremely difficult to get and was needed for the toilet and the floors of the verandah, and sometimes one had to buy it on the black market to finish an essential job before the monsoon came.

Rob left the remainder of his redundancy money for John to get necessary equipment and came home. He then found that although he had paid National Insurance for over 20 years, as he had been out of the country for four months and so had not drawn benefit, he was not entitled to any on his return. It was a blow – and a challenge.

John got a table and a few chairs made for the house. He ordered a supply of 25 basic drugs that WHO recommends and opened the clinic. Gradually patient numbers grew as they found they could get treatment for things they had just accepted before as fatal. John employed a girl, Soumeni, and a tribal boy in the clinic. They gave out the medicines John prescribed and acquired useful skills as well as helping with language problems.

A lad came to John's clinic who had been to hospital for treatment of TB. He was lucky that, while there, he had not been sterilised, as the Indian doctors at that time had to meet their quota of sterilisations. However the lad was discharged with the TB still actively infectious. As it needed prolonged treatment, John suggested he lived in and cooked for John. He was quite a good cook if he was in the mood, but he had an annoying habit of going walkabout as do the Aborigines in Australia.

A couple of years later I went to visit John again. The pepper vines were climbing up the shade trees. It was time to prepare to plant tea and coffee. John's clinic helped a number of the workers on the tea plantations and a Scotsman who was manager of one of the plantations invited John and me out to dinner. He sent a car for us as we couldn't have gone otherwise. They lived in what seemed to us unbelievable luxury – electricity, fridge, bath, a cook, strawberries and flowers from the garden, beautiful tableware. The view, especially the glorious orange horizons of an Indian sunset, the beauty of which induces a sense of awe, provides one of my greatest memories.

These friendly connections with managers of tea and coffee plantations were invaluable. John was given cuttings of the best varieties of coffee and tea for his plantations and instructions for cultivation. To start with, it was necessary to buy 1000 small oblong plastic bags, fill them with a mixture of soil and compost and insert a three-inch cutting, and then construct a nursery with wooden supports to hold up a roof of what looked like bracken to provide shade, under which were placed rows of cuttings that had to be watered twice daily. All this provided paid work for local people.

John began to grow more than he needed, so that he could sell some and help pay the wages. As he gained skill, he began to grow enough to give plants to tribal people to plant up their land. Land is very scarce and expensive in Kerala so people are moving into the tribal area and taking over tribal land – and bringing their diseases with them. Tribal people had no way of proving their ownership, no ability to go to court and bribe witnesses. It was therefore important for them to plant up their land and thus demonstrate their ownership. John supplied plants and the knowledge if required.

After a time, more land was bought, two miles away. John appointed a manager, trained as a social worker by Dr Staley, an Oxfam Field Director. Another problem was the number of people from other villagers that came to the clinic with diseases caught from contaminated water supplies. John would go to the village and realise that a well for drinking water was needed as people were just drinking from a stream. QPS got some funding for this and John was able to employ local labour to dig a deep well for drinking water.

Sometimes I took John's Dobermans for a walk in nearby woods. I realised that pixies were following me, but when I turned round they disappeared. This happened a few times so one day I turned round and started singing 'Hickory Dickory Dock' with actions. A few brave pixies came out to look at me and others followed. The next time they began to join in the actions – especially when in 'Sing a Song of Sixpence' they pecked off each other's noses. I became a public entertainer and they learnt a little English. Some children had something that had once been white wrapped round them, some without anything. It could be very cold at night in the hills but they would be snug in their nest like birds at night. These children did not go to school as they had no clothes. When I came home I gave a number of talks and slide shows and had bring and buy sales in aid of John's work. A school that had supported a Vietnamese orphan until the scheme was dropped, used to have a weekly collection, pennies and halfpennies, to provide pants or a skirt so that tribal children could go to school. The advantages were having a free midday meal provided and mixing with the non-tribal children. A regular midday meal benefited the children and helped them absorb some of the modest education on offer. John bought the material for clothes locally and had the garments made by a useful man in the village who had a sewing machine, thus giving more work to local people. When John went back to visit in 1994, he met some of the tribal children now at school who greeted him by singing 'Hickory, Dickory Dock'! I cherish this, the tiny threads, vibrations, that link us: "the earth is a living web" – (Frijof Capra.)

Occasionally there were tribal celebrations that included fire walking taking place around 2 or 3 am. John and I set out and walked a very long way to one such event. Mothers, carrying their babies, would walk without lingering across a red hot bed of glowing wood embers about 15 ft wide and 40 ft long. John was invited to join them, but replied that it wasn't a propitious day for him – nor for me.

When John first went to the Nilgiris, he went hunting with the tribals and I have a bow and arrow that he used somewhere at home. As the forest has been cut and reduced the habitat for wild animals, wild pig is not now on the tribal menu, a great loss. If a pig was killed all the tribe shared the kill; in any case it had to be eaten quickly as they had no method of storing it. It is a long and difficult process to turn hunter/gatherers into agriculturalists and in the process their diet was impoverished.

When I first went to visit John I was able also to visit friends in Madurai who were working with displaced Tamils from Sri Lanka. From Madurai I could book two days in advance on the overnight train to Madras. There, Mrs Krishna Rao ran Sarva Siva Sangh. She was a most creative, sensitive woman who provided home, work and training for destitute women. It was easy travelling by bus to Bangalore to visit Hema who, though in a wheelchair, started a training centre and school for the physically handicapped. In Mysore I visited Mrs Webb whom I had met at an Oxfam conference when she was helping Tibetan refugees in South India. Later she developed connections with the Holdsworth Memorial Hospital in Mysore. At the time of my visits she was organising and financing four village health workers and ran a clinic for their patients. (There is more about Mrs Webb in my account of my second visit to India.)

Mysore was beautiful with its blue flowering jacaranda and the flame of the forest trees. The Maharaja's Palace and the temples were floodlit during festivals. It was interesting that the Maharaja was a Muslim, but governed his Hindu subjects with amity on both sides ... well away from the troubles of Northern India during partition. I bought some flame-coloured Mysore silk to make pyjamas for my husband. Mrs Webb had found me a small restaurant with guest rooms near her abode. On the last evening we went to one of the luxurious hotels of the British Raj. We sat in the garden under the trees lit up by little lamps, waiters galore to serve us, and we pretended to be memsahibs of the Raj.

Travelling by bus was educational. As a front seat became available I moved forward where I presumed the weight of the engine reduces the bouncing. I was promptly ordered to go to the back by the driver, the proper place for women. Apparently the women are often sick so this was the right place for them! Sometimes a priest would come on board, put a red tikka on your forehead and intone a prayer and accept donations for his services. No opportunity is lost to make ends meet. The rich can be very generous and Indians do not say 'thank you'; it is an honour and a blessing on you if you give. The Indian government has been outstanding in its generosity to Bangladeshi refugees, doing much more than wealthy Western nations contributed. India was also very generous indeed to the Tibetan refugees, providing buildings, land and monthly payments to Tibetans as well as to Tamil repatriates.

When staying with John, apart from fetching milk, taking the dogs for a walk and reading in the shade, I usually spent an hour or so in the morning being entertained in the clinic like the other six or seven who were waiting for treatment inside, to be replaced promptly when one patient left the clinic, by another waiting outside under the trees. All the tribals paid one rupee a year and they got a ticket with their name and number on so their medical record could be checked quickly. Addresses were a problem – past five trees, left, then right by a large tree, cross over ...

One day two mothers came in with their children. They had been so worried they had taken time off from work to go by bus to Sultan's Battery to see a doctor. Steroids were prescribed, very costly and the doctor gets a rake-off from the chemist. The children got worse and when they came to John he found they had rickets, a calcium deficiency. All they needed was milk and calcium tablets. They began to improve and so did the number of people coming to John's clinic. Unscrupulous doctors in the tribal area are a menace.

Another day a woman who looked old came in moaning. In England she would have been in hospital; a pity she hadn't come to the clinic earlier as she had very low blood pressure. John gave her an iron injection and iron pills to take. Suddenly she started laughing, likewise the others waiting in the clinic. I asked John if she had been given some laughing gas – "No, I just got fed up with the moaning so I was a bit vulgar. I told her to go home and let her boy friend rub it." That John should think she had a boy friend cheered her up so much that it was 50% of the treatment. Laughter relaxes and allows the natural healing processes to function more easily.

After about seven years the tea, coffee and pepper were producing a good income. John now had three Dobermans – alas the male was said to have a good pedigree, but the promised pedigree never arrived. The result was that when Rani had her pups their price was much lower as their father had no proven pedigree. One puppy was kept and the three dogs slept on the verandah adjoining my window. It was a great pleasure to see the dawn as I lay in bed. At night one dog would bark to another across the valley, an amiable conversation to begin with. Then suddenly all three dogs would set up the most terrifying musical howling, I presumed to frighten off 'wild beasts' but suddenly they would all stop upon the instant and peace returned. Odd how one can get used to an unholy noise and miss what I called the 'dog's opera' on the nights it didn't take place.

My visits to Indian friends gradually became more restricted; Asian toilets where one squats were a problem and waiting 18 hours at Bombay for a connecting Indian Airways flight to Bangalore made life a struggle rather than an enjoyment. The last time I went John asked me to bring a video as he felt he could use it for teaching his staff. I was asked at the airport whether I had anything to declare. I asked what needed declaration. 'You have a camera?' I answered truthfully 'Yes' and was told to proceed. John was surprised when I arrived with the video, he had written cancelling the request as I would have to pay 100% customs duty! There was a shop in Sultan's Battery with a TV in the window. It was not for sale, but one could be ordered. The 'Come again next week' formula started again. I was there for six weeks and still no TV was available.

John used to buy stock and cuttings from a beautiful area in south Kerala. The father of the business was a Rosicrucian of western extraction who had married a Hindu. They kept up the western tradition of changing for dinner when the old man was alive. I don't know how John managed; he might have had a lunghi with him (a gaily coloured cloth to wrap around the waist). The ritual ended when the old man died. It was the mother's duty to get the daughters married and one of them fancied John. He was asked to visit them to discuss the matter. John had the skills to help them develop their land. An Indian husband often spends periods apart from his wife, which would have enabled John to keep an eye on the clinic even if he was not there full time, and he could get a resident's permit if he married an Indian. A European man expects to 'fall in love' and has no culture of arranged marriages and he felt he would be marrying the girl for the wrong reasons. It must have been a blow to a girl of a wealthy family who had set her heart on him. Arranged marriages can be just as satisfactory and sometimes better than a 'love match', but one can only do what seems right at the time. It is difficult to overcome cultural barriers.

The clinic went on apace, but patients were arriving with what appeared to be leprosy. Tribals were said authoritatively by Dr Narasihman's secretary NEVER to suffer from leprosy. John wrote to a friend 500 miles away who was running a leprosy clinic, to come and give his opinion. It WAS leprosy and a good thing that John had sought advice. QPS got in touch with the Damian Foundation in Belgium as they funded the work of John's friend. They agreed to pay the cost of a trained leprosy worker. For a time he slept in the clinic until a house could be built for him.

It was not only treating people who came to the clinic, but going into the forest to the villages of five or six houses to check on the families and be sure to give follow up treatment to all patients. John went to one village where the people had names so alike he made a plan of all the houses to keep a check, but the next time he went, some of the houses had disappeared.

To cover the distances a motor bike was needed. If you offered foreign currency for it, you could get it six months earlier. Bring and buy sales, donations from friends etc., raised the money and the leprosy worker could go into the forest taking one of the lads in turn who worked in John's clinic. This gave them experience and formed a bridge between the tribal people and their language and the non-tribal leprosy worker. Soon there were over 100 leprosy patients and their families to visit.

Leprosy takes a long time to incubate. The first sign may be a small white patch on the skin and loss of feeling in the feet and hands. People don't realise when they have damaged their feet because it doesn't hurt, but soon cuts get infected and won't heal and patients must wear shoes. A man with leprosy may pick up something so hot that the first indication that something is wrong is when one smells burning flesh. Drugs can prevent the disease from spreading further but cannot put back what no longer exists. Of course we used to have lepers' 'squints' in English churches, so it was endemic here once, before the rise of ICI medicinals for which my husband did research.

Some afternoons, if the motor bike was not needed by the leprosy worker, John would take me with him to visit patients. Tribals would come to the clinic and ask him to visit someone too ill to get there. There was no address but a certain place to be at a certain time. The contact was seldom at the appointed place and had no idea of time. John would find a nearby group of houses and enquire – well, they all had ailments that needed attention and the desperately ill one was elsewhere.

The trust of the Tribals in John grew, but it had some problems. A woman had a huge growth and no baby emerging. John had done some kindness to a doctor who in turn offered to do an operation free. John arranged for a jeep to collect the woman; she had to be carried through the forest to where the jeep was waiting. She was carried into the operating theatre, doctor, anaesthetist and nurse at the ready; but the husband would not allow the operation to take place. Luckily John visited the hospital to see if all was well before the patient and her husband had left. John found that the husband feared he would have to pay for his wife's stay in hospital after the operation. When John agreed to pay the additional charges, the operation went ahead as planned. We visited the woman some time later, the growth removed and she recovering.

It seemed a good idea to get John a motorbike of his own – more bring and buy sales. There is a wonderful ineptitude in India among wealthy people who own a car. If he can afford a car the father never dirties his hands, so neither do the sons, so they learn nothing.

The paid mali does it all. Tribals have never had a car or a motorbike, so they are in the same state. When the motor bike had a puncture or needed attention, the leprosy worker was shown by John what to do, but as more punctures were made in repairing one, John found it less exhausting to do it all himself.

The early death of Dr Narasihman, in part due to overwork, was a great blow to John and the patients in Kotagiri and the little tribal hospitals. Dr Narasihman had become an advisor to the Indian government on tribal affairs, an honour but also a responsibility, attending meetings in Delhi when already overburdened.

The lack of protein in the tribal diet was a cause for concern. We pondered. If the tribals hunted wild pig surely a solution would be to raise their own pigs. John bought four young sows and a hog. They grew apace but the hog did not do what was required of him. To buy another young hog would delay the breeding process so an older hog was bought at great expense as one pays by weight. A jeep had to be hired to fetch the animal who with difficulty was heaved into the jeep. Unfortunately the jeep had a puncture on the way home and the pig, of freedom-loving disposition, escaped into the forest. It was a tremendous job for two or three men to locate him, catch him, and get him back into the jeep again. When they arrived home, he was put in a sty and fed and watered. However, he was a non-violent protester pig and refused to eat for two or three days. John could see he was going to die, so he opened the gate. Presently the pig got up, went outside and relieved himself for about two hours, then came back and ate his food. Do not say pigs are dirty animals, they do not use their sty from choice to defecate. His relations with the young sows was happy and had results. John gave responsible tribal people a piglet. But, as in the ground nut scheme in East Africa, there was much to be learned. Wild pigs had foraged for themselves in the forest but these had to be fed. When it was time to kill the pig, it was too much for the family to eat and there was no way of storing the meat. As it was not a money economy, the chances of selling the meat locally were slender. When all the village went hunting, all shared the kill. The pig scheme faded out.

One year the leprosy relief friend, John Dalton in Madurai, had his mother to stay, so it was arranged that the two Johns and two mothers spent a week going by jeep to Kodaikanal, a hill station of the British Raj, and also visit some projects on the way. The views were wonderful and the hill villages and their self-support systems ingenious and we provided entertainment for the children. I think tribal children are unlikely to go to school. Dr Narasihman once persuaded some tribal people to send their children to a semi-boarding school where they would come home at weekends. One died and all were withdrawn. It was a minor accident that could have happened at home, but the school was blamed. Mind you, sometimes that worked the other way. When John, though not taught maternity work at home, delivered his first baby by the light of a candle and a medical book, it was a boy. He was held in great esteem.

Kodaikanal had a lingering Raj atmosphere. The little bungalows with verandahs and small gardens facing the lake were Indian-English; the shops, some with glass windows; a club and government rest house with faded grandeur, the furniture of mahogany and teak. Once I stayed at a guest house near Sanchi which had a bed with no bed clothes. I was loaned a travelling rug for the night by some other visitors but as they left very early in the morning I had to be grateful for half a night's cover and warmth. Of course a lot of people travelling on trains take their own bed roll with them.

We visited a boys' home administered by a European and funded by a charity in England. It was on a steep hillside, a fine house for the project administrator and dormitories for the boys. There was another large building, a hall, that was very imposing higher up the hill. The boys had to walk carrying soil from the river bed up into the gardens and also carry mud for the bricks. I don't remember any other educational work, well, there was feeding and looking after rabbits. Perhaps I felt uneasy unnecessarily and wondered how much rabbit the children had in their meals. The administrator looked very well fed. In England we provide children with an education and then a dole with no work attached to provide basic training to gain self respect. That makes me uneasy too. It was a merry trip we all enjoyed but sometimes made us stop and think and question.

One thought was to start keeping rabbits ourselves and John bought some from the above-mentioned project. The next time I visited there were several rabbits but we didn't eat any and I didn't ask John to kill one for me. One morning a snake got into the hutch and swallowed some of the baby rabbits and was so fat he couldn't get out again. I felt deeply for the mother rabbit sitting there unable to tackle the snake and knowing some of her babies were inside him.

At a government farm some distance away they had super hens that laid super eggs. John bought four or five and one died of heat stroke on the way back and provided a chicken meal for about sixteen people. Alas super hens required super food not available in the tribal district if they are to lay super eggs – another dead end! Country fowl have little meat on them, lay small eggs and are given little food. In the morning they stay in their hen house and are expected to lay an egg; in the afternoon they are free range and usually come back for their evening meal. Cows did produce manure, a valuable commodity, and a little milk, but racist cows who would not let white faces come near to milk them added to one's problems. A friend milked John's cows and I had to go for the morning milk. She didn't like me either. John's efforts in pig, poultry and rabbit farming were educational rather than successful.

Part Three – A Period of Grief and Frustration

My husband died and John came home on bereavement leave. It was good he came home to be with the family and discuss the changes we were planning including dividing the house, now too big for me. He had a resident's permit which was due for renewal but of course suffered the usual delays in handing it over and he looked like missing his flight. He went again to the office dealing with these matters. "No problem, you can get one at India House in London." "No problem" meant no problem or responsibility to the one who said it. Distress, grief, frustration was compounded when, on the following weekend, India slapped on a requirement for visas for all going to India and hoards of people went to India House where there was no extra staff laid on to deal with the problem. When the flood of applicants had subsided somewhat

John went to renew his resident's permit. "We have plenty of doctors and nurses in India, you are not needed" he was told. True, but these nurses and doctors don't choose to work in tribal areas where no money is made to repay the cost of their education and enable the extended family to finance another member. After much pleading John was given a three months tourist visa to find a doctor and staff to run the clinic, order the drugs and keep the accounts, oversee the farm and its accounts, help the tribals to plant up their land and continue the well digging programme. It was impossible.

As soon as he got back to India, John applied again for the renewal of his resident's permit. At last he got one, but only two weeks before it expired. He then applied for Indian nationality – it took months to get a reply to this request. It was not refused, but the reply said that the British Government had failed to sign some papers they should have done at Independence! Further delay. I immediately got on to our own M.P., Barry Sheerman, who took the matter up with the Foreign Office and the British Embassy in Delhi. All this took another nine months, but at last the agreed forms were signed. We breathed a sigh of relief. This information however was not published in the Indian Gazette so no cognisance could be taken of it. Back to square one in snakes and ladders. John searched his mind; the block development officer that he got on very well with had been moved. John had written very politely to the new officer, perhaps before they knew each other well enough. He pointed out in the letter an area of tribal land which was being encroached on – this may seem innocuous, but not all Indians are sympathetic to tribals and this may be interpreted as stirring up trouble amongst the tribals and when Delhi sends to Madras for a report on the applicant seeking to renew a work permit, this casts a shadow. However, as there was no refusal, John continued as usual.

In 1989 I was staying with John when he had an official visitor, an unhappy man who valued him and his work very much. John was told to leave the country within a month. The yearly accounts had to be done, by John, and sent in, and people persuaded to take on the various projects, and a doctor found. John saw me off the next day and I can still see his grief-stricken face as I waved from the bus. On arriving in England I phoned Andrew Clark, head of QPS, to give him the news. Busy as he was, he flew to John to see if he could help but there was so much to do that only John could do.

After John left a doctor with high commendation from a respected organisation was appointed. Then reports came that the doctor had started another clinic not far away taking drugs from John's clinic where patients were getting poor treatment even if the doctor was there. Soumeni, John's valued woman helper in the clinic, left owing to the new doctor's unwelcome attentions – one does not give up a job lightly in a tribal area. Rani, John's faithful dog, was not fed and this added to John's grief. The other dog's bones were found in the forest, probably eaten by a leopard. The complaints of the patients mounted and at last the doctor was dismissed. He left taking all John's medical books with him. There was nothing John could do but grieve. A cruel and distressing time; it is hard to see the community that has become your family, that you had cherished and given so much love and care to, all shattered.

Then suddenly there seemed hope. An Indian friend in Bangalore was a friend of the appropriate minister in Delhi and he went to see him about John's resident's permit. This is not just a day trip, but about 1000 miles. The minister was sympathetic and said that if he got a warmer recommendation from Madras it would provide him with a reason for countermanding the previous decision. "That's no problem, I went to school with the appropriate official in Madras, he's an old friend of mine." Our friend got home to Bangalore and phoned us the news and said he was off to Madras in the morning. He had a heart attack that morning and died. The door had slammed shut on our hopes and now we had to contend with the sudden death of our friend.

I think it was about this time that John bought a barge in Holland with an idea of taking it to France and converting it into a pleasure boat on the lovely Burgundy canals. I did not approve, he had no skills for this except his good humour and ability to get on with people, which did not seem sufficient. When I saw him go off with a merry challenging look in his eye for the first time in a couple of years, I relented and gave him all the support I could.

By chance the farm manager of John's tribal project met an Indian doctor in Sultan's Battery, who used to help and advise John on difficult cases on Sundays when there were often well over 200 patients to be seen. The doctor had been injured in a car accident and his father had been killed. He was now recovered and had married a social worker. The committee appointed him to take over the house and clinic. The strange thing is that the doctor was called Nevin Wilson, and his brother was called John Wilson. A healing balm came into our hearts, this seemed a happy solution. Dr Nevin wrote to me expressing his amazement at all the work John had done in establishing the clinic and farm and all the other well-drilling and agricultural help for tribals as well as the leprosy programme. As the doctor had qualifications in leprosy work the Damian Foundation was happy to continue its support. The letter warmed my heart.

QPS were wanting a worker in Sri Lanka and John, whose experience in India and ability to speak Tamil was relevant, was appointed for the six months period deemed enough for a time in the troubled area. This suited John, as he hoped at the end of the period to get a visitor's permit for India. I think it was about this time that he was offered a very well paid job by the Red Cross, but it seemed more urgent at the time to use his tourist visa and get back to the clinic. He was told to apply for the next Red Cross job available. When this occurred, it meant application forms had to be sent to Geneva, and officials there did not even take up his references. Odd.

John arrived unexpectedly at the clinic at Ambalamoola just as all the staff were having a meeting in the clinic – a wonderful coincidence. His dog Rani was still alive to greet him. The tribal boys who had helped John in the clinic were qualifying as leprosy workers; their confidence had started when they had been given status by riding on a motor bike which they had thought was not for them; this reflects the attitude of Indians to tribals and outcasts. Wherever John went people stopped to greet him and talk.

The farm was not flourishing. The man in charge was good but a welfare worker, not an agriculturalist. There was no-one to tell him what to do and naturally he had not got the social opportunity to meet the plantation owners and get help, as John had done, and this valuable line of communication had been lost. John's visit helped to restore this, greatly to the advantage of the farm. It seemed sunshine had come after darkness.

On leaving John brought home his video that had been locked in a cupboard and never used, but not the videos of Gandhi I had taken him. I was burgled a few months later, so the burglar got the benefit of this much-travelled video. John now had the satisfaction of getting back to his barge and dealing with the problems that ensued. He is not an intellectual, but can acquire information that he needs effectively which is better than having a lot of useless information. He enjoys a challenge and does not give up. John is not a Quaker as he says he does not want a label round his neck, but he is more Quaker than most I know in his values and practical expression of these and finding ways of helping people to help themselves, and this is all done with a great sense of humour. "Getting on in the world" has a different interpretation in my family. I think it was Clutton Brock who wrote a book called *Ultimate Belief* based on "Truth, Beauty, Love and Compassion". I hope these are the values my family has been brought up with.

The situation in India seemed satisfactory. Then John heard from his friend John Dalton, the representative of the Damian Foundation in India, that they were not satisfied with the oversight of the leprosy work. Dr Nevin Wilson had taken study leave in Madras, then in England, where he had very limited success in adding to his qualifications, and had taken a job in Nepal. Another Indian friend who did welfare work some 20-30 miles away from John's clinic, and who had great standing as the 'Youth of the Year' in India, had tried to help but the distance was too great for daily visits from one of his doctors and it was too much in addition to their usual commitments. He came to London where John talked over the situation with him. In addition the chairman of the Nilgiri Wynaad Committee had just died – he was not very active but that as well as the other problems and the fact that the honorary treasurer wished to retire, disturbed me greatly.

A flicker of hope came. I had left some money in my will for projects close to my heart and as the exchange rate in India was very favourable to foreigners, I had already sent money to these old friends. Surely John's project could be funded out of this 'setaside' money. John wrote to say he was coming on a visit. Imagine his surprise when he arrived and found Dr Nevin had returned the day before after having been away for two years. Apparently he did not like the job in Nepal. As he was occupying the house, John slept in the clinic. I find it unbelievable that people take on a job and care so little for the tribal people who need their care.

After consultation with the committee, and the peripatetic doctor, the very capable 'Youth of the Year' was voted on to the committee and John Dalton, representative of the Damian Foundation, a tower of strength, was also invited. This would mean a 500-mile journey each way for him, so it was no light undertaking twice a year. To brighten up the leprosy workers, John took four or five of them to Madurai to a refresher course put on by John Dalton. As none of them except the non-tribal leprosy worker had ever left the Nilgiris before, it was enjoyed as a merry holiday. John had often arranged modest treats for his workers when possible, but this was a valuable special expedition.

Then the pump was not working and there was no-one to mend it. John found out what had gone wrong; a new part was needed, so he went into Coimbatore to order this, and maybe talk with John Dalton. When the ordered part arrived, he returned with it to Ambalamoola, fixed it, then found another part was worn and needed replacing and had to repeat the performance.

The coffee, tea and pepper plantations needed some oversight; pruning, manuring, getting improved stock. He was kept very busy. He visited my dear friend in Bangalore who founded the Association for the Physically Handicapped, a school and training centre. Rani, John's bitch, seemed to know he was leaving again and died a few weeks after he left.

There are changes, but as far as we know, the clinic is running and certainly the farm is making a substantial income towards the expenses. Leprosy cases have diminished greatly though vigilance is necessary for all diseases. Dr Nevin is in residence. I was glad John went this last time and so was he.

On the way home via Colombo, John visited the Quakers and the Red Cross. The Red Cross asked when he was coming back as they were so short of competent workers and there was a job going. He was given details and applied – to Geneva. Again they did not even pick up his references! Very odd. Apparently they were scaling down their operations.

John is now working for the Quakers in Sri Lanka – for keep and pocket money and a laptop computer. No telephone in his flat yet, no help with cooking, washing, shopping, cleaning. I hear an Irishman has been appointed to join John. At the moment of writing in 1996, John has taken some leave due to him and has gone back to Ambalamoola, taking medicines difficult to obtain in India. He is looking forward to meeting old friends and seeing what progress has been made.

CHAPTER FIVE

Friends World Committee for Consultation in Canada, Lebanon and Kenya

THE FIRST GATHERING of Quaker Yearly Meetings in many parts of the world was held in 1920. This led to the establishment in 1937 of the Friends World Committee for Consultation to promote the better understanding of Friends the world over, particularly by joint conferences and inter-visitation. Triennial meetings are held in different places, with each Yearly Meeting invited to send representatives. The world committee is divided into sections – Africa, India, Japan and Korea, Australasia, Europe and the Near East, North and South America. Some sections held annual conferences but distance made this difficult in Australasia, so Marjorie Sykes, who lived in India, published 'The Friendly Way' to keep Friends in touch with regional news and views.

Besides hoping to deepen the spiritual life of Friends by sharing their joys and problems in different cultures, the FWCC, being an international body acquired the status of a Non Government Agency that could present its findings on relevant issues to the United Nations in New York.

I think my work for Oxfam and my travels in India where I made a point of visiting isolated Friends, as well as projects such as the Quaker house in Delhi and the rural centre at Rasulia and its nearby schools, may have led, in 1975, to my being invited to be one of the London (Britain) Yearly Meeting representatives on FWCC for three years. This was an unexpected joy, especially when the

European section which met annually was meeting that April in Beirut. One's fare was paid, and I suppose other expenses if one needed them. Naturally I made use of the opportunity and with Doris Eddington, went a week early and visited Amman where Quakers had a central office that supported the Quaker workers near Jerash. There small schools, nursery classes and a woman's centre for Palestinian refugees had been set up. The sunshine, the dignity of the Arab women, the happy children and their singing games, the houses and tiny gardens, were a joy on this visit. It was very different from the starving Bangladeshis who arrived at the camps on the Indian/Bangladeshi border. The Palestinians were not penniless but needed help in restructuring their lives when the social amenities they were used to were missing. It was a pleasure to hear the calls to prayer of the Muezzin everywhere.

After a week, we returned to Beirut and the conference at Brumanna. A Meeting House and a boarding school had been built on the hillside above Beirut. The school was on vacation so we enjoyed the beautiful premises and the views, the trees, gardens and hostel and the open air theatre. About five different religious sects including the Druses gave talks as did George Gorman, a well known Quaker. Excursions were arranged to see the cedars of Lebanon and go up the Bikaar valley to visit the remains of ancient cities. We also went on a coach trip along the coast south of Beirut. The scent of orange trees in flower perfumed the way. We visited Tyre and Sidon and saw the huge marble pillars brought there by sea from Egypt. Like geology, this gives one a wider and deeper perspective of one's ancestors.

As we neared the Israeli border the ruined villages which the Israelis deemed to house terrorists were pitiful reminders of the fear and violence which lurks below the surface of 'civilisation'. Further away from the border some training centres in carpentry, carpet-making etc. had been set up and some rehousing to ameliorate conditions. It was rather surprising to be asked by local people if we wished to buy any guns; we didn't of course, but it left questions. These were answered only two weeks after we left.

I planned to spend a few more days before leaving by going to see an old friend near Amman. I arranged to meet some Quakers in Amman and visit Petra, the 'Rose-red city half as old as time'. I went on ahead and was surprised how long it took me this time with all the checks and counterchecks at the two border posts into Syria. From Damascus I took a taxi with three others to Amman. Then I had to get another service taxi to Zerka where Miss Coate lived. The taxi had a fixed route and when I asked how near it went to Miss Coate, the taxi driver and the other passengers said they knew her and would take me there. It was getting dark, so I was in luck. First they took me to her clinic and she wasn't there; then we went to her housing co-operative – not there. Then they took me to the Police Station and the policeman happily came with us to show us the way. Miss Coate was a bit surprised to see me handed over by the police and five other well-wishers.

I met Miss Coate at an Oxfam conference. She had been an inspector of mission schools in Palestine and was Arabic speaking. It seemed right to her to go with the Arabs and she was retiring anyway and had a pension; she felt she could be of more use to them. She had a beautiful but very simple mud-brick house and I was delighted to be with her and hear the latest news. After starting the clinic she noticed that all the men – not the women – were sitting about and saying they were tired. She realised they needed work. The men had skills, so she started a building co-operative and this was working well. The men had gathered one evening chatting – doubtless while the women put the children to bed. One of the men said he was a water diviner, and the others were sufficiently interested to get sticks and have a go! In the morning the foreman of her building group came rushing round to tell her that he had discovered he was a water diviner too. She got out the car and took him out into the desert towards an area where there were the remains of old Crusader castles. The diviner's stick started dancing about even when they were still in the car! The problem was that she needed capital to buy land and to sink a bore hole, and this is where Oxfam came in to help and when I first met her.

Miss Coate was now over eighty and had been honoured for her work by King Hussein, hence my welcome from the locals. The next morning her foreman took me out to see the hundred or so little houses with shady verandahs that had been built. Each five or six houses shared a well and one man was responsible for the maintenance of the pumping mechanism. As each house was completed, the workers had the opportunity to buy it by putting down a deposit. There was also land allocated to each house. With irrigation, this was fertile and they managed to pay off the mortgage within two years. There came a time when increasing numbers of people knew that there was water and came to carry it away in saddle bags on donkeys. One man as he took the water for his ten camels said gravely "Madam, the Lord gave you water so you can give some to me!" The Lord did not give diesel for the pumps so the Huddersfield Famine Relief Committee provided it. I suppose we were also servants of the Lord when we helped drill the wells.

I meant to keep my account of the visit to Miss Coate short, but I suppose I feel like Pirandello in his play *Six Characters in Search of an Author*. I admire her and her practical wisdom so much, I couldn't leave her out.

The next day I picked up the Allotts who were from Ireland and with another friend got a taxi south, along beside the single track railway at Deraa that T.E. Lawrence described. We then turned off before reaching Eilaat, to the narrow defile that led to Petra. There was a large and very pleasant cafe in a cave near the entrance to the narrow passage between high rocks which led to the cave houses of Petra. You could hire a horse at the cafe or walk. As you emerged a cave house with a pleasant façade faced you. I think it was called the Treasury. The other caves were more primitive and those higher up needed a ladder to gain access. You could of course pull this up after you and then you didn't need a front door. Apparently this was a safe haven for caravans and a wealthy trading centre. There was a 'hotel' at Petra, some caves and a few caravans, but these had to be booked well in advance so we couldn't stay. I have seen many cave houses in France and Spain, but this was in a class of its own. It was in the middle of a desert where caravans on which its wealth was based could find protection from marauders once through the narrow defile of the entrance; it was the unexpected wealth and an ancient civilisation after so much desert that was impressive.

We returned to Damascus and had a night there and visited the 'street called straight', the mosque with Saladin's tomb in the garden nearby and a museum showing people going on Haj. The long covered market, or souk, had such a plethora of craft work, particularly in metal and of lamps set with coloured glass. Men walked round with a tea urn on their back, so you could have a drink, non-alcoholic, any time. Near the bus station there was a beautiful small mosque with a shallow blue-tiled pool to allow people to wash the face and up to the elbows before entering. It was time for prayer as we came into the courtyard, so we waited quietly and I hope, prayerfully, as we watched the ritual of kneeling and head touching the ground several times as the prayer was intoned, facing towards Mecca. Islam has much to commend it – no colour bar, no images of Allah that can act as a barrier to the religious life, all going on Haj wear the same white garments and walk the whole distance and then walk round the Kaaba seven times intoning prayers. The days of fasting are kept much more strictly than we keep Lent. There are 'extremists' in every faith but Christians are not in a position to criticise after their appalling behaviour in the Crusades – when Saladin was more humane than the Christians and the Arabs in Morocco welcomed Jews and those trying to escape the autos-da-fé organised by Isabella and Ferdinand in Spain.

Back to Beirut and home before the civil war burst upon us. The school at Brumanna had the standing of a public school in the Middle East. It took exams to prepare pupils for entrance to Oxford and Cambridge as well as Near East Universities. It had a religious ethos nourished by the teachings of the Old and New Testament and the Koran. For a time the school continued, but as the war increased in intensity, parents naturally withdrew their children and finance became a problem. It became a day school for children from nearby villages. At last it was handed over to an educational body in Beirut. This was not a satisfactory solution. The war has ended but controversy about management continues. Other schools, one for girls and another for boys, in Rammalah, about fifteen miles north of Jerusalem, have faced difficult times too, but so far have survived.

The next triennial meeting of FWCC in 1979 was to be held at MacMaster University campus at Hamilton in Canada. There must have been fifteen hundred people there. Friends were very pleased as a very evangelical group of Friends had decided to join and were given an opportunity to take a session. I did not feel on the same wavelength as the three or four evangelical groups who reported on their achievements at a main session. Their main interest seemed to be rejoicing in the number of their converts. However the report from the Alaskan group interested me. People who wait in silence and expectation that their Shaman would speak words of wisdom, felt close to the Quakers who also wait in silence upon the Holy Spirit which might speak through anyone present. This formed a bridge with Quakerism – and with Zen. I would call it activating the deep collective unconscious and sense of oneness of all life.

My other brief pleasure was meeting Douglas Steer who wrote of 'mutual irradiation' as a result of the 'colloquia' he organised with various Christian and Zen Buddhists in Japan, and with Christians and Hindus in India. The aim was to share their experience of their faith rather than the beliefs and formal teaching of the faith. There is a difference, as I found when our inter-faith group invited two Muslims to come and speak to us at my house and they talked of Islam. We then invited them to come again and talk of their own experience and how this affected their lives.

Though I found the main sessions overwhelming, we attended small groups sometime every day; there were morning study groups, but I am not happy in crowds – I don't even like going into a library and facing thousands of books unless I know what I am looking for, then the hunting instinct takes over. I exchanged letters with three or four FWCC members I had met for a few years, but gradually these lapsed. The variety of Quakerism in different cultures gave food for thought, even more when I attended part of the QWCC meetings in Kenya.

As Canada YM followed I booked to go there and was taken by car via Niagara – large and powerful, so I paid my respects. Alma College, where YM was held was pleasantly situated in woods and had a dozen or so old people's modest bungalows in the grounds, rather like almshouses. The old people were invited to school functions and the girls were encouraged to visit and keep an eye open in case help was needed. This seemed a very practical training of benefit and pleasure to all.

The food had been very lavish by my standards at the FWCC so I booked in as a vegetarian in Canada. Imagine my surprise when the main meal was carrot, peas, potatoes, etc., with no protein at all. There were only eight of us at the vegetarian table. We asked if we could have some cheese, so a small bowl of grated cheese was put on the table – a dessertspoon each! Think twice before being vegetarian in Canada. Canadian Friends have enormous distances to travel. It costs Friends from the western seaboard more than it cost me travelling from England. I liked meeting Canadian Friends I had met before at Rasulia, the Quaker farm project in India. The worship groups had a variety of unexpected happenings – they were a bit free range – but the memories are blurred. I enjoyed it and appreciated the difficulties of such a few Quakers in a huge country.

At Toronto the Meeting House has guest rooms. This allowed me to visit an American Indian 'tourist' site and a huge 'condominium' composed of separate flats but with a large lounge-entrance hall where you could sit and chat with your visitors if you did not wish to take them up to your flat. The flats were very luxurious too and there was a swimming bath for residents. I was also introduced to huge indoor shopping centres long before we had such things here. There seemed to be a good reason for these in Canada where the heavy snowfall in winter makes shopping in a warm atmosphere more inviting.

Quakers also have a camp site, Camp Nekaunis, with wooden buildings on the shore of Georgian Bay, part of the Great Lakes complex. The friendly people, the woods, swimming in the bay, all made me wish I could have stayed there longer. What I enjoyed most was the ten days or so when I first arrived in America. Some of us spent a weekend at a conference centre, with wonderful vegetarian food and discussions on world food problems and development. I felt at home. Then we were taken by coach to visit Meeting Houses in New England, sometimes simple wooden structures with a verandah. We stayed the night with local people, then on again to visit the house of Rufus Jones. Some Meeting Houses had a screen between the men's and the women's sections and separate entrances for them. I suppose it concentrated the mind. The Meeting House at Boston was a fine building but I was shocked to hear that Quakers were once driven from the settlement and the death penalty was meted out to Friend Mary Dyer who returned. Not all who went to the New World believed in freedom of religion, except for themselves.

I loved staying in the old farm houses, meeting people in their own homes. As I had taken a record of the Huddersfield Choral Society singing the *Messiah* to give to my hostess, it was a problem when there were so many. However I was invited out to bring my record with me and play it to everyone. I found it odd to be staying with one happy family consisting of 'his and her' children and 'our' children. This entailed 'his and hers' visiting as well as 'hers and his'. Strangely it sounded quite a happy arrangement. There was also a school, Rockwood Academy, we visited, started in 1850 by some Ackworth Quakers. It was smaller, but the architectural style was similar. I flew back to New York to get the plane to England.

There were two other enjoyable European section Easter conferences at Baden Baden and in Belgium. Smaller and a joy to meet friends I had met before.

The next triennial was in Kenya in 1982, preceeded by a conference at Kaimosi. I knew the Oxfam organiser in Nairobi so there would be an opportunity to visit Oxfam projects. The films about wild life in Africa and the outstanding nature films of David Attenborough, had created an appetite in me not satisfied by the wildlife parks I had visited in India and Sri Lanka, where so few animals were to be seen. I booked a safari to the Masai Mara and a stay at the Ark in the Aberdares. The road from the airport was especially beautiful with its flowering trees. Apparently the botanic gardens at Kew and Edinburgh had advised on the planting of the roadside and the park in Nairobi and it was greatly to their credit. The YMCA was economical and the meals were good. Many students from the university stayed there and provided local knowledge and there was an outdoor swimming pool. It was within walking distance of the centre of Nairobi. This was an impressive modern town with fine shops and civic buildings and, as I remember, a very beautiful mosque. I acclimatised for a few days and was taken to visit the slum areas on the outskirts. Some homes were little more than tents but there were also small houses with little gardens where people were growing a few vegetables. Voluntary agencies were running weekend courses for teenagers and mother and baby clinics and classes for young mothers. There were slums but the people seemed cheerful and well fed, due to the voluntary help given, and much, much better than the slums I had visited in Bombay and Calcutta. Further afield visits were planned for when I returned from the Masai Mara.

On Sunday I went to Quaker Meeting at the Ngong Road Meeting House. There were about forty people present, an unprogrammed meeting, and I think mostly white people. There was another centre at Ofafa which I think was more of a settlement where Walter Martin and his wife spent some years. He was remembered with great admiration. He was very sensitive to African aspirations as more African countries at this time were gaining independence. He had a number of personal friends among the new heads of the African states, which was of great value during peace negotiations in London when he became Clerk of Quaker Peace and Service.

I was lucky to be asked out to lunch after Meeting on Sunday by two Friends who lived a few miles out of Nairobi. They had a beautiful house and garden with unusual African trees – Erythinia, Battle Brush, etc. One tree had a cluster of orchids growing out of it. The wife had been a student of Ikebana (Japanese flower arrangement) so we had a common bond. Most valuable too, they gave me their telephone number.

A safari minibus carrying about eight passengers came to collect me at the YMCA and we had a long day ahead going down into the Rift Valley then travelling on dusty roads which at times obliterated the scenery. The driver could spot different birds though travelling at speed; it was good to know they were there even if one couldn't see them. We stopped for lunch and could see many unusual birds and naturally were surrounded by Africans offering their crafts for sale – unusual and attractive necklaces, carvings, etc. At last we arrived at Kiswa Tembu – great trees along the drive to a huge single story hall with windows – usually wide open on one side so that we could look out onto grass and trees and sometimes see animals and always, birds. I was taken to my tent. It had a verandah with two cane armchairs looking onto a stream. The tent was opened and I could walk upright. There was a bed with a reading lamp, a 'hall stand' for hanging my clothes and a little table with tissues and toilet necessities. I was further amazed when I unzipped the back of the tent to find a flush lavatory, a wash basin with hot water supplied by my own oil drum containing water with a fire underneath it. I had never been camping like this before.

We had dinner in the main hall, sometimes followed by a display of African dancing or singing and then we were conducted to our individual tents as occasionally lions wondered around looking for a meal. At six o'clock a tray of early morning tea was brought in. At 7am we were taken off in a small touring minibus with a roof that could be opened. Once seven or eight gazelles came leaping across in front, their grace was a joy to behold but I hadn't got my camera at the ready. Sometimes we would stop and look at a lion a few feet away and he would contemplate us. Then he would just turn round and look the other way as if he didn't like what he saw — I'm not surprised. What surprised me was that he didn't run away, as other animals did. Is this the basis of our pride in British bulldogs and British lions? After watching the Mara animals wake up, we returned to breakfast under the trees, then to be taken to another area.

I have never seen so many animals, hundreds and hundreds that move up into the Mara from the Serengeti and then return when the rains arrive. Cape Buffalo are the fiercest and should not be approached although they are herbivores. I saw a lioness leave her two cubs and speed off to catch a young zebra, but the buffalo barred her way. It was unusual for a lioness to hunt alone and I wondered if one herbivore was protecting another herbivore, or was there some other reason? Some tourists walked in a single file, silently, led by a game warden with a gun. Apparently the wild animals don't attack unless they are attacked or they fear for their young, or if they are hungry, but are unlikely to attack a disciplined group in broad daylight. After lunch it was siesta time; then another exploration. Wildebeest, zebra, okapi, gnu, lions, lionesses in groups with their cubs, giraffe that can eat thorn trees, gazelles, wart hogs, ostriches, impala and a few elephants, and wallowing, yawning hippopotamuses that spend most of their time in the mud. There are so many varieties of deer, but when they are grazing there will always be one or two posted on little hillocks ready to give a warning if danger threatens.

Kiswa Tembu was extremely well run, I thought it must be an American who organised the excellent plumbing for campers and an Englishman who arranged early morning tea served in bed. I found out later that this surmise was correct. The African staff shared their culture with us too – a successful combined effort. The five days safari came to an end all too soon.

Soon after we left Kishwa Tembu we stopped at a Masai Village where a Masai warrior in tribal dress offered to show us round for £10 a head. Nobody wanted to stop except me, so we continued our journey. I think it was here that we encountered a Masai warrior who had graduated at Nairobi University but found it more acceptable, and possibly more profitable, to live at home and, with good English, speak proudly of his tribal culture.

Most of the party were taken back to Nairobi but I had booked a few days in the Ark in the Aberdares. However I was offloaded at a beautiful hotel with sleeping chalets in the garden. It seemed odd as I expected to go straight on to the Ark. The hotel was full of many groups of tourists and it felt a little lonely sitting at my table alone. I had my soup and then saw a young man sitting across the room eating and reading a book. Perhaps he felt as I did but was reluctant to face a snub. I weighed up the situation, plucked up my courage and went across to him. I pointed out that I did not enjoy eating alone and if he cared to join me, I would be delighted. He jumped up with alacrity and joined me. It was a happy meeting. He worked for Pan Am and therefore had free flights and he had a few days' leave. He also had a small vehicle with him and was planning to go to Masai Mara. Coffee was served in a spacious lounge with an open fire. We talked and had so much in common it was a joy. One of the waiters came up to us and asked us to turn out the lights before returning to our chalets. We looked round and everyone else had retired. He conducted me to my chalet, although I don't think there were any lions there. I saw him off regretfully, but it had been such a happy meeting I was grateful.

The next morning I wandered around the grounds, looking at the birds, including the sacred ibis, and saw Lake Naivasha; I was wondering when my driver would come. Time passed and I was getting anxious. One of the other tourists joined me in the garden and asked where I was going, so I told him my problem. He went to speak to the head of his party who was organising this very prestigious safari and therefore well up in the safari hierarchy and knew the boss of the firm I was booked with. He phoned up and reported that a car was now on its way to take me to the Ark. I relaxed and enjoyed the garden but too soon a car arrived – apparently to take me back to Nairobi. There were further discussions but I refused to move. At last the promised car arrived and we set off post haste to the Aberdares, the road taking us over the equator twice. When we arrived at the Aberdare Country Club, the coach taking the visitors had left for the Ark and only very limited traffic is allowed into the Aberdare Game Park. More discussions – at last the car was allowed to take me in. I found out later that the modest accommodation I had booked had been overbooked; with the 'boss man's' intervention I was given a luxury suite that was vacant.

One left the car and there was a catwalk to the hotel. Visitors were allowed on the catwalk but no further. There were good viewing verandas on the other side looking over a shallow pool and a salt lick. At night the pool was gently floodlit and a bell would ring in your room; the idea was – one ring elephant, two wart hog, three leopard, four ... so you knew when to leap out of bed when it was an animal you particularly wanted to see. It was restful in a way, no running about unless there was a bell you wanted to respond to and plenty of interesting people to talk to and lovely meals.

Well, all too soon that came to an end and I went back in the tourist vehicle to await further transport at the Aberdare Country Club. The club was an illustration of the fact that some people had in the past a very high standard of living and some were still enjoying this. The garden had exotic trees and birds but even that began to pall as we waited and waited. Then we heard that a small group of officers had staged a coup against the President, Arap Moi. A car at last arrived for me and we drove quickly until we came to the Blue Post Hotel. The road into Nairobi was closed at the Cahaier Barracks and this prevented further movement. There was a wonderful waterfall nearby but it is surprising how after a time one loses interest even in that. Evening was coming on, so I paid for a bed at the hotel and gave my driver money to get a bed in the village. How glad I was that I had not spent £10 visiting the Masai village! As I had paid in advance all my main expenses, I had taken little money out with me and the result was that I had no money for food. However someone noticed I wasn't eating – quite likely I had a lean and hungry look – and I was invited over to share at a table with a small tourist group who said one more didn't make any difference. How very kind of them. It made a lot of difference to me and I also shared breakfast with them.

We continued to wait. Then I remembered the telephone number that I had been given by the Quakers with whom I had had lunch. I rang them and asked for news. Apparently it would be easy for my driver to leave me at their house as soon as the road was clear past the barracks. So we waited for that ... and waited, until at last the road was clear. At last we could continue and I arrived safely amongst hospitable friends.

They were uneasy. There were a number of ruthless killings and alas, when law and order break down, the lawless elements come out to profit by the occasion. The servants lived in a house nearby, they were frightened too. I was surprised when shown to my bedroom on the ground floor that the windows were barred and I was told that all possessions were kept out of reach or put in drawers or cupboards as 'fishers' came with a long rod with a hook on the end of it and could catch a lot in this way. We said a short prayer with the staff and went to bed. After a few days order was restored – I suppose force was used but I was glad of the results. I am not a complete pacifist. I approve of the use of a police force and feel a prompt restoring of order is in the same category. A revolution means that injustices have not been dealt with and it is a question of listening to complaints and doing something to remove the tension early, rather than ignoring early signs.

Back at the YMCA I found many foreign students had returned home but others were pleased to tell me all about it. All the Asian shops had been ransacked – though what that had to do with Arap Moi I don't know. The banks were still closed so I couldn't get any money. Luckily I had left a small amount with my passport in safe keeping at the YMCA. The man in charge of the YMCA, I think he was a Quaker, understood the problem, so allowed me to delay payment for board until I returned from the FWCC at Kaimosi, when we expected the banks would have re-opened.

Some very ancient coaches were laid on to take Quakers going to Kaimosi, which is not far from Victoria Nyanza. The scenery was magnificent – the hills, the flowering trees, the lakes, one of them pink with flamingos. We arrived to find police at the entrance. The Kenyan government was taking care of us. It was evening when we arrived but there were problems – rooms not ready, catering under strain. Apparently there had been a number of cancellations. We were bedded down for the night and then moved to different rooms when they were ready. There were a number of toilets and wash basins in what might be called a large bathroom if there had been any baths – I don't remember showers. If you wanted hot water you took a jug and went outside where a wood fire heated some water. Gradually arrangements were sorted out. The long queues for meals were memorable, but as it was sunny and warm, except in the afternoon when it rained, queuing was a social occasion. It seems to be part of the culture in Africa, that when there are guests and food, everybody joins in. I think it is a relic of tribal culture, but the strain of catering for 1000 guests and large numbers of uninvited guests, was difficult in the extreme. Meat killed had to be eaten the same day, no time to 'hang' it to tenderise it, no fridges or freezers. I suppose guests expect a higher standard than the locals did. Meal times were a great opportunity to mix and talk.

In this way Barnabas Lugonzo heard there was a Quaker from Huddersfield present and tracked me down. Barnabas had stayed with us when he was studying architecture at the Polytechnic. QPS knew he would be in a senior position in the Kenyan administration when he returned, but his wife needed to share some of his experience to play her part and feel at ease in her position. They therefore financed her to come to England to join her husband. Then Barnabas left her with me while he went to London to study. Ziporah's English was very limited. She was studying catering including French patisserie! She became poorly and I took her to the doctor who could find nothing wrong. I went to see her tutor at the Polytechnic who said she just could not cope and her English was inadequate. Friends had intended Ziporah to be with Barnabas. When he came to visit her I told him what I thought, but he said she must do as she was told. I got in touch with Friends

House and she was moved to London to stay with Barnabas. Before they returned to Africa she produced her first child. It was good to meet him again and talk.

The Quaker settlement at Kaimosi included schools and a college for boarders. There was a huge dining hall, assembly hall, a hospital and a vocational training centre. It was founded by American Quakers who expect a much higher standard of living than indigenous Africans. After some years the Americans felt it right to hand over to local administrators and withdrew. There was great competition to take over the well-paid posts and the big houses of the departing Americans. Some local Quakers wished to divide up the assets and establish two Yearly Meetings instead of one. I have seen comparable trouble in India when an extended family takes over. This also applied to British Quaker projects, but not to the same extent as the discrepancy between local and expatriate standards of living was not so high. This causes a lot of trouble and bad feeling and should be taken into account when a project is established.

A Yearly Meeting was held while we were there. It was in the open air under the trees. There was a lot of singing and speeches, but it was not easy to conduct the finer points of discussion. Our day began with breakfast and queues. Meeting for Worship followed in the big assembly hall. This consisted mainly of different African groups following one another in singing and swinging, praising the Lord. Few Africans feel really at home with silent worship. Study groups followed – there were about twelve in my group, seven or eight of them local people. We had been given questions to discuss, arranged by one called Noake; this gave a framework to our discussions. The only one I remember was 'What was your one most transforming experience that has altered your life?' One African said that "If I didn't hit my teacher, he wouldn't hit me", another that "If I became a Quaker I should get more education." The simplicity and honesty of the answers staggered me. They were practical and based on experience. A Hindu would have talked for half an hour taking off into the empyrean. A Chinese would be practical I know, but so simple? It was a learning experience for me although 'transforming' is too weighty a word.

The groups also divided up into twos, one of whom was blindfold and had to be led by the other, then after twenty minutes we changed over. That was good training in sensitivity and awareness. We had some large assemblies in the great hall with a speaker and smaller 'special interest groups' that I enjoyed as I met people interested in similar things. There was a special African day when Africans showed and played unusual musical instruments; they also sang and danced their own dances. Missionaries, as in Puritan England, had barred dancing. This would not have suited me and I was delighted to see real African dancing. Africans move beautifully. A teacher in a nearby senior school in Huddersfield taught creative dance. Those of African descent excelled in this greatly; it added to their self-esteem and their school work also benefited.

An impressive figure at the conference was Ham Soc Hon, a well-known Quaker from Korea, who had served a number of prison sentences for his criticism of the government. I was pleased to meet again Barry Wilshire who for a few years organised a Peace Caravan that had visited Huddersfield and Bradford on its journeyings. They arranged talks and role play, dramatic presentations in Meeting Houses and schools, which made a valuable contribution in getting the ideas of conciliation and its methods across to young and old. We naturally visited the farm and hospital – the monkeys swinging from tree to tree keeping us under surveillance. The grand finale was a 'banquet'. Groups of African women carrying baskets on their heads walked to the kitchen area where the feast was being prepared. A huge marquee was erected and African tribal culture took over. The crowd was so great that Alan Crosby and I sat outside talking and watching the scene. We went in briefly at the end.

Those who wished to were invited to stay with an African family for the weekend. Diana Simpkins and I went to stay with the Mirembe family – seven children and all the neighbours coming in to look at us and share the feast. It was hard work for the housewife. The Mirembe children went down to the stream to collect water. The kindness of the family was unbelievable. They knew we found squat toilets difficult to cope with, so had made some boxes with holes in the top for us to sit on. The boxes were much too small so there were problems, but the thought was appreciated.

We went to Meeting on Sunday, where I was asked to speak. The translator could always modify unsuitable utterances. We were taken by car to Victoria Nyanza where two fine boats lay rusting in the harbour at Entebbe. They had been brought from England in sections to Mombasa, by rail to Nairobi, then by lorry to Entebbe, where they were assembled. These boats used to run an efficient service between Uganda, Kenya and Tangyanika, but when independence came, the three states could not agree on the management so they remained as rusty relics, memorials to a bygone efficient age. We then went on to visit a Quaker overseas volunteer, Judith Hinch, at an agricultural training centre at S'angalo. She had got a pond dug and had stocked it with tilapia – a fish that thrives in salty water. She showed us two huge sophisticated machines sent by a firm in Europe intending to be helpful. They stood rusting – a monument to European ignorance and inability to find out the needs of a peasant culture. I found out what was needed and with the help of the Huddersfield Famine Relief Committee and the Young Farmers Club that Judith belonged to in England, we were able to be useful donors whose gifts were appreciated. It is a lovely feeling when you are able to start the process of helping and seeing it grow.

Barnabas had insisted that Diana and I should visit his shamba. No official in Nairobi could maintain his dignity without having a shamba – an ancestral home and plantation in the country. Women were working there picking tea leaves to be sent away for processing. We had an indoor toilet we could flush – a lad climbed up a ladder outside with a bucket of water to pour into the cistern. I visited Barnabas in Nairobi where he lived with his wife and five children in a lovely house. I asked if Ziporah always did as she was told now. There was laughter and I gather that discipline was easier. Barnabas showed me the low cost housing he was erecting for the government. We were also taken to the World Wild Life orphanage and hospital for sick animals at the entrance to the nearby national park. We were not allowed to visit the park as some insurgents were thought to be hiding there. I was sad that the rest of my Oxfam programme could not be undertaken as people feared to leave their families and risk going far.

There was disatisfaction over land. Many of the big European estates had been divided up and farmers/peasants resettled, but the top echelons of the administration were anxious to hold on to the well run estates where export capacity improved the balance of payments and of course was not without profit to them. When the parents die the shamba is divided equally among the children, so the share gets smaller each time. Six or seven children is usual in African families, but when I suggested it would ease the problem if they had fewer children they were shocked. "But this is part of our culture!" Well, it is their problem, and my solutions will not be useful.

After a visit near Kaimosi, some old coaches were laid on to take us back to Nairobi. The coaches broke down, first one, then another, so it was two hours after curfew that I was deposited at the YMCA. The next day I was able to go into Nairobi, view the damage to the Asian quarter, go to the bank and visit a few attractive tourist shops. Barnabas came and took me out, I paid up at the YMCA and had a last swim in the pool. I was quite relieved it was the last time I had to cross the garden to a very pleasant dormitory building with so many keys, and where the automatic lights always went out before you found the right door and the right key. I was sad about the cancelled Oxfam visits, but I had seen and experienced so much of the beauty of Africa and its wild life and so many friendly people, it is a treasure I have in my old age to look back. I think it was Villon who wrote: "Où sont les neiges d'autant?" ... the snows of yester year melt but live in the memory.

CHAPTER SIX

Hong Kong Action

(Based on an article in To Asia in Peace, *Edited by P. Arrowsmith, Sidgwick and Jackson, 1972)*

IN 1968 I joined a Non-Violent Peace Action group going to Cambodia and hopefully, on to Hanoi, to demonstrate against the war in Vietnam. Earlier I had turned down the opportunity as I felt it was impractical, but when, a couple of weeks before they left, they were short of volunteers, I agreed to go and pay my own expenses.

In the two peace groups I have joined, this one and the other which was Anglo-French with the Ark community, both contained people who had strong personalities, did not always act in a committed way and were less than peaceful and supportive of each other. (In the Anglo-French group these were, unfortunately, mostly English.) This group planning to go to Vietnam however, had several very aggressive members and unity of purpose or action was never achieved. In fact, the group spent most of the time in Asia as the somewhat unwelcome guests of the Cambodian government, before splitting up to different destinations, and never arrived in Hanoi, as originally planned. My first estimate of this group as impractical had been the correct one, but as so often happens, it led indirectly and in a completely unforeseen way, to a demonstration against the war in Vietnam, helped by Hong Kong Quakers.

The NVAV had come to a halt in Phnom Penh, unable to proceed further because of the difficulty of entering Vietnam, and had begun to disintegrate; some had already returned home, and others could not agree on a course of action. Meanwhile the Cambodian

Government was playing host to the group and occasionally arranging expeditions to various sites, including one to the Vietnamese/Cambodian border, which was under attack from South Vietnam troops.

I was sent to Hong Kong by the group to see if we could arrange a joint project between our Non-Violent Action in Vietnam group and the American Quaker Action Group. Fourteen people (out of twenty-four) in NVAV said they would be willing to join in such a project if it was feasible. The AQAG had a boat, the *Phoenix*, they were using to take to Vietnam. Likely participants were asked what skills they had that might prove useful – only one had any sailing experience. Having myself observed some of those who claimed to be swimmers in action, I thought they had over-rated their skill in that direction. This was important because it had been suggested that the *Phoenix* should sail to within the three-mile limit and the mined zone, from which we would swim ashore and demonstrate at the nearest US base. Some degaussing equipment to repel mines might have been useful.

The team was somewhat divided as to whether we should just demonstrate at a US base. I myself felt that most people would be better satisfied if the action included taking even a token quantity of relief supplies to the Buddhists, NLF or Red Cross.

When I arrived in Hong Kong, the day after the *Phoenix* crew, they were all busy unloading supplies they had not been allowed to land at Da Nang, and loading up with medical supplies for Hanoi, where port clearance had been promised – so it was 'all hands on deck' until late the next evening. It was a great relief to be with a small experienced group of Quakers, sharing concerns at a deeper level. Our discussions revealed the following:

1. The boat might be available, if the owner agreed, until May, after the monsoon. (This was in January.)
2. There was some concern about which crew members might stay on.
3. The area within the three-mile limit is heavily guarded, and the possibility of a repeat landing less likely now that the US navy had been alerted about the *Phoenix*; in any case, the proper authorities should be informed at the time, so that a confrontation should take place.

4. A crew of four would be essential; in addition, a maximum of eight demonstrators should be taken. All of these would have to be carefully vetted by the *Phoenix* crew.
5. Permission to proceed would have to be obtained from the boat owner and from AQAG in Philadelphia.
6. £4,000 insurance would be needed for the boat.

After attending the *Phoenix* press conference in the Hilton, as I was unable to make any useful contact over the phone with Phnom Penh (where the remainder of the group were located) I flew back there to report direct to the group. Deciding factors about the proposed project were the lack of contacts in Vietnam to give support, the problem of raising the £4,000 insurance, and failure to evolve a good plan of action – all things needing a lot of time to deal with adequately.

During my three days' absence (before the others had heard my report), I felt the climate of opinion had shifted. The group seemed to be at least half way to Singapore, in spirit, en route to take direct action in Saigon. [Another alternative plan that eventually proved impossible.] It appeared unlikely that any of the group would be able to move about in Vietnam. As I disliked the idea of jumping into the dock at Saigon and was sick of prolonged meetings, I decided to quit the team and, making use of the close contacts I had with other organisations, see something for myself of the situation in Vietnam – which might prove of value. I felt uneasy on account of the rapidly changing attitudes in the group, also because people unwilling to take direct action were being sent home. There was evidence of pressure being brought to bear by stronger personalities. I must admit that I do not know how we should have resolved such a situation, in which moderate, not very effective people were devouring the currency, thus limiting the activity of the direct action group. [The whole project had been somewhat underfunded from the start.] The point was that the direct action group was not as united as it appeared to be on the surface.

From then on, financing myself became an immediate problem. A member of the group lent me sufficient US dollars to buy my air ticket from Phnom Penh to Hong Kong. My husband repaid this in England, and transferred money to the S.E.Asia Bank in Hong Kong for my use. A society, for which I had worked voluntarily for many years and whose director I knew well, advanced me some money for immediate needs. Having already worked to get reasonable accommodation in the event of the NVAV group going to Hong Kong, I was able to go direct to the newly opened Chinese YMCA in Kowloon. There I stayed for a week, then spent a week or so with Friends. The YMCA was reasonably central and provided some of the essential services for organisation in a foreign land – information, telephone, fixed address, meeting place and shelter. Before leaving Phnom Penh, I had arranged that the group, that is, Rachel Blake [the person who managed communications in the group], should keep in touch with me by Poste Restante at the G.P.O. This meant daily pleasant, but time-consuming, trips across the ferry to Hong Kong Island. A letter from Phnom Penh from me to Quakers in Hong Kong reached them a week after my arrival.

The bitter winds, low cloud, drizzling rain and low temperature after the heat of Phnom Penh made me all too aware of my physical limitations – moreover I had no winter clothes with me and was suffering from a mild throat infection.

The very day the Tet offensive broke out, I had returned to Hong Kong to get my visa for Vietnam. Saigon was cut off by phone, and only American transport planes were flying there. Projects that I was going to visit there were now in NLF hands. The Quaker teams withdrew to Hong Kong. Visas were not available unless one had a return plane ticket to and from Saigon, and there were no civilian flights or transport operating within the country. After three weeks of frustration, it became apparent that things were no better. Some kind of peace demonstration in Hong Kong (which previously would have prevented my getting a visa to Vietnam) was now possible. I had already had contact with Quakers, young Americans at the University who had demonstrated on the steps of the US Embassy, (where they had tactfully been allowed to post themselves when the police came to arrest them as they were standing on a public footpath). This meant I could get help over press and television coverage, also with writing the Chinese inscriptions on my banner and having photographs taken when apprehended by the police. There is no doubt that it is invaluable to have people with local knowledge around in such situations.

David Gillett, a member of the group left in Phnom Penh, now joined me. I was glad to be supported by such a pleasant person – moreover we had a common Quaker background to form the basis for an action. Since the Communist riots of the previous year, public meetings and demonstrations had been banned in Hong Kong. Even the public showing of the Quaker film about the *Phoenix* was not allowed. It was important to inform the press and news media about our demonstration only a short while before the event if we wanted to avoid being joined by hordes of Communists and police. So, on Sunday at 2pm, air tickets around our necks, we stood at the entrance to the Fergusson Pier (where, so a local supporter had told us, the American troops disembarked for 'rest and relaxation', with our banner. On it was inscribed: "We support U Thant's Peace Efforts in Vietnam" – relevant because U Thant was making special peace efforts at the time. We also had leaflets addressed to American Servicemen. But alas – no troopships were disembarking that afternoon. Only six policemen in a van demanded to see our pamphlets, then sat waiting for trouble. Newsmen and television reporters came along too. After an hour, we moved, followed by the police, to the Spring Gardens, where crowds were listening to the band. Many people came up, took leaflets and expressed support. David took some leaflets into the nearby Hilton Hotel. After two hours, we were driven by a friend to the airport where – joy – an American transport plane had just come in. Without waiting to unfurl the banner, we dashed down the lines of soldiers queuing up for coaches, and gave them our 'Green Beret' and 'US Servicemen' leaflets. They accepted them and we saw them reading them in the coaches. Overjoyed that we had got the leaflets into the right hands, we waited for the next transport, due two to three hours later. Unfortunately the coaches were then moved to another side of the airport, and the few soldiers who passed through the main hall refused the leaflets ... presumably warned not to accept seditious literature. As it was now 9 pm, we withdrew our faces, but saw them again on television news that night after the latest Vietnam newscast. There were also brief accounts of the action on the front pages of the papers next morning. We gave our remaining dozen leaflets to the Quakers to help them continue the anti-war propaganda in other ways.

There can be no doubt that small, mobile groups of two or three people can be effective, provided they share a basic common concern and are reasonably mature personalities. However, it is exceedingly difficult to keep in touch with other mobile groups – or even static ones – when posts are slow and erratic; letters get lost, and telephone calls booked hours ahead are costly and merely add to the confusion when the line is so bad that only odd words can be heard.

Local contacts, that you can make quickly, and with whom you share a common background, are very valuable. They can help over finance, hospitality, the gleaning of information about strategic demonstration points, information about local press and television personnel, photographing and observing events in terms of knowing how to act effectively if arrested, providing quick transport, etc. It is not desirable that these supporters, who are often UK administration employees, be involved in this kind of demonstration themselves – they have their part to play in other ways, and can make an invaluable contribution. In fact, we had been offered some leaflets to be printed in Chinese, but the sudden confirmation of our return flight booking on Saturday for early the following Monday morning meant that the printers had gone home for the weekend before we could contact them. We therefore had only the two or three hundred leaflets addressed to American Servicemen to give out.

As a result of articles in the local newspaper (Huddersfield) and other papers and journals, I was invited to speak and show slides on my 'Visit to the borders of Vietnam' to schools, UNA branches and Quaker Meetings in places as far apart from each other as Aylesbury and Ayr. I received invitations to address Townswomen's Guilds and business and professional women's organisations. This provided me with the opportunity to give a brief background to the conflict in Vietnam and in SE Asia as a whole, as well as describing NVAV as such, using slides to illustrate my talks. I was able to sell a considerable number of peace movement leaflets and many copies of Thich Nhat Han's book on the situation in Vietnam, *The Lotus in a Sea of Fire*.

[The remains of the NVAV group finally managed to demonstrate against the Vietnam war at an US Air Force base in Thailand, where they were imprisoned briefly, then taken to Bangkok where they were kept in prison for another two weeks while they waited for a return flight to England.]

FURTHER EXPERIENCES OF HONG KONG

Hong Kong consists of Hong Kong Island and part of the mainland called Kowloon connected by ferry and now by underground. There are also a number of smaller islands; the biggest is Lantau, with a beautiful Buddhist temple on its central mountain and on the shore a village devoted to fishing and its processing which spreads a strong aroma. When I first went there were lots of floating villages with floating 'shops'. I think many sold drinking water. Large families lived on the boats together with chickens and other pets. There was usually a shore-based clinic not far away. A little train ran from Kowloon to the Chinese border, passing many rice paddies, duck ponds and ponds for rearing carp – three layers in each pond, differentiated by their differing feeding habits. It was beautiful in its economy and simplicity and the peasants tending the ponds in their flat broad-brimmed hats. I'm sad this simple beauty has gone. Now the land is mostly covered by high-rise flats inhabited by people who used to live in boats.

One can still see some boat villagers at Aberdeen Harbour on the far side of Hong Kong Island and can stop for a swim at sandy shores where at festival time families visit in the moonlight, let off crackers, light lamps and have a picnic. At the Bon festival you visit the family grave, burn incense and remember your ancestors. Most of the bigger boats, small gardens or inside the homes will have a shrine to ancestors. There is a sturdy background of Confucianism in Hong Kong as well as in Japan and China.

A bus takes you up through thick woods, past the Japanese internment camp at Stanley (read William Sewell and his and his family's experiences there during the 1939-45 war) then down to villages on the sea shore where smallish snakes are for sale. I'm not sure if they are pets or to be fattened up for eating. One can ascend the peak on Hong Kong Island by a lift or walk up through the woods, with printed advice in English of suitable exercises to do every couple of hundred yards before you proceed further. The view across the bay to Kowloon and the islands is breathtaking and as the sun goes down and the sunset colours turn gradually to a purple velvet, there is mystery and a sense of worship, never to be forgotten.

Quakers meet in a room at the Archbishop's Palace, mostly expat and one or two Chinese. The place used to be easy to walk to, but when I went again a few years later, modernisation of one way streets with no connecting paths for pedestrians meant I lost my bearings and had to take a taxi. The new underground from the island to Kowloon has station names written only in Chinese and so I feel safer going on the ferry – it's lovely to see the view and the boats, especially on my first visit when there were many sampans sailing about their business.

At the end of the war the Japanese left, but as Mao Tse Tung took over in China, thousands of refugees came, including Pastor Stumpf, a Lutheran businessman who provided the materials with which the refugees could use their skills by making pincushions, tea-cosies, wind-chimes and so be self-supporting. It was World Refugee Year and as I was speaking at many meetings I took my samples with me to get orders. At first imported goods had an 'estimated customs tax' to pay, but when the size of the parcels increased, in response to demand, the Customs became very difficult, wanting to know the percentage origin of the material used in every item in each consignment. I persuaded my MP, J.P.W. Mallalieu, to ask a question in the house and as the volume of goods coming in this way continued to grow, another MP did likewise and customs were relaxed. With Rob, my son trained as a financial analyst, we battled on for five years or so until Oxfam realised it was worth taking over and developing into its 'Helping by Selling' or Bridge scheme. On one range I was making 100% on cost price and still underselling any such goods sold in local shops. The profits, of course, went to the refugees.

The voluntary agencies and the Hong Kong government worked extremely well with one another. High-rise flats were built with nursery schools on the top floor. There were training schemes for adolescents and care for the elderly. Many agencies such as Oxfam and Save the Children Fund, as well as individuals came to help after the showing of the film *Like Paradise* which shows how fire swept through the tents and makeshift homes on the hillside one Christmas. The late influx of boat people from Vietnam was too heavy a burden; other countries took a few but nowhere near enough.

The New Year is I think the most colourful festival with its banners, lights, fireworks, giving of presents and the streets even more crowded than usual in the evening. Everyone calls 'Kon Hei Fat Choi' to their friends and friendly dragons wend their way adding to the festivities.

There is a revolving restaurant at the top of a tower block in Kowloon. You eat lovely food and see the whole panorama of the bay and islands unfold before you in the changing light. There are some lovely temples in gardens where people come to pay their respects and burn incense. There is a wonderful upmarket shopping centre near the ferry terminal where craftwork in porcelain, jewellery, carving, embroidery and quilted satin Chinese jackets are for sale, and an Oxfam shop on Hong Kong Island.

I visited the Buddhist headquarters in Hong Kong to find out what help they were giving the Buddhists in Vietnam, but they did not want to become involved. I realise it was a difficult situation for them. When they heard I was visiting relief projects in Hong Kong they urged me to visit their home for homeless old women. It was a lovely place with gardens, greatly above the standard of most people. The women did their own cleaning, gardening and catering. They loved cooking and would cater for visitors and of course be paid for it. They seemed to love serving me with vegetarian food of delicate flavours only comparable to one other such meal I had in India prepared by the housewife herself. Everyone seemed busy and happy. I wish I knew old people's homes of the same quality in England.

The last time I visited Hong Kong was for a few days at the end of a tour organised by the Society for Anglo-Chinese Understanding. I went again to Macao, where some Portuguese architecture still survives. Oxfam was running workshops to ease the poverty and a Catholic priest, Father Luis Ruiz, was doing amazing work helping the poor with his clinic and children to get schooling. When he came to England a large audience at our Famine Relief AGM were spellbound. I meant to visit him again but the YMCA delayed giving me his letter and when I returned from Macao it was too late.

A new, South-East Asia, University has been built on an island connected by a long bridge to Macao, largely funded by Chinese businessmen. The verandahs, courtyards at different levels and all facing different directions across to hills, islands, woods and bays were overwhelming in their variety and beauty. I had been visiting a Quaker from Walsall who had been lecturing and teaching for many years and looking after her elderly mother and father. In her spare time she had taken further qualifications and when they both died she had spread her wings. I admire this loyalty to her parents and her dedication to further study. In the morning we went for a good walk on to a smaller island where a TV mounted under the trees allowed evening viewing. We were going to look at the old Portuguese area in Macao, but I fell asleep and didn't wake up until it was too late to go. The Friend and the environment were just right for relaxing. I sent her Cronin's *A Wise Man From the West* about Matteo Ricci, a Jesuit priest who went to China and studied the Chinese classics. The Empress became a Christian. For his scholarship, skill and devotion he was given a state funeral by the Chinese. The next two Jesuit priests were turned out as ignorant trouble-makers. A Jesuit also went to India (see *A Pearl to India* by Cronin). He studied the Veda and Upanishads, became a vegetarian and lived simply as a Brahmin priest, unlike the Christian missionaries. The Inquisition visited him and also Matteo Ricci and found nothing contrary to Catholic discipline. I find this amazing, but Jesuits are well educated men, in learning and a deeper understanding of Christ's teachings. It was they who started the 'Reductions' in South America where runaway slaves were given shelter and training. This did not please the slave-owners and at last even the head of the Jesuits in Europe had pressure brought to bear to dissolve the 'Reductions'. A sad but heroic story. The role of the Catholic Church in South America is shameful; they extracted gold from the Indians taking their leader Montezuma as hostage. They took the gold given to them to free him, but then put him to death. The gold is to be seen in crucifixes and such like in Granada Cathedral for the Christians to contemplate. Just saying 'I'm a miserable sinner' is not enough. I would sell these horrors and with the proceeds see that the street children in South America were well cared for and trained, and introduce free birth control, but that is not anywhere near enough to outweigh the shame. Alas, I digress again. Can America ever compensate for napalm falling on the bare backs of children and of 'agent orange' and its effects on forest and soil, land mines that go on mutilating people years after the breaking of International Accords on SE Asia contrary to International Agreement?

It was with sadness and nostalgia that I watched the ceremony when Hong Kong was handed back to China, though I knew it was right to return our ill-gotten gains of the Opium War. The lease of Kowloon on the mainland of China had ended, and Hong Kong was not viable without Kowloon. By infilling shallow bays, the island became much larger than when we took it over. When floods of Chinese fled from the communist takeover and later desperate people escaped from the Cultural Revolution, the efficiency with which the government worked with relief agencies was outstanding. This, followed by the Vietnamese boat people, was too much. Other nations took a few of the boat people and had time to prepare and select a few, but Hong Kong shouldered most of the burden. Certainly the streets and little public gardens were extremely crowded when people left their high-rise flats to take a little air and exercise in the evenings. I am happy that under British rule it was able to help so many desperately unhappy people. An island and islands of great beauty, a flourishing international port – one of those jewels in the British crown, has been handed back to China. I pray that they will treasure it and its people.

Chapter Seven

Travels in Vietnam
September 1973

I HAD FIRST TRIED to enter Vietnam in 1968 but the Tet offensive had just broken out and, although I reached Hong Kong, I was not allowed to continue. This time it was different. The US were beginning to withdraw from Vietnam and leave the South in what they hoped would be a secure position.

Saigon airport was busy with American planes and my plane was delayed ... no-one to meet me as I expected. At last I got transport to the wrong place, but they were able to send me to the house where the Quakers were living. Saigon must have been lovely once with its wide tree-lined boulevards, but now the trees were shattered. The ring, given me by the National Liberation fighters and made out of bits of American war planes, turned black from the pollution. The Quaker Peace and Service Group were mostly running crèches and play groups for orphan babies who were left in their cots and a bottle put into their mouth at feeding time, because the helpers could not cope with the numbers.

I spent a few days with the Quakers then visited a number of Quaker and Buddhist play groups in hospitals and orphanages, and the Buddhist School of Social Service on the outskirts of Saigon. It was arranged I should fly to Hue, with a student from the University to travel with me and act as an interpreter. The roads were dominated by the NLF and were not safe.

I awoke to the sound of a gong, the big one in the pagoda courtyard which has a heavy beam of wood swung against it to make the sound, then heard the chanting of a single nun, the sound growing in intensity as others joined in what seemed a strange cacophony. The light was beginning to filter through the windows of the sleeping room that adjoined the temple and no shadowy forms of nuns were to be seen within the mosquito nets. Thank goodness for mosquito nets which enabled a few light breezes from the open windows to keep the air moving, unlike Japan, where even in the humid heat of August the paper screens are kept firmly closed at night and one is stifled with the stillness of the air. A fan is essential there, not a coquettish frivolity.

The mind graduallly comes into focus and remembers the previous morning when we started out at 6 am by jeep to travel up Route One, the boulevards of horror, where refugees fleeing from Hue had been machine-gunned and bombed as they fled. One remembers with humility the courage of the Buddhist monks and nuns, who, wearing saffron robes, had walked in long lines on either side of the road supporting the refugees in the middle and trying to arouse the compassionate One that resides in the hearts of soldiers on both sides in this war. The road was still strewn with the remains of tanks, lorries, shell cases and rubbish.

Then we had turned on to the rutted track where the dust rolled up to envelope us and stick to our sweating bodies. In Quang Tri province we came to the area of the heaviest fighting where 95% of some of the villages were destroyed, where people were living under awnings attached to an odd wall of a house that was still standing. We met a man now over forty-five years old and demobilised, who was digging out the shell cases and levelling the bomb craters where his mother, wife and children had been killed. Some children were clambering happily on the ruins of the pagoda, a natural junk playground.

The pagodas, even those largely destroyed, still act as social centres and advice bureaux. The Buddhists gave land to the government for the resettlement of refugees, cared for orphans and the old, gave food, seed, hand-tillers and sometimes tractors to returning refugees, but the need remained enormous and their resources were very limited. Officially the government gave 2,500 piastres' worth of material, rice for six months and some corrugated iron sheets to each returning family. Some had received part of this. The army was very slowly clearing fields using mine detectors but it was sad to see soldiers spending their precious time hanging up banners for President Thieu's two-day visit to Hue. Some villagers showed us with pride the area they had been able to cultivate and their first rice crop that they were harvesting.

I was very impressed with the Buddhists arranging that refugees returning to their villages should be encouraged to take orphan children from that village back with them. Maybe lost relatives would return to claim the children, who would meanwhile have been learning the skills necessary for survival as a village child, something they could not do in an orphanage. As the refugees were so poor, a monk visited the adopted child once a month and paid a small amount to his/her upkeep. When I returned to England I was able to involve five or six schools in Huddersfield who each sponsored one of these children – whose photo they had and they received an occasional report, so I was able to raise money for this for a number of years. In addition I showed slides, spoke of the needs of Vietnam and sold copies of Thich Nhat Hanh's *Lotus in a Sea of Fire*. It was a joy to help and good training in caring and compassion in our schools. Hudfam also ran a gift shop, some of the proceeds of which went to Vietnam.

The Buddhists gave a hand-tiller to many villagers to enable the young and old to get on with cultivation when all men between eighteen and forty-five are in the army and 70% of the draught animals have been killed. But they pointed out that if a hand-cultivator sets off a mine the man walking with it loses at best a limb if nothing worse, whereas with a tractor a man is more protected as the plough is behind him and he is moving away from the area of explosion. Shell cases, hopefully exploded, were collected in huge heaps in every field. Some farmers were bedding them in nose down to make the foundations of a new house. One village showed us with pride the little school they had built of thatch and bamboo, another the one-piece seat and desk made with considerable skill and ingenuity from old munitions boxes, where every nail had been straightened out and used again.

"How can we be sure that what you have told us is true if we can't read? We want our children to have education and a better life than we have had. Help us with our day care centres." It was dangerous for the children to be playing in the fields alongside working mothers and as there were not enough places for all the children in government schools, only those who could read and write and do arithmetic by the time they were five or six were accepted. As an infant school teacher I was horrified. To refuse to help meant no education and its further opportunities for thousands of village children. I turned over the problem ... the chanting had stopped, clappers and gongs were silent and I was not ready for the breakfast of bread, vermicelli, vegetables and pickles. Sometimes one was offered French bread and the mind wandered off again to coffee. Had I become a coffee addict without knowing it?

Soon we are all off again visiting more pagodas or village headquarters where gifts, loans and development plans for each village are shown. The Buddhist School for Social Service supervised the students in their care who were provided with very simple food, shelter and a small amount of pocket money. They tried to make their projects self-financing after the initial help, and to start village co-operatives so that the wealth – if that is the right word in these circumstances – is shared by all. At the Tay Loc orphanage the boys went to school for half a day and the rest of the time was given to self-finanacing projects such as filling tea-bags, making vermicelli and doing carpentry. At another orphanage fruit trees – guavas, oranges, coconut – were grown as well as soya beans and rice and this could in time make the boys self-supporting. I was glad that Oxfam had appointed Andrew Clark, a community development officer who travelled with me for part of the time to work with the Buddhists and liaise with Oxfam.

As the few buses that ran from Hue to Da Nang were terribly over-crowded and as there was no queue to give some hope of being able to get on sometime, we took a service taxi with eleven on board to travel along the coast, up over the mountain spur that jutted out to sea and down innumerable hair-pin bends with a dare-devil driver whose skill and luck amazed us all as we clutched wildly and swung with brakes screeching down into Da Nang. We went there to the rehabilitation centre run by Quakers for people who had lost limbs. New limbs were made of simple available materials; these were not sophisticated but enabled people to be mobile. I remember seeing a small child with no legs sitting on a little wooden 'buggy' with four wheels, propelling himself along.

Here we visited a huge regroupment camp where people were waiting to be sent back to their villages, which is likely sometime provided their area is not in disputed territory. Also on the sand dunes there was a nursery school. The sea looked beautiful from a distance until you realised it was the main sewer for the area. Around the perimeter of the nearby abandoned American camp stretched a ring of temporary shacks and muddy alleyways where people who once scraped a living supplying the needs of American soldiers, were left like the flotsam of the receding tide. Barbed wire stretched in endless coils from north to south of the country, enough to encircle the world in a parcel of misery or a crown of thorns. One wonders who had made a fortune supplying thousands of miles of wire in which the barbs were flattened into razor sharp edges. Vietnam is an enormous scrap yard of American rubbish. Some is being collected and exported but there is so much that is too heavy or that nobody wants. It is also a graveyard of many American products, of American aspirations but not of their miscalculations ... they live on.

We flew from Quang Ngai to Saigon, that once elegant French city, ten years ago of half a million inhabitants, now swollen to three to four million. The housing and sanitation has not kept up with its growth. The polluted air spewing from the exhausts of thousands of Honda motor bikes as well as lorries and cars using what must be dirty petrol, chokes one. Lost or orphan children who lived in alley ways or slept in baskets near the markets found life more difficult without the American soldiers who were often very kindly disposed towards the children. A few homes had been opened where children, often no more than seven or eight years old, could sleep or get a meal. Those that showed some signs of settling down were hived off into smaller homes and sent to school. Those were the few lucky ones. There were many orphanages for younger children in Saigon and I was glad see that some had play groups run by the Gordon Barclay Quaker team. They had trained nursery nurses and provided toys for children who previously had been left in their cots all day with a feeding bottle put in their mouths at intervals. Children deprived of love, nursing and play become physically and mentally retarded. They put out their arms or clutch your legs, needing love so much. Lucky are the children who can be found foster homes.

I think when I visit Oxfam-supported projects I am looking for the best way of meeting people's needs, but I am also looking for beauty. This is hardly to be found in the appalling destruction in Vietnam. The beauty here is not in the surroundings but in the courage of the people, in the faces as they came to greet us, palms together, bowing then silently vanishing into the darkness again. There is the pride and happiness on people's faces as they showed us the desks they had made or the canal they had cleaned out, and the quiet happiness of the Buddhist monks and nuns who shared their meals with us. I guess many were followers of Zen as they had a simple arrangement of bamboo on the table or in the temple showing heaven, man and earth in harmony. Is that not what is needed in this war-torn world?

We heard many stories of the torture and imprisonment or disappearance of those who stood out for justice or peace by negotiation, many of whom still lingered in appalling jails with little hope of release without considerable pressure from foreign governments or such organisations as Amnesty. That this had some effect was encouraging as two trade union leaders released the day before had told my contact, who shall be nameless. They attributed their release 70% to outside pressure and 30% to pressure within Vietnam. It takes great courage to do this in Vietnam and this should encourage us in Britain to do more.

The Royal Tombs in Hue look neglected and forlorn, but Bao Dai the last king refused to co-operate with the policies of America and her puppet Diem, so went into exile rather than be the cause of further bloodshed. He still lives on in the hearts of the people.

CHAPTER EIGHT

A Visit to Japan

THE JAPANESE CONNECTION began when I started studying Ikebana as a way into Zen meditation under Stella Coe at the Buddhist summer school. Stella advised me not to go to Japan as the old Japan was changing and I would be disappointed. I was glad of the warning. In addition Oxfam had some contacts during World Refugee Year and was happy for me to follow these up – at my own expense, of course. Two Japanese Quakers staying at Woodbrooke had stayed with us. One of them, Toranosuki Sakuma, was very anxious that I should visit his family and other Quakers in Japan. There was also a Quaker centre and guest house in Tokyo.

The journey was eventful. Japanese airlines are very good but the price of United Arab Airlines was much less, so I chose the latter. We changed planes in Cairo – a huge bewildering airport. After waiting some hours we were told our plane left next day, so we were taken by coach across Cairo The coach broke down, but at last by 3 a.m. we arrived at the Garden Hotel for an overnight stay. Staff rushed around shouting "Don't panic" as they put up extra beds. We had not expected an overnight stop, so we had the minimum of toiletries with us. It was blissful to get into bed at last. I don't know why we were called at 6 a.m. for breakfast. It seemed cruel when later we found that the coach was not coming for us until mid-day, but as we looked out of the window across the garden, the Pyramids stood before us – an unexpected thrill – so we were able to spend the morning riding on a camel and interviewing the Sphinx. We had a few hours' stop in the Philippines, where tourists could visit the airport shops and buy large straw hats and bags and other beautiful handicrafts.

I was met at Tokyo airport by Sakuna and his family. Happily, unlike most Underground stations in Tokyo, there was an escalator rather than stairs. Sakuma's house was on the outskirts of Tokyo not far from the underground railway and a busy main road. He had inherited this very valuable land and had rebuilt the house about a year before. Houses are built mainly of wood and have to be rebuilt every twenty years. As this cost him about the same as my house that has so far lasted over eighty years, I was shocked. It was a pleasant 'modern' house, two stories, large windows, a small front garden with shrubs meticulously pruned, some stepping stones and a tiny lawn that Sakuma 'mowed' with scissors. Japanese houses are very small and intimate and usually they prefer to take friends out to a restaurant, so it was a privilege to be allowed to stay. The porch before the front door allowed one to deposit one's outdoor shoes and put on house slippers. These were changed for others at the benjo (toilet). If one went in to the tatami room one wore no slippers at all because this was a kind of 'holy ground'. Most Japanese homes retain one tatami room. The size of the room is described as a six-mat or eight-mat room. The mats are thickly woven of straw and are very precious. The windows used to be paper screens, but in towns they are now made of more durable material that allows a gentle light to filter through. At right angles to them is a recess, a low dais, a tokonomo (shrine) against the wall, where a scroll hanging is counter-balanced by an Ikebana flower arrangement which is linked to the season or festival and/or a haiku. The rest of the wall was covered by a large cupboard which contained the futon (mattress) and bedding for the night, and space for clothing, etc. This was my beautiful and simple room for a week.

As we were 'modern' we sat at table with chairs for meals (prepared by his daughter-in-law, who never sat at the table with us). Meals were artistically served. There were so many, to me, unusual foods such as seaweed and fish delicacies to taste, each meal was an adventure. Like everything else in a Japanese home, the bathroom was small and compact. I was told when taking my bath to wash first, then get into the bath that looked like an electric washer with a built-in seat. The hot water covers your shoulders, and later, when I had to do a lot of sitting on my heels, Japanese fashion, it did relieve the aching muscles. The first time I used it I got out and washed my smalls in the water and let the bath water run away. This was a mistake – I had deprived the rest of the family of their evening bath. I then saw the point of washing first, and not doing my smalls in the bath water!

Sakuma came with me when I visited my Oxfam contacts. We travelled after 10 a.m. to avoid the rush-hour. There were no escalators, so many steps up and down in the humid heat, and the very crowded trains – I couldn't imagine what the rush-hour was like. Large blocks of buildings were named, but not streets with a sequence of numbers, so I found this very difficult to cope with and was very thankful for Sakuma's help.

We also visited the Meiji gardens where Ikebana is taught, also the tea ceremony. The Ikebana class was for two hours. I had to pay for the lesson, buy a book giving instructions, buy wrapped branches and flowers, and was loaned a pin holder and dish. I had already got my third certificate, so I was astonished to be told to do the simplest arrangement I had learned when I began Ikebana. The 'instructress' went and chatted with a friend. When I finished, she came and said that in Japan one often used a flower instead of a branch for the third placement. The she asked if I wanted another lesson. I pointed out that I had come for a two-hour period. I had to buy some more branches and flowers for the second arrangement and the same for the third. Time was getting on and I knew Sakuma was waiting so I prepared to pay up and leave. I found I had had three lessons. It was a very expensive morning, so I'm not surprised I was the only student present.

There are many schools of Ikebana in Japan, some classical, others more modern, but all keeping to a basic theme and placement of branches, of Heaven, man and Earth in harmony. As I had been trained in the modern Sugetsu school I went to their headquarters in Tokyo for lessons. Kasumi, the very gifted daughter of the master of the school, gave a short demonstration. Then some eighty pupils were lined up at long benches, according to their grade, and followed their book. A teacher walked up and down. I chose to do a 'free style' this time Being a member of the Ikebana International, I did not have to pay an entrance fee, only a class fee and payment for wrapped branches and flowers. Towards the end of the period Kasumi walked up and down the lines occasionally pausing to speak to a foreigner. She bowed. I bowed. She spoke encouragingly, then bowed and I bowed. This was an interesting experience. In the old days it was one teacher and one pupil, who had to watch and imitate or perhaps sense what the teacher was doing but not saying. Now the Japanese had gone into mass production. I must say I preferred the teaching in England that I had experienced, with words, examples and explanations and the stimulus to interpret phrases such as: 'Opposites are equal' or 'The futility of utility' which is difficult but stirs the inner life especially when practised under the guidance of Stella Coe. This is where the way into the inner life develops, as in archery, kendo, the tea ceremony, etc. I deeply regret that in Japan and in England training of Ikebana is being lost and is just becoming 'arranging flowers'. It's like the coming of new light into the world at Christmas getting smothered by the Christmas bonanza and its religious significance is lost. One day Sakuma and his son took me to visit Nikko, a Shinto shrine. After the underground into Tokyo we travelled a long way in a train through built-up areas that at last gave way to paddy fields. The very tall cypress trees made photography difficult, as they cast so much shade. At the end of a long avenue was a Tori (gateway) – two huge cypress trunks capped with upswept finials – the entrance to the shrine. There were a number of 'Treasure Houses' built of intricately carved wood – natural treasures themselves, containing treasure. They are re-built every twenty years, so the craftsmen's skills are passed from one generation to the next. We then came to a raked gravel area, removed our shoes and entered the shrine. It was very ornate with rich carving and colouring, quite unlike the palace in Kyoto I was to visit later. We had a picnic which consisted of rice balls wrapped in seaweed. We got on a single-decker bus to take us up to a famous lake. It was an astounding road, long bridges swinging across deep ravines. It was so dangerous that another road of the same variety was used for descent – one-way traffic. Arrived at the top we were greeted by a tremendous thunderstorm which caused the buses to be cancelled. At last when the storm eased we were glad to get the first descending bus without seeing the lake.

The heat and humidity took its toll and I fainted on the stairs coming up from the underground. As I came round four Japanese with smiling faces were there with a stretcher and in no time I was in hospital where it took an hour to track down what the Hospital for Tropical Diseases in London took many days to find out. I had to pay a lot for necessary pills and attention, but everything was very expensive in Japan. We went home by taxi – a long way. I ran a temperature of 104° for a few days, which prevented our going to see the great Buddha of Kamakura. My hosts were so kind and I was sorry to be such a nuisance. Sakuma's son wanted to improve his English, so from time to time we talked English conversation pieces. Sakuma then took me to stay at his house in Mishima, about a hundred miles away. It was a tiny house with a tiny garden, a tiny pool, stepping stones, austerely pruned shrubs and azaleas. The house had a main room with a family shrine, where I slept, and a small room at each end, a tiny kitchen and bathroom. Everything had to be put away with the utmost care into the cupboards provided. Here we sat on our heels at a low table for meals. I am sure the habit of sitting habitually on one's heels affects the circulation and is responsible for the short stature of elderly Japanese. The younger generation who more often sit on chairs are taller. The little shopping centres charmed me with their gaiety, colour and cleanliness. The tiniest patch of space became a garden, maybe only a rock and an evergreen. The railway stations would have a large arrangement of rocks and pine or cupresssus growing from them. I did not appreciate the garlands of artificial flowers in the shopping centre at Mishima. The shopkeepers were delighted a foreigner visited their shop and one insisted I accept a yukata (cotton kimono) as a gift. Sakuma said it would be impolite to refuse. We all bowed – profusely. A friend had brought Sakuma a gift of fruit – she bowed to give it to him, he bowed lower when accepting. They chatted. She bowed again on preparing to leave, Sakuma bowed lower. A little more chat, the friend bowed lower than Sakuma, who had to bow lower. There is excessive courtesy as well as excessive ruthlessness. Children are brought up on a very strict code of behaviour – never thought of as just children. So I suspect that when the code may legitimately be broken in adulthood they go beyond the bounds we would accept here. However, behaviour patterns are changing the world over and this may no longer be true. The heat and humidity of August produces few flowers. Basically there it is the time of the cherry blossom, of the iris, of the water lily and of the chrysanthemum – upright and cascading varieties. This I think accounts for the artificial flowers in the shops in August, and for the few flowers – uchis – used in Japanese flower arrangements. This is changing as it becomes westernised, which I regret.

The Emperor heard of a wonderful garden of many different varieties of iris and came to visit it. The Zen priest cut all the flowers but one – the most perfect – wanting to teach the Emperor it was not mass and quantity but perfection that was the aim. The wealthy had a tea house in the garden. Stepping stones lead to the low door, a small stone water trough fed from a bamboo pipe allows visitors to rinse their hands before bending to enter. The four- or five-mat tatami floor has a small pit in the centre where the kettle of water hums as it boils. The two or three invited guests enter silently and sit on their heels. The host then enters from another door bringing the green tea, a great luxury. The movements are few and stylised as the tea is made; the green tea is whisked to a froth. One lifts the cup without handles with both hands and drinks three times, the last time making an appreciative noise. The first guest is then allowed to show some appreciation of any special treasure – something small and unostentatious that has been put on display. A chabana arrangement of one flower and leaf or small spray hangs on the wall. The house is a simple tiled roof construction with windows that look like vilene and allow a soft light to enter. Some houses have folding screens that may be drawn back at different times of the year to show the spring garden, or the autumn garden with especially planted trees and shrubs showing the variety of autumn colouring.

There is what is known as giri in Japan, where all owe allegiance to the Emperor, to the overlords, to the local clan leader, and to the family. At times these clash and then it is honourable to perform hara kiri, ritual suicide. A noble, finding this is required of him by the Emperor, would invite a few intimate friends to a tea ceremony. The quietness and awareness of the ritual, the scent of the tea, the sound of the water boiling in the kettle and the pouring of the tea, the minutiae of small every day things is given attention and reverence and a fond farewell, beautiful in its simplicity and dignity. The guests then would leave ...

There is a time for moon viewing, sitting viewing the cherry trees in full bloom and sharing evocative haiku amongst a few friends. Perhaps this is the old Japan that is fading. It was Sakuma who introduced me to the Abbot of a famous Zen monastery near Mishima and arranged for me to spend a week there, as described in Chapter Nine. When my week there was completed, he collected me, rested and refreshed, and put me on the train for Osaka where I was to spend a few days with the clerk of Quaker Monthly Meeting. I saw a strange figure squatting at the station, with long hair tied in a bun and very long finger nails. I turned away and felt a tap on my shoulder. The strange being was John, the American husband of my hostess Yukiko Baches. He consorted with a very odd group, much to his wife's dismay. However he was very courteous and helpful to me, and my record of the Huddersfield Choral Society singing The Messiah charmed them both. They had two girls and a boy, friendly and attractive children. The mother was a teacher and the father taught English. Many foreigners supported themselves by teaching spoken English.

We slept in the main room, which had air-conditioning, for which I was grateful. The father had his own room, a futon on the floor and everything else piled up round it. Having stayed with Sakuma and seen how meticulous the Japanese are I was staggered to see what happens in a small house when one isn't. I do not think American and Japanese culture combined very well.

It was holiday time so Yukiko took me to Nara, the old capital of Japan where the great Todaiji temple with its huge Buddha and surrounding shrines and museums and pagoda are visited by thousands. The huge gateway with its sacred deer leads into a long avenue of cypress and pine, a lake on the right hand side, then another huge screen or gateway onto the raked gravel space before the main temple with its tiled roof and upswept finials. People were reverently moving slowly and looking carefully as they do in York Minster. There are no rows of chairs as in a church. People go to the Buddha Rupa and bow and stand there meditating or praying, sometimes burning incense, then bowing and moving on. There was a reverent atmosphere which was deeply moving. What I remember most vividly are the adjoining shrines and museums with their carved wooden eighth century stylised faces of holy avatars in meditation and others of real people that emanated life and wisdom. The latter were eleventh century and seemed to have more character than the beautiful sculptures of Greece, but of course did not have the athletic grace.

I had hoped to travel by boat on the Inland Sea to Hiroshima. I was told firmly that this sea which I had longed to visit for so many years was now so polluted that nobody, simply nobody, went by boat and I was to travel by the famous bullet train. It was certainly very fast. My ticket told me where to stand on the platform to get to my seat most conveniently. A ticket collector came round and bowed, looked at my ticket, bowed and departed. Then a very smart hostess in European uniform with a white bowler hat and white gloves arrived, bowed and asked if I was comfortable. On being assured that all was satisfactory she bowed and departed. This was not a weighty job but helped to solve an unemployment problem and kept people busy.

Hiroshima was surrounded by low hills, which to some extent restricted the area of the atomic blast. A few gaunt ruins were left to remind people of that day in August 1946. The rebuilding had made it easier for me to find my way to the International Centre, as roads now had names and houses were numbered. The International Centre was a single-story Japanese house where a core of people lived who made a point of visiting and caring for those who suffered from the effects of the Atom bomb. Foreign visitors were welcome to come and support the work, staying a few days or a few months.

A large area of the devastated city had become a memorial park, where walkways led to a huge stone arch under which a perpetual flame burned in memory of the dead. At one end a huge museum housed pictures and artefacts so grim and awful one was glad to get out into the fresh air again. Here – it was most unusual – a Japanese girl came up and started talking to me. Usually if I spoke to anybody they said "I don't speak English" and rushed away. They were afraid of losing face. As I was told there might be eighty pupils in an English oral class you can see that they had little opportunity to speak English. The girl was very friendly and pleasant and showed me one huge tree like sculpture hung with paper cranes that children in Japan had made in memory of the little girl who was told that if she could make a thousand cranes she would live. Alas she was unable to do so, but it gave hope and occupational therapy.

I was told at the International Centre that I should not only visit the horrors but should take the little single track coastal train to the jetty for the island of Miyajuma. The little jetty was undoubtedly Japanese with its gay tiled roof with upswept finials. The boat took us about two miles to the island where on our right I could see huge deep orange toriis standing with their feet in the water, beautiful with its shimmering reflections. At the jetty I noticed a large pagoda like the one in Kew Gardens. To the right there was a wide path entered through a torii with a pine wood on the left and a few intermittent pines on my right interspersed with stone lanterns. They are about five feet high with a space beneath the elegant stone roof where a lantern could be put on feast days. These lanterns were given by the faithful in gratitude for favours received – the recovery from illness of a close member of the family or the birth of a child. This path led to the Shinto Temple, where the beauty of the stone lamps, pines and the sea beyond with its toriis standing in the water made one approach the shrine with a feeling of reverence.

The platforms going out into the shallow sea were the place where ritual dances were performed at special seasons of the year, which the public could watch but not join in. The main shrine was again a single-story wooden building where the priests in black and white robes performed the prayers and rituals. It was customary to clap your hands or ring a bell to alert the spirits to your prayers. If it was something very important like the return of one of the family from far away places, you would ask the priest to intone the ceremonial prayers suitable for the occasion. The whole family would stand in a line and listen. They would then bow and leave, having left an appropriate gift, elegantly wrapped. Shinto is the national religion of Japan. It is a nature religion in which reverence is given to mountains, especially Fujiyama, to lakes, waterfalls, trees and so on, which all contain Kami the inner spirit. The sun goddess Amaratsu from whom the Emperor is considered to be descended was very angry with her brother who caused thunderstorms, so she hid in a cave and refused to come out. Lack of her sunshine caused problems, so a festival was held. Toriis were built on which exotic birds were perched. At last the goddess had to come out to see what was going on and was prevented from going back into the cave. This explains the toriis at the entrance to Shinto shrines.

To say that the Emperor, Fujiyama, waterfalls and trees are 'worshipped' means that they are given respect and reverence, just as Hindu gives respect and reverence to the cow that gives milk, the bullock that ploughs the land and both give dung for fuel (which also provides the comfortable, clean and wholesome flooring in Indian ashrams). I wish that we gave more respect to animals instead of using them as non-sentient machines. This links up with present day creation spirituality, which I accept. Shinto, besides being the national nature religion of Japan also contains a system called giri, mentioned before in describing the tea ceremony. It is considered right to fight to the death and not allow oneself to be taken prisoner. This is one reason why European prisoners were treated so badly during the war – they were 'dishonourable persons'. It is interesting that marriage rites are conducted by a Shinto priest. The bride and bridegroom wear ceremonial Japanese dress. The rites completed, the bride and groom disappear and reappear in western evening dress for the reception and feasts. A strange mixture of western and Japanese culture.

Leaving the Shinto shrine was a little bridge, a smaller and more colourful edition of the Bridge of Sighs in Venice. From the little bridge, which led on to the mainland, hung a number of copper lanterns covered with verdigris, gifts of the faithful. On the mainland, turning right, one came to a large pool with huge rocks. Swimming between the rocks were many large goldfish. Further on one walked to a very large pool where porpoises leaped out of the water, an additional attraction as well as the shrine. The village had a small deep river flowing through it, on one side bordered by little restaurants with tiny gardens overlooking the river. I went into one of them where there were tables and chairs, but went through this to an inner room where there were cushions and low tables. This looked on to a tiny courtyard perhaps ten by twelve feet, with huge rocks, tiny pine trees and azaleas, a small pool with a bridge and stepping stones across the raked gravel. The tall rocks were symbolic of heaven, the shrubs of man and the water, bridge and stepping stones of earth. It was a whole world in miniature, refreshing to the spirit as was the Japanese tea. I went up through the clean and tidy narrow village street to where a chairlift took me part way up the steep hillside. You then continued up a wandering path, stopping at different shrines on the way to pay your respects and to have a rest. Arrived at the top there were huge rocks and a wonderful view of the many islands of the Inland Sea. I forgot about pollution! Returning to the mainland, I noticed the tide out so the toriis did not look quite so glamourous standing in the mud. I'm glad I remember so clearly the beauty of the scene in the morning.

Next day I went to the Hiroshima docks and found there was a boat going to Osaka. Of course it took much longer than the train. The boat probably held about three hundred passengers, but there were only twenty on board. It made me feel I was not moving with the times. There were futons where you could lie down and rest, but while it was daylight it was much more pleasant to be on the deck looking at the many little islands. But, sad to say, we did not call at any of the ports. Arriving back in Osaka, my hostess who was secretary of the Osaka B & P Club told me we were invited by the chairman to visit her for the day at her flat at a mountain resort where the heat and humidity were more bearable. We took a coach which wound up through the heavily wooded mountains to the hotel and we were shown up to her flat where a dozen members were gathered. We sat on our heels around a low table, were served tea and Japanese biscuits and chatted – Yukiko translating for me. Oddly enough, only two women were wearing kimonos. The others wore European short dresses and tights. In that humidity I felt tights unbearable, but this did not trouble the Japanese. Later in the afternoon we went down to the hotel restaurant for an evening meal where we sat on chairs at a table but used chopsticks. The Japanese are liberal in these matters – as with their wedding ceremonies. The drive back to Osaka, winding through the towering woods, was a wonderful experience

The next day I left by train for Kyoto and then took a little electric train to Yamashina where I was to join the Itto-en community,

which I have written about in Chapter Nine. Ayako Isayama is an established member of this community and she speaks English fluently. She was forty-seven when I first knew her. She attends interfaith conferences on behalf of the community and has visited Rome where they were addressed by John Paul II at the opening of the conference, when representatives of sixty-five countries were present. She has also visited Cambodia, Vietnam, Korea, Nepal, India, America in the same capacity. I feel she is one of my daughters, like Cao Ngoc Phuong, a Vietnamese, whose life is dedicated to the service of the community, not personal gain, though it does enrich the inner life. I heard from Ayako this Christmas; still after twenty years we correspond. One day I booked an Ikebana lesson at the O'Hara school, some two hours' travel away from where I was staying. As I got off the bus there was a cloudburst. The awning under which a few of us were sheltering gave way and we were soaked. What to do? It would take me two hours to get back to the community, so it seemed better to go to my lesson. A place had been reserved for me at the front. The class had started, so I squelched to my place, to the amusement of all. An attendant brought me a thin towel about a foot square, so I wiped my face and watched the master at work. Container, pinholder, branches, and a few flowers were on the table before me and one tried to do what the master had done. Luckily I'd had previous training. I don't think he spoke but if he had I wouldn't have understood. At least it was a test of observation. I must have concentrated hard, because at the end of the lesson I found I was dry. I paid for my lesson, but they graciously presented me with the branches and flowers, saying they were honoured to have a foreigner. The buildings had been a palace and had a huge lake. The owner had given this historic lake and palace as a centre for the study of Ikebana.
There are many palaces in Kyoto. They were called 'detached palaces' in a restricted area. A few of the essential servants lived in, but most lived outside and came in daily, a bit like the forbidden city in Beijing. *The Tale of Genji* by the Lady Murasaki and *Confessions of Lady Nijo*, written about the time of the eleventh century, give some idea of the background of courtly life. Lady Nijo was a concubine of the Emperor whom she had loved very

much, but I think court ritual and doubtless intrigues led her to become a wondering nun. It is a moving story.

There are many luxury hotels for westerners in Kyoto, but also some older Japanese guest houses where one lives in the old Japanese style. They are extremely expensive and exclusive. There was also what is called a Gion corner, where tourists could experience a much cheaper and devalued taste of Japanese culture. A Japanese silently arranged a few flowers, not giving any explanation of the basic ideas; there was some dancing, a little playing on Japanese instruments and a 'tea ceremony'. As I had been with Ayako to some of her lessons on the tea ceremony, I was nauseated by what I saw at the Gion corner. A fat American was invited to join in the detailed ritual. He sat on a chair while the others sat on their heels and it became a laughable travesty. To the Japanese the tea ceremony has a quality of our Communion and yet it was the Japanese who invited him to take part as a tourist attraction. I found it distasteful.

Buddhism and Shinto now interweave in Japan. Many religious seekers had travelled from Japan to China where they had been influenced by Buddhist teaching and Buddhist monasteries had grown up as at Nara. It was in the seventh century that a Japanese Buddhist monk was impressed by the huge arrangements some twenty feet high, of rocks representing Heaven, trees and larger shrubs representing man and small shrubs and water representing earth. Five or six monks might work prayerfully on this for a fortnight. You will still see in the courtyards of hotels in China these landscaped structures. The monk took the idea back to Japan where it was seen as a useful training and as so often when Japanese take over ideas they improve and refine them. The idea of expressing one's beliefs in a practical way day by day is good training and I realise how much I valued doing an Ikebana arrangement for Quaker Meeting every Sunday. The twenty-foot arrangements gradually became smaller. Many monks took up the art and developed rules or guidelines for interpretations, Heaven being the main branch, man two-thirds of that, and Earth a third of the height. It should enclose a space – 'the Void' – be three-dimensional, use one or two flowers only in the heart of the arrangement, preferably an open bud to show impermanence. There is more about Ikebana in Chapter Nine.

When I left the Itto-en community I had to return to the heat and humidity of Tokyo where I stayed at the Quaker International Centre. The department stores in Tokyo were sumptuous but because flat land in Japan is used for growing rice and most of the country is mountainous, the land is very expensive. The large department stores have a basement and another basement below the first. Even in 1973 I couldn't help wondering what would happen in an earthquake. Unless a cavity opened up I suppose the basement would not topple down, but if the water mains were cracked and electricity cut off by tremors, there would be too much water, no light and no electricity for the lifts. Shock waves run through me at the possibility of such a disaster.

Some of the Oxfam contacts came to visit me at the Quaker centre and we sat in ceremony in the tatami room. I was disappointed with the results. Oxfam has so many centres in America, Hong Kong, Australia – but I felt this did not seem to be fertile ground. Japan was doing its own thing – which I regret to say seemed to be helping other countries in SE Asia to set up industry which moved pollution from Japan. Although we have an excellent Oxfam in Britain, which raised £98 million in 1994, I do not think our government record is beyond reproach when I think of the shame of third world debt and our sale of armaments to third world countries.

The Quaker Centre was a friendly place and I enjoyed my stay there. The Meeting House is close by so I expected to go to Meeting there on Sunday. I tried to phone to confirm my flight to Hong Kong, but three times by the time I got through my money had run out before I could speak to the right person and I knew no way to cope with this problem. I went to a travel agent for help who told me I had been wrongly booked by my United Arab Airlines in London and there was no flight from Japan to Hong Kong that day. The next flight was five or six days later, which meant I would miss my flight from Hong Kong to Saigon, so I had to leave on Saturday. Alas, but UA Airlines was half the price of Japanese Airlines, and I had seen the pyramids.

CHAPTER NINE

Encounters On the Way

I WAS ASKED by a friend to write 'notes' on what contribution other faiths have made to my spiritual growth. These writings are the result. How far all this is spiritual, I leave others to decide. This is really an adventure story that gradually unfolds, a 'who done it' of seeking and finding, of losing one's way and facing one's failures, learning from them and moving on or rather, deeper. I'm not sure how one separates spiritual growth; it is intertwined with all growth, with everyday experiences in which one can see a depth that is part of a greater whole. Looking back is what old people can do easily; one can relax over difficult and dangerous situations, knowing you survived; one can see the stepping stones and interconnecting threads one never noticed at the time that were guiding one – sometimes timeless moments when one suddenly sees the sun on a white cherry tree in full bloom – the white radiance of eternity that draws back a veil and brings illuminations to one's pondering. Sometimes it was books, people or dreams that opened an inner door. I'm speaking with hindsight – I don't feel the journey has ended yet. My temporary complete loss of sight for a few months began to develop intuitive knowing and unexpected synchronicities followed. Perhaps when I have written this – which I am not restricting only to 'other faiths' – I shall be able to see what has contributed to my 'spiritual growth'.

My mother was the headmistress of a church school so we went regularly to church. There was a communion table, not an altar, no crucifix or candles – that was thought to smack of popery – a bad thing. We were low Anglicans. I had an objection to being preached at, so during the sermon I pulled down my earflaps and decided to think my own thoughts. If I showed unwillingness to come to heel in spiritual matters, my pocket money was reduced. 'Answering back' and 'impertinence' were serious offences at that time. This was an added incentive to keep quiet and think my own thoughts. I was fed up with God and I remember when my mother and father were out at a meeting I sat cross-legged in front of the fire and whispered "I don't believe in God". I don't know why I whispered, but I sat waiting for divine retribution with some anxiety. I was an only child and later found the companionship of the Young Crusaders cheerful. I remember singing "I'm H.A.P.P.Y, I'm H.A.P.P.Y, I know I am, I'm sure I am, I'm H.A.P.P.Y," on Sunday afternoons. I suppose it was uplifting in its way and I was confirmed when I was about fifteen.

I must have been speaking in an authoritative manner as a result of my new status as a confirmed Anglican, to a young undergraduate from Cambridge whose English parents lived in Peking. He pointedly asked me what I had read of Confucianism and Buddhism. As I rather fancied the young man, I immediately set about to remedy this defect. I have an old notebook from that time marked 'very private' in which I wrote extracts from the Dhammapada: "For never in this world does a hatred cease by hatred: hatred ceases by love, that is its nature". I was fourteen or fifteen at the time and when others in my class at school were reading Scott and Dickens and George Eliot, I was reading Buddhist sutras or the Analects of Confucius. I thought I would establish a church where Christ, Buddha and Confucius were worshipped. The presumption of this amazes me now.

When I was eighteen I went to Homerton Teacher Training College in Cambridge and stayed a third year to take the Cambridge Geography Diploma of the university. Somehow I found my way to the Unitarian church where Dr Flower, the minister, was a man of deep spirituality and learning. On Sunday afternoons a light tea was provided in the adjoining hall which gave people a chance to meet socially, attracted many students and led them to join the Fellowship of Youth (FOY) which provided discussion groups, occasional dances and picnics on the Cam. To me the joy of evening service was that people such as Gandhi and Dr Rhadakrishnan, philosopher and president of India, who wrote *Recovery of Faith* and other books, and other people of spiritual standing who were visiting Cambridge, were invited to speak. I felt I had come home. I was glad to belong to this community. FOY led to my going to Easter conferences at Manchester College, Oxford, a training college for Unitarian ministers, and to Flagg, near Buxton, where summer camps were held. There were other summer camps – one where our tent blew away so my friend and I took refuge in the marquee – and that collapsed on us. I thank ... God?... for a friend who had a great sense of humour and could always find something to laugh about in our many near disasters. She was the most generous and caring person, but not a churchgoer – her faith was practical and rooted in day to day living. I bought a Singer Eight car with a hood and a 'dickie' and I used to travel with friends to Executive meetings of FOY at Unitarian churches all over the country. Comradeship, laughter, facing difficulties, contribute to one's spiritual growth and learning of 'the way'.

On marriage in 1936 I moved to an industrial town – Huddersfield – of woollen mills and chemical factories such as ICI where my husband was a research chemist. After living in Richmond, Surrey, with its river and terrace gardens, Richmond Park, the Old Deer Park, the old palace where Queen Elizabeth the First had died and nearby Kew Gardens, followed by three years at Cambridge, the Backs at crocus time, punting on the lower and upper river – Huddersfield was a shock. However I went to visit a friend who was doing social work in the slums of Manchester and then I realised how lucky I was to have hills and valleys and moors within walking distance and to live in the home of the Huddersfield Choral Society, valued from Japan to America, and with people who could not enjoy Christmas without hearing or singing the *Messiah*. My friends felt anywhere north of the Wash was barbarian country though they were pleased to come and stay with me for rest and relaxation when London was being bombed.

There was a very large Unitarian church here with a very small congregation that I suppose had not accepted the 39 Articles but had not the wider vision nor the opportunities to develop it that the church in Cambridge had. One young minister, Dudley Richards, made an impact. He held 'book services' where he preached on a book at the evening service and we were invited to stay and discuss it with him after the service. Alas he did not stay long and moved to London HQ.

It became a lonely time. My husband and I had a great deal in common in socialist matters, but as a research chemist his seeking went into his work. I turned to books. As my husband and I had registered as conscientious objectors and I was involved with the Peace Pledge Union, I organised the selling of *Peace News* in the town on Saturday afternoons and a few Quakers came to help me. They had started a children's class at Meeting, so I started going there on Sunday mornings to sit with like-minded people quietly while I had my children minded. I didn't apply for Membership for about ten years as I had problems with 'God'.

In 1943 my husband and I and a number of other like-minded people started the Huddersfield Famine Relief Committee (Hudfam) of which I became the organising secretary. This included organising concerts and Any Questions evenings to raise money, shop displays of comparative rations, flag days, clothing appeals, packing the clothing and sending it to a depot in Manchester – first run by the Quakers and then taken over by Oxfam. As an inexperienced organiser struggling with a new committee, one had to learn who talked big and whom one could rely on. It was a learning period with two small children and no time for reading. My one relaxation was one night out doing advanced French at an FE course.

Though Hudfam had Europe in mind when it started, the immediate horror of the Bengal famine stirred our conscience. An enthusiastic young scout master offered to organise a flag day for it. I had permission from the mayor for this but was unable to make contact with the young man. At last I got in touch with his father about a week before the date to be told his son had done nothing! I got a printer to print 'flags' but they had to have pins stuck in the bits of paper, so I collected pins – not readily available in wartime. Students at Avery Hill College, evacuated here during the war, and school children helped to put the pins in the flags. I made about 60 telephone calls in three days, finding that I needed to have special collecting tins and where to borrow them, printed wrappers for the tins, special permits for each flag seller available from the police – ringing members of Hudfam to rally round. It was a wonderful co-operative time with so many helping in so many ways and the £200 we made on a cold January day – that was a lot in 1943 – not only helped the Bengal flood victims but also established Hudfam as a working group of people who knew they could rely on each other. This is a valuable asset.

When the children started school I had more time for reading. Dean Inge's *Mystical Christianity* opened a door and I knelt in gratitude. One afternoon, reading Henry James' *Varieties of Religious Experience* and pondering over it, something said to me "Take the skin of the snake and make a path to walk on." I had a horror of snakes and as a child kept one large friendly snake under my bed to keep the little snakes under my pillow in order. Odd I could make friends with a big snake – certainly under the bed and not in it. Even the bath water as it curved into the waste pipe moved like a snake. I began to realise I must face my fears of snakes and going down into the cellar at night; were they the symbol of something else in my psyche? Was there something that was imprisoning me and yet acting as a challenge?

I had started going to the Buddhist Summer School and learning about meditation. One night I woke up and felt I was being attacked by devils. I thought I must be having a nightmare so I switched on the light. It was 2 am. My terror increased and I wondered what Christians did when they felt beset by the devil. I clutched an imaginary cross, desperately holding on and very gradually the fear and tension eased. I wonder if I had said the Lord's Prayer or sung a hymn, would this have had the same effect? Happily this has not happened again, so far. What to me is interesting is that I turned to something I felt primitive, but it worked. When I see gospel choirs, mostly of African descent, singing, swinging with such fervour that Jesus is their saviour and friend, I feel their confidence is a helpful shield in danger and distress. "Yea, though I walk through the valley of the shadow of death, thou art with me ..." I wonder where those devils sprang from? My collective unconscious? The Tibetan *Book of the Dead* tells the pilgrim to walk courageously and face the hungry ghosts he meets on the way. One is grateful for support when trying to be courageous.

I dreamed I went down into the dark depths and brought back the old primitive dances that nourished life; that I must go down into the long, dark tunnel. With care I should be safe from the huge death-dealing high-tension cables on the right and should emerge into a garden full of sunshine. In another dream I had a tiny boat with an unknown destination. On my right was a huge luxury liner with crowds of happy people aboard about to start on a cruise – but I knew this was not for me, so I plucked up my courage and set sail. I still find large noisy crowds are not for me.

These dreams made me realise that there is something much older and wiser in me than my head knowledge. Reading W.P.Martin's *Experiment in Depth* provided an introduction to Jung, who had studied the symbolism of Asian religions, seeking answers to his questions on depth psychology – an interfaith connection looking at the world-wide inner promptings of the Holy Spirit. I was changing the beds one Monday morning – six to change and the washing to do – when suddenly I looked up, and framed in the large bay window was a white cherry tree in full bloom lit up by the sun. White cherry trees had made me want to dance before, but this time a veil seemed to be drawn aside and I realised that my odd unease with some people was caused by a current which linked us in some mystery. I knelt and wept for joy, my little Sheltie nestled to me and quivered too. I wrote to one of the people in a very guarded way and what a joy it was to have my intuition confirmed.

As organising secretary of Hudfam I was invited to go to Oxfam's first conference at St Edmund's Hall, Oxford. After the war, when the refugees were repatriated, all the other two or three hundred famine relief committees had closed down, but our first flag day had been for Bengal and the need to help people in distress was still there, even if the war in Europe had ended. It had been a struggle to keep our committee together and a number of members retired. I knew that there must be someone at Oxfam who had kept Oxfam active and felt as I did. It was a wonderful conference and I made contacts with such people as Pastor Stumpf which led to my importing craft work, made by Chinese refugees in Hong Kong, that he had started. On the last evening an elderly shabby man whom I had not noticed before came and sat beside me at dinner – not the appearance of a millionaire! We shared our experiences step by step of keeping our committees alive and active. What a joy to find someone on the same wavelength! He later

ENCOUNTERS ON THE WAY 173

started 'Help the Aged' and he became a good friend for many years until his death.

Hudfam were then sending grants to Quakers, Catholics, and Save the Children fund in Morocco during the Franco-Algerian war that was on. The Quakers were setting up training centres for mothers and children on the Algerian-Moroccan border. The Catholics had a feeding programme. Save the Children were helping in the aftermath of an earthquake at Agadir. My mother had recently died and left me a little money so it seemed a good idea to take my eldest son, who had just left university, to go and see what was being done and to take photos to show at meetings on my return. Then I began to ponder. I had always wanted to travel and perhaps I was just finding an excuse. If I really cared should I give away the money I planned to spend on travelling to Famine Relief? I had a dream – an Arab on the left and Dr Flower of the Cambridge Unitarian church on the right held a large golden orb – a grapefruit? When it was cut in half the inside was as beautiful as the outside – so I felt free to go. It was my first opportunity to meet so many dedicated people working in the field whatever the name of their faith and organisation.

My dreams continued to tell me my roots were not reaching the soil – hanging in a void – dreams became more and more insistent. They even indicated the psychiatrist to go to – one of those connected to the joy of the white cherry tree in full bloom. I felt if I did not respond I should just be an empty shell. Oddly enough it is easy to go to a doctor for medical care but much more difficult to ask for psychiatric help. My doctor arranged an appointment for me three months before that psychiatrist retired. No wonder my dreams were so urgent. What a joy and relief it was to talk to somebody who understood and could help me interpret my Jungian dreams, so it opened another door.

I had been on a number of Aldermaston and Weathersfield marches with my youngest son and taken part in the march to Holy Loch. Now I felt free to go and demonstrate. There were inner questions about my responsibilities to home and famine relief activities. I dreamed I was holding a tray and more and more was being loaded on it and I said, "Help, I can't carry any more" – but when I looked underneath it was not my arms that supported it, but large sculptured hands and arms like those in Henry Moore's sculptures. I felt free to go. I acquired two convictions for demonstrating two days running and finally after considerable delay ended up in a maximum security women's prison.

This experience taught me a lot that I hadn't read about in the Howard League journal. After much dawdling hoping I would pay the fine, the Huddersfield police rang me and as I still refused to pay, they had to take me in. I asked if I was wanted straight away but I was told they would call for me at 4pm, as that would still count as a day of my sentence. I heard later that one of the J.P.s had refused to sign the warrant for my arrest, so I suspect they treated me gently; also they were glad I was not going to be difficult to arrest – no protest drama. At 4pm the police came, we had a cup of tea and I was escorted to the local lock-up. Anything that I might use to hang myself was removed. In the morning a man and a woman police officer who had travelled from Scotland came to escort me to Gateside maximum security prison for women, situated near Glasgow. The officers I travelled with had been given money to buy me lunch on the train, but they were embarrassed about taking me to the dining car, so I agreed with them that they should give the money for my lunch to Oxfam. This started us talking about my recent visit to Morocco, Quakers, etc. When we parted the woman officer said that if I was out in time, she would like to take me to the Highland Games. So far I had enjoyed friendly encounters, but the warders in prison had a very different attitude – it was Them and Us, where I belonged. After a long wait in a cubicle, all my clothes were taken and I was given prison garb – as I remember it – a vest, a cotton dress that reached my ankles (later I discovered that it was designed by Vogue) and two shoes, one with a pointed toe and one with a square toe. My feet were large, so they posed a problem.

I had read in reports of the Howard League of the training prisoners were given to make them better citizens. As 80-90% of the women prisoners were in for petty crime – drunkenness, prostitution, theft, etc., and had sentences of less than six months, there was no training. There was a 'no talking' rule except on the few occasions when we had exercise – walking round the prison yard in twos – and the heavy Glaswegian accent, sometimes whispered in the slopping-out queue, was difficult for me to understand. My work in the morning was to scrub the stone floor of the lower gallery and clean the toilets. In the afternoon I scrubbed the upper galleries that had been scrubbed by someone else in the morning. I asked for some disinfectant to put in the very stained lavatory pans and the officer put a lot of something into the pail when I was scrubbing. As I rinsed the floor cloth my arms stung and turned red, so I went posthaste to pour the liquid into the lavatory pan. Alas, I had forgotten the scrubbing brush – it certainly had the shortest bristles I had ever seen, and it went down the drain. I had to report to three officers, each giving me a good telling-off – I had damaged the waterworks of the prison, but wet and bedraggled in my Vogue dress, I survived. One old lag was sorry for me, bless her, and brought me a mat to kneel on the next day. Another one brought me a small piece of cheese she had saved from her meal. Can sympathy do more? I accepted it with grateful humility. Again, reading about prisons, I was surprised how much money was allocated for food. I could have done a lot better than that at home, on the same budget. My request for unsugared tea had to be referred to the doctor as it reduced the calories I was supposed to have. Porridge with sugar instead of salt would have met that deficiency if it had been allowed.

I could hear my neighbour weeping at night. Gradually I got round to speaking to her. Her husband was in prison, her children were in care, she was illiterate and so had no contact with them. She had stayed clear of the drink for nine months, then an old friend came to visit her; they drowned their sorrows and now she was a guest of Her Majesty again. I felt so sorry for her. She would return to the same situation she came from, with no hope. Maybe there was some aftercare, but sadly inadequate. The same situation applied in a different way to many of the prostitutes, who needed to learn another trade to support them and their offspring. George Fox said we should have a sense of all conditions. Once a week we had a film. No speaking or turning your head around – infringement of rules meant we should all be marched back to our cells. Here was an opportunity to experience courage, laughter , beauty, joy in and gentleness with animals and children. But the first film was a Western where a man and his son were killed and pushed down a well; a few more murders followed. The next film was about jewel thieves. I expect the prisoners learned a few more tricks, but I think the thief was caught in the end, so it was a 'moral tale'. What a lost opportunity! I recently sent my video of *The Inn of the Sixth Happiness* to a woman's prison in Scotland. It was one of my treasures, but I hope that perhaps one woman, maybe more, will take its message to heart.

I was allowed to go for a very brief visit to the library to take out one book. Luckily I found a copy of *Christian Faith and Practice* left by another Conscientious Objector. Prison gave me the time to read and ponder; I felt upheld by it and part of a greater community. It was extraordinary the cards I received from the most unlikely people, who though not protesters themselves, respected others who stood by their convictions. I learned much and was thankful for the experience. I had been nominated by the Labour Party to be a J.P., but my prison sentence scotched that. I was more useful working with Oxfam and community relations than sitting on a bench.

I had attended a number of Inter Faith conferences including those of the World Congress of Faiths. With the increase of Asians into Britain especially in Bradford and Huddersfield, and such events as World Co-operation Year, from time to time I organised Inter Faith services planned by members of all the faiths. The next big door to open was the result of being invited to join the Council of Management of Oxfam, then the Executive and later the Asia Grants Committee when field staff were beginning to be appointed. I took my duties seriously, encouraging the setting up of an Education Unit and starting a Young Oxfam in Huddersfield – which Oxfam later followed. I did not approve of grants being made only to missionary projects – we were not a missionary society. My mother's modest legacy came in useful. It is easier to go on a missionary tour when cars and telephones are easily available – otherwise it is the local bus, a bullock cart, occasionally a 'lift' by someone who has transport. It meant the great advantage of staying with Indian families who proudly showed me their projects but also wanted me to see the beauty of their country not just the poverty. These were people who, in spite of the pull of the extended family which takes the place of the welfare state in India, still reach out to those outside the family that need help. They were not missionaries who could return to England to tell us what they were doing and raise money for it, so we mistakenly thought they did nothing.

The culture of India became alive when I attended a Hindu wedding in which all the village participated, saw the home ritual and the travelling story-tellers, acrobats, the priest who performed the morning ritual at the family shrine of a strict Brahmin family, or the housewife at the shrine in the kitchen, or reciting prayers and anointing the tulsi plant in the courtyard. The morning bath had its ritual – one is given a bucket of hot water and a little water pot so that a Hindu can anoint the god within as s/he pours water over the head and sings bajans – songs of praise – when so doing. One morning I was out in the fields when a Muslim came up to a small shrine and paid his respects. I was told the shrine was in memory of a Muslim pir – a Holy Man, who had left his land to the village. Presently a Hindu priest came up and prayed there. I asked my companion why a Hindu priest should pray at a Muslim shrine. He looked surprised at my question and said "But he is a Holy Man!" I thought of William Penn – "The humble, the meek, the merciful, just and pious souls are everywhere of one religion". I'm glad to be a Quaker with Zen Buddhist teaching intertwining and underpinning it. I like Douglas Steer, an American Quaker who writes of his sharing of experiences with Buddhists in Japan. He calls it 'mutual irradiation'.

A great experience was being taken twice to the rock temples of Ajanta and Ellora. The thirty cave temples of Ajanta are excavated in the side of a semi-circular escarpment overlooking a narrow gorge and small river to which steps led down from the monasteries and prayer halls. These were constructed between the second century BC and the seventh century AD. The 'walls' or vertical surfaces are painted with stories from the Jakarta tales about the life of the Buddha. They are elegant, sophisticated and often deal with courtly life, and are a great treasure. The only Buddhist rock temples and abris I saw in China provided a much more down to earth teaching of respect for elders with a young man carrying his aged parents in two baskets hung from a pole across his shoulders and a mother caring for her little child that was wearing the split pants with a little apron at the back that young Chinese children wear today ... a distinct cultural difference in attitude.

Another afternoon I was taken to visit a swami who lived under a tree. A small whitewashed temple had been built nearby by his devotees. As the swami was meditating I was left overnight to be collected the next day. One of the other two visitors there who spoke English took me to a very old, partly underground shrine to meditate. Imagine my horror when the symbol one fixed one's gaze on was a snake sculptured in bronze. I had once had a dream about going to a snake pit and I wondered if there were any live ones lurking nearby. I felt my end had come and it added to the depth and quality of my meditation. After about an hour my companion said to me, "You were meditating on death, weren't you?" I certainly faced my fears and didn't run away. We then went to visit the swami who after greetings said, "Ask me a question!" I said I feared my questions would be trivial and childish. He said with authority, "God looks into the heart of the devotee." So I relaxed and we had an interesting discussion, but 35 years later I cannot remember much. We later had a simple meal and I faced another trial. I was taken into the jungle not far away and a lamp was left on the path so that I could make my way back to it having relieved myself. I was glad to get back to the lamp! The two men and I slept in our clothes on charpoys in the little temple. I think it was at the urging of the English-speaking Hindu, I was accepted as a devotee and I was given a cotton blanket to remind me of the swami. I use it as my underblanket still. We kept in touch for a few years and he asked me to send him a sculpture of my head. Finding a willing sculptor was a problem and when I did, the sittings required, the cost and transport, seemed out of proportion to me as a Westerner that supported Oxfam. If I had been a Hindu, I would have been sure that becoming more enlightened I would do better in caring for others as a result, but it is difficult to free oneself from one's own culture. I sent him some large photos I had taken of him that he had asked for to give to his devotees as he was moving away from that area.

Staying at the Gandhian and Kasturba ashrams and their Peace Centre in North Lakimpur in Assam was a joy. The Gandhians work among the poor, the outcasts and the tribal people in remote areas. They run schools, community projects such as establishing a rice bank after the harvest so that needy villagers can be fed instead of borrowing money at exorbitant rates from money lenders. The Gandhian rejection of the caste system, their respect for the writings of other faiths and their asking me to contribute made me feel welcome. My offering was modest, singing "God be in my head and in my understanding ..." I'm not sure who wrote it but for people who try to serve God and remember that Jesus said, "To the least of these my children, you have done it unto me", it seemed appropriate. I still use the word God occasionally, but I prefer Holy Spirit, Inner Light or ground of being. Allah is said to be closer than one's jugular vein – obviously immanent and transcendent.

The art and architecture of a country especially when it is so different from one's own, makes an impact at a deep level. The Mogul emperors of North India made a tremendous contribution in science, astronomy, architecture and in their many universities. The wonderful organisation in London of the World of Islam festival was in 1976 when there were exhibitions in the British Museum, the Museum of Mankind and the Science Museum. Arts and Crafts, paintings, calligraphy, musical instruments, medieval lore, engineering etc. were shown. There was also an exhibition at the art gallery in Manchester.

In Delhi and Jaipur there are open-air observatories with structures that were used for studying astronomy that you can walk around and test for yourself if you are able. The breath-taking beauty and refined austerity of many mosques and madrasahs in Isfahan, Iran, the minarets and golden domes, the blue purple jade and ochre of the faience tiled surfaces touched my heart. I loved the long bridge with its niches for residents to sit in the heat of the day cooled by the spray from the river when it was in flood that was both beautiful and practical. Most people know the Taj Mahal in India and Fatepur Sikri nearby – alas the latter had to be abandoned when there was insufficient water to support the royal court and its entourage ... not a success story but they learnt from their mistakes. There is so much about Islam that I admire and one has only to hear Kenneth Cragg, Islamic scholar and then Archbishop of Jerusalem who wrote *The Call of the Minaret* and other books to know where his heart is. I think the Sufis were the Quakers of

Islam, wearing undyed wool, with their commitment to frugality in living. One of the Mogul emperors was a Sufi, who did a daily stint of work with his hands, lived simply and was buried simply in the courtyard of a mosque beside a tree. Only Islam has managed to prohibit the making of statues of Allah or the servants of Allah which can entrap people who cannot break through to the spirit behind the form, but one remembers that Ramakrishna was enlightened when contemplating Kali whose mouth drips blood and who holds a skull in her hand, and he was a Holy Man and a seeker. I find it puzzling, but I can't put myself into his culture. Zakat is the giving of part of one's income to the poor, the discipline of prayer five times a day, the discipline of fasting at Ramadan and the teaching of no conversion to Islam by force. These are the 'teachings' but of course they are not always followed. This is true of the followers of all faiths. Islam at the time of the Crusades was more 'Christian' under the rule of Salal el Din than the so-called Christian crusaders and more Christian in practice than Ferdinand and Isabella in Spain when they thought they had done well to get rid of the infidels by burning them. One notices that each faith does not live up to its highest ideals all the time, though individuals in that faith keep the Holy Spirit alive and are witnesses to that life. When I read *Reveille for a Persian Village* and *A Well* and *Three Widows* by Nazme Nagfi I felt I had found a kindred spirit as they linked with my concern to help people help themselves.

Christians have a vestigial 'fast' in Lent and on Fridays. Alas! the lenten lunches – coffee, bread and cheese and watercress based on 500 calories which was a reminder of lenten fasting and raised money for Famine Relief which I started 30 years ago, is now in decline, partly as the church hall where it was held is being demolished for the site of a super shopping centre.

Guru Nanak, born into a Hindu family, had a wider vision which made him aware of the beauty and simplicity of Islam. The Sikhs were pacifist for many years but they were decimated by later Mogul rulers until at last Guru Gobind Singh felt they should protect themselves and their families. When the Kailsa was formed, Sikhs let their hair grow and wore a turban, wore short trousers not a dhoti, wore an iron bracelet and carried a knife for protection only. One is sad that their witness to peace died out. One thinks of

Gandhi and Martin Luther King with admiration and reverence in our own times.

The destruction of Hindu temples in the north of India by the Moguls left the gopurams of southern India untouched. There was a tank for ablutions in the courtyard as a mosque had, but high oblong towers ornately carved with many statues of myriad gods that are all aspects of Brahma, are all strikingly different. There are many courtyards and shrines. I first visited the great temple at Madurai at 7am when I was waiting for a train connection. There are many huge temple complexes in southern India. Of the three main gods – Shiva, Vishnu and Rama, Shiva Nataraja dominates with its magnificent statue of Shiva with four arms dancing in a ring of fire, where death and life are part of the eternal dance. It is closely akin to Sidney Carter's Lord of the Dance – "They put me on a cross and hung me high, but I am the Lord that will never, never die. I live in you and you live in me – I am the Lord of the Dance", said he.'

There are a number of shore temples and seven Ratnas – shrines – at Mahabalipuram south of Madras. This place is close to my heart, where there is a rock carving I treasure. At the top of a rocky outcrop there is a lake well filled during the monsoon and water cascades down a cleft in the rock. On either side of the cleft are carvings of people and animals coming to drink from the same source. There are devas, some people practising 'austerities' – standing on one leg with hands clasped above the head – elephants, snakes ... and at the bottom a small animal also doing 'austerities', a gentle loving humorous touch which contains an insight into the unity of all creation. Of course at the festival of Nagapanchami Hindus put out milk for the unwelcome cobra recognising that even what they fear, has a right to live. I must admit that when a cobra rose up swaying near me in my son's tea plantation and he felt he had to kill it to protect his tea pickers, we were sad for we had encroached on his territory. There are many museums containing sculptures near ancient temples and palaces. One notices the differences in the Gandhara sculptures from the north where there is a considerable Greek influence.

In Sri Lanka the very high standard of ancient sculpture is shown in the remains of cities of Anaradhapura and Polonnaruwa supported by an efficient irrigation system, as well as Buddhist temples. An offshoot of the original Bodhi tree at Bodhgaya under which Buddha gained enlightenment grows in a temple courtyard. In Kandy is the Temple of the Tooth – Buddha's – where drums, chanting, masses of flowers and incense are overpowering. Nearby in a hall one can see ritual dancing. At Sanchi, near Bhopal in India, dated about 3rd century BC is one of the oldest stupas, built by Ashoka the Buddhist king of that period. Later a processional path encircled the stupa and carved arches provided entrance. It is interesting to note that the Buddha was always indicated by a footmark, an umbrella, or the Bodhi tree at this period – later Hindu Buddhists reverted to their ancient ways and Buddha rupas grew apace. I feel a kinship here with my 'low' church of England upbringing – no altar, no cross, no candles. The Ramakrishna Mission in Calcutta is still struggling with the problem of Ramakrishna rupas – only the Muslims seem to have been effective in dealing with this problem.

I was staying at a Gandhian ashram that had an effective biogas plant for cooking and went to visit some schools run by the Gandhians. Life is simple – children wash their own clothes and help with the needs of the school within their capabilities which is also a good training in community living. (I think that my involving five schools in Huddersfield to support Vietnamese orphans, is also part of their social training.) The children were taught basic agriculture and village skills as well as ordinary school subjects and as they demonstrated to me, their folk dances and songs. I felt happy with this.

Nearby was Bodhgaya with its Bodhi tree under which Buddha gained enlightenment. There is a main shrine and many temples and guest houses attached, built for the different Buddhist nationals who come on pilgrimage. At the main shrine devotees made progress towards the entrance by prostrating full length and then moving forwards as far as their hands would reach. Recently on TV a Holy Man in India had rolled all the way there and back to a distant shrine. He had some supporters with him to protect him from the lorries on the road and presumably supply him with food and water. A friend of mine spoke unappreciatively of this. In a way I agree with her, but to a Hindu this was a witness to his faith and would be treated as such by his followers. I remember reading about Quaker women in England who walked naked through a town as witness.

My youngest son John had set up a clinic and house and plantation in south India. Rob my eldest son went to help him and we all met in Sri Lanka where we spent ten days sightseeing. As the house in India was not finished when we arrived, we camped out in the partly built clinic. When we were about to move into the house, it is the Indian custom to have a puja and pray for a blessing on the enterprise (see Chapter Four).

I know a swami of the Ramakrishna Mission in Calcutta very well. We had a common friend in the Khasi hills in Assam and both the swami and I had been involved in the Bengal Famine in 1942. He showed me round the swamp villages and projects that the Hudderfield Famine Relief Committee had supported. I queried why models of the gods were on a rubbish heap. He said there was a festival the day before and they helped people to concentrate – but a stone, a tree or a flower could do just as well. The aim of putting the models on the rubbish heap was to prevent people using them as idols. RKM shows the face of modern Hinduism. Swami Lokeswarananda became the head of RKM in Calcutta. Their headquarters at Gol Park is an international guest house and a centre for students and had two meditation halls – one with a rupa of Ramakrishna, the other with just a beam of light on a large stone. I was asked to give a talk there which was printed in their magazine. I think he was interested to find one who appeared to be a Christian, willing to reach out beyond the outer forms. He told me that at Christmas, a lecture was given at RKM on the contribution of Christ and his teaching. "We also celebrate but do not kill any animals for celebration." Touché. The swami could not understand how we could worship a man being tortured. It is a challenge to look at our culture through alien eyes.

In Benares I stayed at the HQ of the Gandhians in their ashram. I was welcomed and asked to tell them why I had come. I told them about Oxfam and as I saw it, the need to support Indians who were helping their own people rather than missionary societies. This led to Oxfam and Gandhians working together during the Bihar famine, when Gandhian and Oxfam water engineers worked alongside bringing into cultivation land given to Vinobe Bhave on his land gift campaign. It also gave me an opportunity to talk about Oxfam-supported health clinics for mothers and babies which included family planning. Although they listened politely, Gandhians believe in abstinence to control births. Visits to the burning ghats where very old people sit nearby waiting to die and have their ashes thrown into the Mother Ganga is very different from Americans who have their corpses deep-frozen so that with increasing medical knowledge they may become alive again. I prefer the Indian attitude and if anyone believes in rebirth or resurrection, surely that is better than having an old body being jerked into another century having lost all friends and family.

The Gandhians urged me to visit Sarnath a few miles away, so early one morning a Gandhian took me by rickshaw. The garden where Buddha had preached his first sermon has a large stupa, a number of other buildings, including a Jain temple. In the main Buddhist temple, large, cool and spotlessly clean, with stories of the Buddha painted on the walls, we sat cross-legged and meditated for some time – the only visitors. When we got up the custodian asked us to come up to the shrine where there was a Buddha rupa and I was given one of the red roses from the shrine. I treasure it in my memory.

In 1986 I joined, with some reservations, a Peace Group that was going to Cambodia, paying my own expenses. The account of this project is told in *To Asia in Peace*, edited by Pat Arrowsmith. In Cambodia one is in a Buddhist country where the monks in the village pagodas do most of the social work. If a school is needed the monks will call a meeting of the village folk to discuss the matter and villagers will offer labour, materials and equipment to carry this out. The pagodas and little temple adjoining are the centre of worship and community service. When I was there for three weeks in 1968 all young men spent about two years training in a monastery – including Prince Sihanouk. A useful national service; in the towns the monks provided hostels for country boys so that they could continue their education. I feel much of this has altered since the tragic Pol Pot regime, where doctors, teachers and educated people were hunted down and killed. I found Cambodia a happy, beautiful country where Cambodian and Vietnamese citizens lived in peace. Sihanouk's official wife was Chinese, but the mother of his children was Princess Monique, a Vietnamese. There were no lepers lying in the streets as in India, as they were taken care of and given treatment. The beauty of the royal palace with its golden roof and upswept finials, the cleanliness of the streets, the growing university providing skills for developing local industry, and the cité sportif where we stayed, which had been built for the Asia games, all this gave an air of joyful expectancy and development. A number of the French rubber planters who had stayed in Cambodia after independence, said it was better governed under Sihanouk than under the French administration. We visited some of the areas that were being bombed by the Americans and slept in houses built on stilts. In the evening the village band came to an area under the trees and we danced the ramvong. In this you and your partner circle round each other, responding to each other's hand movements, and all the dancers are moving in a large circle. In a way it was very intimate because you had to watch your partner to respond. As an addicted country dancer I loved it. When bombers came over the lights were extinguished and the music stopped ... only to start again when bombers had passed.

We spent three weeks in Cambodia but before we left I used a £5 traveller's cheque left over from my summer holiday to go to Ankor Wat near the Thai border. There is one main temple of outstanding dignity and beauty and many others built at different periods, also shrines, palace, lakes. Walls were heavily sculptured with scenes from ancient history. Basically Cambodia was Buddhist but when there was a threat of attack, Krishna's advice to Arjuna was recalled about doing one's duty but taking no pleasure in slaughter, being detached and finding ways of making a just peace. The temples were Buddhist but a Hindu influence was there.

The royal Cambodian ballet in which the princess and princes took part was a royal responsibility in which ancient myth and cultural teaching was kept alive, but Sihanouk had opened it up to other gifted dancers. I used to stop and watch members of the Royal Ballet School practising about 7am in the morning when it was cool, as I went on my way to the GPO to post a letter to England. At special seasons they danced before the main temple at Ankor Wat, sharing their ancient culture with tourists. This reminded me of the Ramlila in a park at Delhi where the story of Rama and Sita is performed in dance and music on a huge well-lit stage and the audience could relax in the warm dark night, in chairs I am glad to say. Rama and Sita were unjustly banished to the forest but there they were helpful to the villagers and animals. When Sita was kidnapped and taken to Lanka, birds told Rama the news and the monkeys made a bridge to Lanka so that Sita could be rescued. When the period of banishment had ended, Sita and Rama were welcomed back to their kingdom by citizens carrying little lamps. This is the origin of Diwali. My Hindu neighbours used to put these little lamps in the windows at Diwali. Alas, they don't now. I still have a large Christmas tree lit up in my window at Christmas. I value the story of Diwali that includes birds and animals as part of our community – I would include trees as well. Our nativity story that is enacted in schools at Christmas of a baby born in a stable with animals present at the birth, the visit of the simple shepherds as well as the wise men, has the same quality as Diwali. We are also trying to keep alive a story of universal significance of humility and oneness of all creation, a loving, caring family where new life and light is welcomed.

I loved Cambodia and its people. Americans who crash-landed were shown the old temples and new developments and then sent back to Saigon as ambassadors. Sihanouk replaced bombed houses on the frontier and had large Cambodian flags painted on the roof, hoping to avoid mistakes on the border. The destruction of Cambodia by the Americans in Vietnam, the ensuing horror of the Pol Pot killing fields was heartbreaking ... and Pol Pot was still active in 1995 – no Nuremberg trial for him! When those who caused the original disaster left, only the impoverished Vietnamese came in to restore some kind of order. When Germany was defeated in 1945, Americans gave considerable help to restore and re-equip industry. They lost the war in Vietnam, and the humiliation and the excuse that Vietnam had overrun Cambodia allowed them to sit back and just leave two countries they had destroyed. I don't think this can be termed a spiritual insight but an insight into human psychology! I am still angry and appalled by Britain who armed the freedom fighters of Vietnam to fight the Japanese invaders and at the end of the 1939-46 war, armed the Japanese to fight the

Vietnamese freedom fighters. Is there any place for this in my seeking an Interfaith connection? I think anger has its place if the energy can be used to fight 'skillfully' against a wrong. All I could do was to demonstrate in Hong Kong (see Chapter Six).

Recently there was a programme on TV about Cambodia, which I had loved so much and which had suffered so much. I looked forward to the programme, expecting improvements. I knew the head of state, Sihanouk, was in hospital in China being treated for cancer, but with United Nations intervention, I hoped the political situation would be under control. It is fashionable now to denigrate public figures, but even if Sihanouk was a playboy, his gifts included the ability to establish a prosperous and happy country – before America moved in. Certainly he played football with his friends at his holiday home, a lovely bungalow in a wooded area near the sea, and sometimes he and his family with a minister or two made films. His films he showed to the peace group after dinner were beautiful. How sensible to enjoy life with your family and friends. He also established a university and started small modern industries.

Pol Pot is old now and rejected by his followers, but they are still a threat to the stability of the country. It is said that the elections, though supervised by the United Nations and costing £2 million, were rigged. Prince Sihanouk's son, Rianarad, has now been deposed in a violent coup, so there is another ruler, with many factions against him. Cambodia endured the terrors of Pol Pot's regime, when doctors, teachers, monks, lawyers and educated people were singled out for destruction and the horrors of the killing fields, followed by years of uncertainty and threat. After nearly forty years of horror and torture, I feel heartbroken for a country and people I loved. How long, Oh Lord, must the suffering and destruction continue? How long?

Returning home, I talked to many groups all over England where I showed slides, sold copies of Thich Nhat Han's *Lotus in a Sea of Fire* and supported the work of the Buddhist School of Social Service in Saigon that I visited in Vietnam in 1973.

I had been studying Ikebana – Japanese flower arrangement – and had taken two or three exams, so hearing that the Buddhist summer school had classes in Ikebana I was happy to go. It was a rich time for participants as Tibetan monks were invited to the summer school; their English was very limited but their quality of serenity and humour was expressed in so many ways. I remember particularly their chanting in the Oak Room at High Leigh Conference centre at 9.30pm each evening; their vibrations were not the shattering ones of a West Indian Steel Band, but reached a more profound level. Within a year their English had improved enormously, due I think to their early training in concentration. At the Buddhist Summer School we could attend classes in Zen, Theravada, and Mahayana as well as Phiroz Mehta's class: he was born a Parsee but had discarded labels and had written such books as *The Heart of Religion*. He was a religious teacher of much depth, learning and understanding. In the evening we had visiting speakers such as John Bloefeld, a writer who was particularly close to Taoism, Anne Bancroft who wrote *Religions of the East*, and Ronald Eyre who produced an excellent TV series on *Living Religions*. He joined our Ikebana class. There was a rich experience of variety and depth fostered by the chairman and founder of the Buddhist Society, Christmas Humphreys. One realised this only too acutely when he died.

In the afternoons one of our classes was taken by Stella Coe who had studied Ikebana in Japan for a number of years when her husband was a member of the British Embassy there. She became a Buddhist and was honoured by the Emperor of Japan – and became his 'Precious Royal Apricot' – for her services to Japanese culture. I was indeed blessed by having insight and instruction from her. Ikebana is a way into Zen, that is putting into daily practice the teachings of Buddhism and leaves room for inner growth and discovery. There are three main placements which may be branches, wood, or rocks. Shin/Heaven is the most important, Soe/Man is 2/3 of Shin and Hikae/Earth 1/3 of Shin. In the basic upright style – Rissenkei – Shin curves up to $10°$ of the vertical Soe, coming forward at $45°$, and Hikae is on the right – 1/3 of Shin at $75°$. There are two other basic styles – windswept when Shin is at $45°$, and cascading when Shin is at $75°$. There are about seven variations of each of these styles – one in which Soe may be omitted; all are required to be known for exams. All arrangements have space – a void – and all are uncluttered; there is depth – a three dimensional quality; there are a few flowers at different stages of development, preferably including a bud or seed pod, expressing change or impermanence. The main flower looks towards Shin, the others talking together or shyly facing the viewer. In Japan an Ikebana arrangement would be arranged on a tokonomo, a low daïs a foot high built at right angles to a window. The arrangements relate to a season – New Year, Autumn, Waning Moon, Boys' Day – with suitable scroll hanging on the wall.

Buddhism teaches you to look at anger and grief and watch moods arising, using the energy roused skillfully by directing it into channels that are creative and peaceful. Stella Coe taught us to make an Ikebana arrangement expressing these feelings, contemplating what we had done and having projected it, let it go. This method is part of Vipassana meditation.

For the last few years I have taught Ikebana at the Buddhist Summer School and know how much easier it is for Buddhists than the non-Buddhists at a U3A class. To develop it into a way into Zen requires one to use one's training to be able to interpret anger, sloth, fear, tranquillity etc. The more advanced students are given Haikus or Buddhist texts such as 'opposites are equal' and 'the futility of utility' both of which exercised me greatly. One holds the theme in one's heart and goes for a walk in the woods that surround High Leigh, the conference centre (not neglecting the garden rubbish dump) with an open awareness. Usually a branch, some wood or a piece of old metal, a toadstool or a tall stem of cow parsley will speak to you. You just collect them and take them back, play with them and then look at what you have done. You may take two or three suitable flowers from a container in the room. Your arrangement has been activated by a deeper level of consciousness and is an expression of the inner life of the arranger. You then share this insight with your teacher. This is when the way into Zen is being learned.

Ikebana has meant a great deal to me. I used to 'do the flowers' for Quaker Meeting every Sunday, but got the feeling that others would like to do them too, so I reduced my turn to once a month. It was only then that I realised that the simple arrangement of heaven, man and earth in harmony with materials from my own garden was a preparation for Meeting for Worship that I missed. I gave a number of demonstrations of Ikebana in and around Huddersfield, as the teaching tied up with my beliefs and my environmental campaign. I was either given a donation for Famine Relief or the club would bring me unwanted Christmas gifts or bric à brac to sell in our Famine Relief gift shop. It was spreading the message of care for the universe and its inhabitants. There are about eight chapters of Ikebana in the British Isles, but most are supported by flower-arrangers who are not Buddhists. This is a loss. There is less training in the basic philosophy, less interpretation to activate the deeper levels of the psyche and the excuse of 'free style' allows one to break the rules one never knew. Alas this is also true of the Japanese who have become westernised. Stella Coe was invited to go back to the Sogetsu School in Tokyo to conduct a series of lectures and demonstrations reminding teachers of the great heritage they were discarding. I hope it had some effect, but there are tides in the affairs of men which Buddhists recognise – impermanence and change is one. Perhaps someone in a hundred years' time will rediscover Ikebana as a way into Zen and the flame will rekindle and we will remember we must live in harmony with our environment and not destroy it; but it is urgent to act on this now.

It was interesting that at the Buddhist Summer School I met a very ordinary Welsh woman who attended a Quaker Meeting but was not a member. She told me she had such strange dreams that she had written to the Buddhist Society. They explained that the dreams were using the symbolism of Tibetan Buddhism. One begins to wonder how deep the collective unconscious of Jung goes to collect its material. Is this part of the DNA programme that we all carry? There is no doubt in my mind that exposure to the art, music, sculpture, architecture, drama, home rituals and festivals – the whole of a culture – has a deep impact at a sub-conscious level when anyone is open to it, especially if it is strikingly different from one's own. The British Raj, with a few exceptions, was closed to this, as it requires humility and a willingness to be aware and listen. Those who think they know form a barrier to further understanding.

I have a great respect for the many Tibetans I met at the Buddhist Summer School and in India. The Indian army had vacated a large property in Darjeeling for a Tibetan refugee children's school. Many of the parents were working on Indian roads and the Dalai Lama had set up a number of schools to protect the children and help them maintain their Tibetan culture. Conditions were deplorable, broken floorboards, the roof of the main dormitory partly blown down, but the Tibetans were cheerful and making new latrines, of which there was a great need, as well as doing repairs to the neglected buildings. There was one smallish room that touched my heart. An ex-Raj washstand had been painted with Tibetan designs; on this stood a Buddhist rupa, butterlamps, incense burning and tankas hung from the wall – all the treasures they had managed to carry with them over the mountains on their perilous flight from Tibet. It was a place of comfort in an alien society. The only thing I didn't like was the mug of Tibetan tea with its layer of yak fat, which was not improved by the many hairpin bends on the road down from Darjeeling that followed.

If you walked up through the tea plantations at Darjeeling, you would reach the area where a relation of the Dalai Lama, Mrs. Thondup, had a centre for the elderly. Small houses in a compound, with lots of prayer flags guided you to a hive of activity. The old people were making Tibetan rugs. I should love to have bought one but they were too heavy to take on travels. They wove aprons, table mats, belts, in typical Tibetan designs, and I was able to bring some of these back. By selling crafts they were able to contribute to their support. The Indian government, in spite of the poverty of many of its own citizens, provided Tibetan refugees with a small monthly allowance and grants of land. They had a problem as they could no longer collect the vegetable dyes available in Tibet. My husband did research at ICI and was working on dyes, medicinals, etc., so with the help of ICI I was able to send them some good stable dyes. I also visited Tibetan schools and a monastery at Missouri, north of Dehra Dun. I walked through the snow at 7 am to see all the monks and students sitting in lines on the floor of a long, low building, a low bench in front of them, on which their heavy oblong books of Tibetan scriptures rested. Each one read aloud or chanted from his own book so they could hear themselves and absorb the teaching.

At Hublai in the south of India near Mysore, an area of barren land was allocated to the Tibetans. Water was scarce, Indian diseases for which the Tibetans have no immunity were rampant and the death rate appalling, but the monks worked hard and cheerfully. I suppose if you believe in reincarnation you will hope to be born in better circumstances if you have earned it in this life. The settlement was run by a capable young Tibetan who had married an Australian volunteer and between them they were now doing a very good job of resettlement and getting a few young Tibetans ready to go to an Indian medical college. This would save them being dependent on the two Indian doctors provided by the Government. Again, one small hall was home; there was no Buddha rupa carried that far, but in its place was a throne on which the Dalai Lama sat to give discourse when he came to visit – a visit they all spoke of with tremendous reverence.

It is interesting how the Tibetans are able to choose from an early age, five or six onwards, children who have the qualities to make good monks. They study the same subjects as the other Tibetan children as well as their priestly training. They are free to leave in later years if they wish to, though for various reasons this seldom occurs. The Jesuits thought they could mould a child's mind by the time he was seven and I am sure a secure loving moral family contributes much to a healthy development in later life; but I am also sure that some children at a very early age are more sensitive and aware than others. One could spot a policeman's son in a class of children – so often like his Dad in attitudes.

Writing chronologically and as insight unfolds, we come to the visit of Seshie Agashe, the wife of Diwarka Agashe – one of my contacts from the International Friendship League Christmas guests. She was a teacher in the school set up by her husband where the children were taught to do voluntary work as well as academic subjects. She was only allowed to bring £2 out of India but I got a little help in sending her to London for a short course that I thought might be useful. She stayed with us for four months and I arranged visits to schools, youth clubs, family planning clinics and 'outings'. She was not at all impressed with our youth clubs where she saw young people sitting around, playing ping pong or listening to pop music. She saw well fed youngsters doing no voluntary service as the boys did in her school in Buldana. It was winter and she felt the cold, kept very strictly to her vegetarian diet but never caught a cold in all that time.

It was the day before Christmas Eve and when I came home from shopping a stray dog was hanging about at the back door. I felt sorry for the dog and invited him in, to the chagrin of my pedigree Sheltie when she saw this outsider stretched out on the hearth rug in front of the fire. The next morning I took him to the Police Station, but by the evening he was back again. My Indian guest said in a solemn voice: 'It is a god who has come to test your compassion' – the god was invited in for Christmas. I have never known a dog so quick to learn from my dog. Luckily I had an old dog basket in the cellar and brought it up. I am sure he never had one before, but he soon learnt. In the morning my Sheltie always came upstairs and jumped on my bed and had a cuddle. The god in disguise jumped on the bed for his share of a cuddle. He had a happy Christmas and so did we; it added an extra dimension to our Christmas festivities and I think that there was that of god in him. I took him back to the Police Station after Christmas. He remembered the way and ran ahead of me up the steps. At first the police did not believe me, as they had never had a dog escape before, but on checking their books they found it was true. As he looked very scabby a vet checked that he had nothing infectious that he might have passed on to my Sheltie. I would have kept him if I could and was sorry to see him go, but perhaps he had other 'god in disguise' jobs to do.

There is a Hindu story of King Yudisthera who set out with some companions and a dog to visit Mount Meru. The way was long and difficult and for one reason or another only the King and his dog reached what we might call the Pearly Gates. The janitor said the King could come in but not the dog. Upon which the King said that his dog was more faithful than all his companions who started out with him and if there was no place for the dog, it was no place for him. The janitor looked again at the dog and saw the embodiment of Vishnu, so he entered with the King. Such a story means a lot to me – we have them in our culture too, like the 'Dog brother of the Order of St John of Jerusalem'. There is an acceptance of One Life or what is called 'Creation Spirituality' by Matthew Fox.

The enormous number of gods in India is bewildering to a westerner, but the teaching of the one behind the forms is readily accepted and fostered. A school for tribal children run by the Gandhians at Dadghaon north of Bombay put on a short play for me in which a woman worked with such humility and dedication spinning, fetching water and preparing meals for her family that people noticed it and came to pay homage to her, as they saw that of God in her. Of course as one pours water over one's head during the morning bath and sings bajans, one is anointing the god within – a reinforcing of one's beliefs through ritual. One greets a Hindu, palms together, bowing and saying 'Namaste', recognising that of God in him or her. Ritual has its place, but like everything else, in moderation. I feel at one with the Indian classical dancer who offers a short dance prayer to the gods before she begins her main programme.

In the 1960s many Asian immigrants arrived in Bradford and Huddersfield which presented many problems in culture, language and education. It seemed illogical to be only concerned with problems in India – the first flag day I had organised was for the Bengal famine, so I became more and more involved in community relations, started the Home Tutor scheme, where English schoolgirls and later women, visited Asian homes to teach spoken English. In 1968 we started the International Women's Society for Asians who spoke English. To extend the knowledge of social workers, teachers and other interested people, we put on a Diwali festival at the Town Hall. A member of our IWS who was a classical dancer trained the solo dancers and a school that had a wonderful teacher of creative dance, trained the villagers, monkeys, birds etc. An Indian member with good English told the story so that the audience could follow the stylised actions. Many people came and it was a great success as we not only celebrated Diwali, but children, parents and others learned to appreciate Indian culture. Another school with many Asians helped to paint the background scenery.

The problem of teaching such a large influx of Asian children was acute. They spent a couple of months at a day reception centre and then were bussed out to different schools, so that no school had more than 20% of immigrants. The problem was the need for extra teachers. My Indian guest, who was a teacher, stayed on an extra month and took a class. This gave her better insight into the running of a school than day visits and also provided her with money to buy presents for her family. When she left the headmistress asked if I knew anyone else and as I had done some supply teaching I agreed to work three days a week, overlapping with an Indian teacher not trained in this country. This gave me time to attend the Oxfam Executive and Asia grants committees in Oxford.

The most rewarding time was when I had half a dozen backward English children in the class. They were my 'helpers' and this gave them a status they had never had before. When I said 'put away your books' or 'put on your pumps for PT', they did so, and the Asian children learned the basic phrases very quickly and they gained by hearing the English children ask questions and talk about classroom activities. It was most encouraging to see what progress both groups had made by the end of the year.

The problem for me came in scripture. Should I only tell stories about Jesus? Our hymns and songs in the infant school were 'religious' in that they were thanking God for rains, flowers, lambs, etc. This prompted me to get books from the Delhi Children's Book Trust which contained stories such as that of the little boy who had taken home a baby squirrel and was thrilled with it, he took it to bed with him but the mother squirrel came to the window and tried to get in. The boy was angry but the mother squirrel would not go away. Then he remembered that the baby squirrel had had nothing to eat and perhaps the mother wanted to feed it. He was glad that no one had taken him from his mother. He got up and opened the window and mother and baby were reunited. There is a story very much like this about John Woolman, when a child. He threw a stone, killing a baby bird. When he realised what he had done, this was to me clearly a religious awakening.

A little Indian girl selling door to door realised that one of her customers had mistakenly paid her too much. At great personal inconvenience at the end of a tiring day the girl retraced her steps and returned the extra money without expecting thanks.

An elephant that was supposed to put a heavy pole into a pit to support some structure at a festival, refused to do so. At last his mahout got angry as onlookers were laughing at him so he slashed the elephant with a knife. Naturally the elephant got angry and the mahout and onlookers ran away to a safe distance. They watched the elephant go to the pit, pick out a little cat that had fallen in, then pick up the heavy pole and put in place.

I also read up stories from the *Tales of the Companions of Mohammed*. As Mohammed passed a certain house each morning, a woman who was sweeping deliberately swept the dust towards him. One morning he missed his dust bath. He enquired about the woman and heard she was ill, so he visited her and gave help. Once Mohammed's servant was given money to buy his master new clothes and bought some more expensive clothes than his master usually wore. The servant was sent back to change them and to buy two simple garments, one to give away to someone in need. When a caravan in which Mohammed was in charge was setting down to rest, one camel was complaining loudly and Mohammed asked the reason. He was told by the other camel drivers that it was not getting properly fed as its driver was selling some of its food. Mohammed told the offending driver that the camel worked hard and should be given its due and if it happened again, the driver would be dismissed.

It is told that the Buddha saw sheep being driven to the temple for sacrifice. One ewe had two lambs and as one was lame and lagged behind, the other one was way ahead. Seeing the distress of the ewe, Buddha picked up the lame lamb and carried it to the temple. There he preached a sermon pointing out that the life of animals was not theirs to give. What was required was their giving their own lives in compassion and service to all creation. He was so convincing that the animals lived – Buddhists are vegetarians and the taking of life is forbidden. This is really a development of the story of Abraham and Isaac and the ram in the thicket.

All these are stories that mothers tell their children. They have basic themes of honesty, frugality, 'turning the other cheek', caring for the underprivileged and a loving responsible attitude to all that lives, including animals. Trying to instil these virtues and practice in carrying them out is the mark of a religious attitude to life: 'religio' meaning a binding together. This is embedded in all religions though some give more emphasis to one aspect than another. It is the responsibility of parents and teachers to practise this in their daily lives, not just by preaching and showing artefacts of the different faiths, but by opening up an awareness of what a religious life means and an open attitude to other faiths and culture at an early age. It was interesting that when I said I had told a story from Buddhism when talking in the staff room the consensus was that I could tell such stories in 'storytime' but NOT in scripture time. Wisely I did not argue but continued as before.

Later I was told that another school was celebrating Diwali and why weren't we? Luckily my class had already been acting out the story of Rama and Sita and making a collage to put on the wall. I invited a Hindu friend to come and dance for us and show us some of the stylised hand movements for flowing water, birds, etc. The children enjoyed it and as we talked together in the classroom afterwards one small child said to my friend "You're a wog aren't you?' She laughed and said we were all different, some children had fair hair, some dark or auburn, some brown eyes, some blue, some darker skins, some curly hair, some straight – we just opened our eyes and an awareness of our variety grew. I'm sure the child who asked if my friend was a 'wog' would realise what a friendly happy person this 'wog' was.

For Diwali we put night lights in jam jars and made coloured paper screens around the jars. The hall looked mysterious and attractive on a dark November morning. My class acted out the drama and I told the story as they did it. I had put some Indian music on to create an atmosphere at the beginning – not all the staff appreciated it, one saying a Christian hymn would have been better. I know this is not really only about what I have learned from different faiths, but the reaction of people at that time to 'other faiths'. I think a greater understanding has grown in the last twenty-five years. My little dancing children reminded me of the small children I had seen in a Gandhian nursery school – a balwadi – they were the milkmaids that played with Lord Krishna when young and they danced and sang praises to Lord Krishna with little pots for milk on their heads.

The school where I taught had no trees, garden or grass anywhere near. I encouraged the headmistress to get the Education Committee to approve the building of a two-foot wall, three feet from the main wall at our end of the playground. This trough was filled with soil and a few shrubs planted. I planted climbers against the wall and of course all the discarded bulbs from our bulb show were planted there. The Asian children helped me, and when a flower was in bloom, came running in – 'Meess, meess, there is a white flower – yellow flower...' One day they came running in – "Meess, meess, there is a little snake." I saw a little worm, fallen from the garden and stranded on the tarmac, in danger of being trodden on. I picked it up, told the children what a valuable little hard working creature it was, and put it back into the soil. I think that was one of the best 'religious' lessons I gave, dealing immediately with an ordinary day to day experience and an appreciation and respect for all life. The little children did not pick the flowers, just shared their enjoyment with me. Alas this headmistress died and a new one was appointed who said with her methods children would learn to read three months earlier. Wisely, as it turned out, I left, but used to go back twice or three times a term to look after the garden. Plants became trampled on and broken. I told the headmistress that I was sad, but she said it must be the dinner ladies who did the damage! To me, developing in a child a caring attitude and respect for other children, animals and plants is more important than learning to read three months earlier. This social training might also guide them in the books they read in later years.

A Japanese Quaker Buddhist who was studying at Woodbrooke spent a short holiday with us and urged me to visit Japan. This coincided with some Oxfam contacts that needed following up and my desire to study Ikebana in Japan. Here I found a culture based on Shinto – a nature religion, where each tree and waterfall had its own kami. Shinto is closely intertwined with Buddhism that arrived later, and intertwined with western secular culture and each has its place.

There was a time when foreigners were not welcome. They were called 'foreign devils'. Foreign traders and missionaries presented a threat to a strictly ordered society. This was based on 'giri', a network of honourable responsibilities. All have a loyalty to the Emperor, to provincial warlords, to the clan and family and if one works for such firms as Hitachi or Mitsubishi, loyalty to the company is part of the training in the firm, which looks after its employees. I feel there is something here which we in the west might take heed of when firms in this country making large profits, cast off their workers as expendable rubbish in the name of efficiency and higher profits. I also admit that I don't know of any workers in this country giving up their summer holiday to help a firm over a difficult period.

With the help of my Japanese friend who was friendly with the Roshi of a Japanese Zen monastery, I was able to spend a week in one. One took elegantly wrapped gifts of money for the Abbot and the monastery. One left one's shoes at the entrance to the monastery. There was the ritual presentation of gifts and introductions, then the sitting on one's heels and the drinking of green tea. The bowl was lifted to the lips with both hands, finishing the tea in four mouthfuls and on the last mouthful making appropriate sounds of appreciation as one did so. This had needed practice beforehand. It was all very courtly and elegant. I was given a beautiful and simple room with sliding screens looking out on to a pond full of huge goldfish and a hillside of azaleas and cupressus. A tokonoma, a low daïs adjacent to the screens, provided a place for Ikebana. Along the rest of that wall was a large cupboard to put my bedding during the day and where clothes etc. were kept. I wore a yakata – a cotton kimono.

At 6am a gong aroused me to dress and go into the adjacent meditation hall where I knelt on one cushion and had another to support my buttocks. Wooden clappers or gongs signalised the periods of chanting or meditation that continued for about one hour. A gentle light filtered through the paper screens. Then silently we went to the dining area where we knelt at a long low table, facing another long low table with a gap between the two. This allowed the heavy pots of rice and vegetable broth, hot water, etc. to slide along a wooden plank so that people on both sides could serve themselves. We each had three bowls, chopsticks and a napkin. Two wooden clappers announced the beginning and ending of the meal. As I was the only woman present and at the end of the table, and therefore had a late start, I became more proficient at holding the bowl to my lips and shovelling the rice in as others were doing. We washed our own utensils and put them away in an appointed niche. As it was a Zen monastery, we all worked at cleaning, gardening, preparing meals, etc. I was assigned to the kitchen where I and two other monks had to peel small potatoes with something like a hatchet – a great discipline for the wrist. After a simple midday meal there was meditation/rest/free time when I could explore the wooded grounds. A light evening meal was followed by meditation and chanting before the shrine in the meditation hall for an hour or so. Bath time followed. As I was the only woman I went last. I was told to make three obeisances to the Buddha, to undress and wash all over, then get into a very large hot bath where there was a seat all round the inside of the bath, so that hot water came up to one's neck. It was all so soothing and relaxing to stiff joints due to unusual postures. The day I left I talked to two western men who were spending a year at the monastery. For them it was a physical and spiritual endurance test. They felt they could not face another winter at the monastery with its bitter cold and long periods – 18 hours a day of sesshin – that took place at special periods of the year. I know that yogis in Tibet are said to melt the snow around them by their special tumo breathing, but to keep warm by this method was a very difficult challenge for westerners, accustomed to central heating, to develop. My brief stay in summer was a great pleasure to me and had a timeless quality.

After my exhausting time in Tokyo, where as a result of all the heat, humidity and stress, I had run a temperature of 104°, I was delighted with this period of rest and relaxation and enjoyed to the full a new experience. I had spent a week of silent retreat at a Buddhist centre near Hindhead. As in Japan, no speaking except when the Roshi came to visit you briefly once a day. It was difficult at first, especially at mealtimes, but one began to develop an awareness that didn't need speech. At the end of the week I went to visit an old friend not far away who lived alone, was pleased to see me, and wanted to talk. I couldn't bear the noise. I apologised and said I had a headache and went to bed very early.

Apart from my staying with a Japanese Quaker and Monthly Meeting Clerk, married to an American at Osaka, visiting Hiroshima and staying at the International Peace Centre, I also spent a day at the lovely island of Myajima where vermilion painted toriis stand in the shallow sea, welcoming one to a Shinto temple. My next main visit was to the Itto-en Community at Yamashima near Kyoto. I had read about this in a book and had written to the author for the address. Here I was looked after by Ayako Issayama who spoke English fluently and a deep bond developed.

This was not a Buddhist or Shinto community, though rooted in both. They were Children of the Light, hoping that their light would reach out into the world, and the light of the world would enlighten them. In their large meditation hall where one would have expected a shrine, was a very large window looking out on to a lovely wooded hillside. Tenko San, the founder, was dissatisfied with just making money and decided to spend his life giving service to poor or ill people in need. After a time people realised the value of his services and came to work with him. A rich widow gave them some land on the outskirts of Kyoto to establish a community and headquarters where they could be found when needed. There they developed a garden, grew vegetables, built a meditation hall, a communal kitchen, a conference centre and houses where families shared facilities. Later a school was built for their own and local children. They continued their work for the poor and needy in Kyoto, including schools, playgroups, etc. They had a small touring theatre group On my recommendation a Japanese friend of mine went to visit at the time of 'humble ritual cleansing' of benjos – latrines – in poor areas. He was a bit surprised but performed humbly his allotted task.

About 6am we went to the meditation hall and did some physical exercises before settling down to meditation. After about an hour we walked chanting slowly in single file to the dining hall where a simple and adequate meal was served as at the Zen monastery. Work followed and I was allocated to the kitchen where heat and humidity took its toll. Half way through the morning there was break for tea. I was told to lie on the floor, where I experienced the rigours of Japanese massage – it was daunting but I felt the better for it. In the afternoon I was shown around by Ayako Issayama who spoke English fluently and was taken to some of the classes she was attending on the Tea Ceremony. The simplicity of listening to the water boiling, the detailed ritual of folding or unfolding a napkin in one movement, the time when first guest may speak of some small ancient treasure placed casually for inspection, the ritual of drinking the tea ... it takes a lot of learning until practice becomes beautiful. This, like Ikebana is also a Way into Zen. Ayako and I have so much in common, I still hear from her at New Year, even twenty-four years after our meeting. This year she told me of her attendance representing Itto-en at Interfaith conferences, the last one in Italy where they were welcomed by the Pope. The free afternoons at Itto-en gave me the time to visit Kyoto and take Ikebana lessons in an ancient 'detached palace' bequeathed by its owner for the study of Ikebana. At Itto-en, as at the Zen monastery, it was the quiet order, discipline and humility, the frugality in housing, clothing and food, which left time and money to share with the greater community of those in spiritual and physical need. It is amazing what a comparatively high and rich standard of living can be enjoyed by communities where a simple life style is practised. Facilities were shared of telephone, electric washer, care of the children and their education, healthy food and simple clothes not dependent on changing fashion. Everybody ate communally during the week at Itto-en. It was a better use of man/woman power when there were so many calls on their time. However, at weekends families could go and get rations from the kitchen, which gave the families a chance to cook and be together. This is an improvement on a Kibbutz. The space for the children to play, the woods with pines and azaleas, vegetable garden, bridges and streams of a Japanese garden, daily discipline of contemplation made it a place of beauty and peace and yet a hive of activity – of this world and yet not of this world.

I have four daughters – Erica, who with enormous courage has faced and made the best of so many difficulties as well as showing such care and compassion for others. Then I have three adopted daughters: Hema, a Hindu who had polio when young, lacked the necessary care available in this country and is confined to a wheel chair. She learned light engineering, set up a workshop and later, a school for disabled children. Oxfam was helping when I first visited her. Difficulties and red tape abound in India and I asked her how she coped with so many setbacks. She replied that on Sundays, a free day, she sat in the garden and read the works of

Gandhi and learned faith and courage from him. Ayako Issayama of the Itto-en community in Japan is another daughter and the fourth is Cao Ngoc Phuong, a Vietnamese and now a nun. To know more read the book she has just written called *Learning True Love* published by the Parallax Press, Berkeley, California. She was a great source of inspiration when she came to Yorkshire Holiday School for Young Friends. I have stayed with her and Thich Nat Hanh, who was leader of the Buddhist Peace delegation in Paris, first at their small Buddhist centre south of Paris, and more recently at Plum village near Bordeaux where two farms and barns have been converted into meditation halls and simple living accommodation. There Vietnamese Buddhist teaching and culture is kept alive for the families of Vietnamese expatriates and others wishing to share in the Buddhist way of life. I call all these women my daughters as they must be thirty or forty years younger than I am. In quality of life or service they are my teachers.

My three weeks in China was with a tour organised by SACU – the Society for Anglo-Chinese understanding. We were prepared by being given a book list and by spending a weekend together with lectures and discussions. The visit was well organised – Beijing, the Great Wall, Xian and the terracotta warriors, going down the Yangtze Gorges, Guilin, schools, many co-operatives, shrines, a mosque, Buddhist temples. I looked for vestigial signs of Ikebana, heaven, man and earth in harmony, that originated in China. In the courtyards of some hotels there were pools with groups of rocks and water plants representing this harmony. The cave temples and rock abris were Buddhist but Chinese in their practical teaching of the Way, unlike the cave temples at Ajanta in India. Here I was just a tourist staying in tourist hotels with very little contact with local people and their homes and families and I realised how lucky I had been in other Asian countries I had visited and how deprived of this I was in China.

The very rich, ornate colouring of painting, carving, furniture in palaces in China was in striking contrast to the simple sliding screens, perhaps painted with a branch of pine, a bird or butterfly, the screens opening onto a Japanese garden, with its misleading simplicity of pine, shrubs, water, rocks in harmony. My visit to China highlighted the differences and similarities between Chinese and Japanese culture, just as the teachings of another faith stimulate one to think and question one's own. I couldn't reach out to Taoism except through the books of John Bloefeld and a few passages I had copied out from the *Tao Te Ching* seventy years ago. Of course books have opened doors into the lives and teachings of all faiths. This is particularly true of a book translated from the French and written by René Grausset called *In the Footsteps of the Buddha*. It is the incredibly moving story of a Chinese monk, who, without the Emperor's permission, escapes and travels along the Silk Road to India and the Buddhist centre at Narlanda to get copies of the Buddhist sutras not available in China.

There is also the story of Matteo Ricci, a Jesuit priest whose story is told in Vincent Cronin's *A Wise Man from the West*. He went to China, became a Chinese scholar, able to interpret the teachings of Jesus and Confucius and Taoism. He became a 'holy man' who converted the Empress to Christianity but not the Emperor. So well respected and valued was he that he was given a state funeral. The Jesuits who were sent out to take his place did not become Chinese scholars and the Emperor refused to have them in China as he felt them to be ignorant trouble makers. I expect they were! *A Pearl to India* is about a Jesuit priest who went to India, studied the Vedas and the Upanishads, and lived as a Brahmin, behaviour unlike, what was felt by Indian holy men, the lax behaviour of other Christian missionaries.

Two other books that have moved me in the last few years are *The Tao of Physics* and *Turning Point* by Frijof Capra. As my eyesight was so bad, a most blessed woman put the whole of *The Tao of Physics* on tape for me and read it as if she understood it all. I felt more at home with Hinduism, Buddhism, Sikhism and other eastern faiths than I did with the physics and quantum theory, but the overlap between mysticism and physics opened windows that look out on to horizons dimly perceived, of that subtle, fragile, intricate web of all life.

Learning True Love by Cao Nguc Phuong, published last year, is a most moving autobiography of a young Vietnamese girl, a student at the Buddhist University of Saigon, who put her Buddhist faith into action during the war in Vietnam. That she could do so much and pass exams, go to Paris to study for her doctorate, return to Vietnam and help set up a department of the University, training village development workers in war-torn areas is outstanding. I don't worship her but the Holy Spirit in her. The courage of people who seek and strive no matter whatever the 'outer cloak' they wear – one worships the Holy Spirit as shown in their lives. I'm thinking of St Theresa of Avilar in her struggle to establish a stricter order of 'discalced' nuns. Her humour, practicality and tenacity in spite of ill health and in face of strangling Catholic officialdom – it is breathtaking.

At Father Bede's ashram in South India, we had 'mass' every morning but in an Indian cultural setting. Prasad, a mixture of dried milk, sugar and flour, was passed around instead of bread; we put a red tikka on our forehead. The hymns were not 'Moody and Sankey' but Indian bajaans giving thanks and praise. In the afternoon when I was there Father Bede gave talks on the Gita. We lived very simply, vegetarian Indian style. The nearby river flooded and destroyed some nearby villages. Members and visitors helped to mitigate the worst of the disaster. This was frowned upon by the nearby 'Christian' communities, who felt no need to help the 'heathen' in their distress! Alas for Christianity. Douglas Steer, an American Quaker, spoke of 'Mutual Irradiation' of his experience in Japan when he arranged a sharing of spiritual experience – not doctrine – with a number of Japanese of other faiths. I feel this is what I have experienced in no small measure.

I appreciate the attitude of Buddha when he said that one should listen to him and then try to put his teaching into practice – not just 'believe' it but find out from one's own experience. When taking the precepts you undertake the rule of training to help you follow them – in everyday life – not to take life, not to take what is not freely given, be honest and refrain from sexual immorality, falsehood and liquors that engender sloth. Right speech, right livelihood, simplicity and frugality are encouraged. All very Quakerly, I feel.

I find it interesting that Taoism, Confucianism and Buddhism can work in harmony in China, while Buddhism and Shinto are accepted as partners in Japan. I find it sad that Christianity looks upon itself as the only way and the rest are heathen. The Christians have also spent a lot of energy fighting amongst themselves –

Protestants and Catholics, the Albigensian heresy, burnings at the stake, Crusaders to 'free' the Holy Places – a dreadful record. Of course Christianity has its saints too, but I suppose all religions have their Holy Ones as well as their fanatics who use religion as a cloak for greed and power. I think that if Christ, Buddha, Laotze, Confucius, Mohammed, Guru Nanak all met, they would find they had more in common than many of their followers and the structures built on their teaching would make them weep.

The religious sculpture, painting, music and dancing, in particular the meditation circle dancing, the sharing of experience of people who are humbly seeking and finding ways of helping their own people in need, and sharing their culture has enriched me beyond measure. Allah is said to be closer to a Muslim than his jugular vein. The Atman within the Hindu, the Buddha nature in the Buddhist, that of God in all as Quakers believe and as Carl Jung wrote to Van Der Post 'I can only say that my work has proved emphatically that the pattern of God rests in everyone .... and has at its disposal the greatest of all energies in the transformation and transfiguration of his natural being'.

Seeking the way, unconsciously, then consciously, has guided my life. I have been helped by dreams. 'God' was so long a problem as I could not accept a Him up in the clouds, but I have seen 'that of God' in so many people of many faiths and I prefer to talk of the Holy Spirit or the Ground of our Being or the pattern of God.

A couple of years ago, before I had trouble with my eyes and was for a time blind, I had been reading a book by Matthew Fox which was a problem. His words were heavily wrapped in Christianity, but when I succeeded in unwrapping them, the ideas went beyond Christianity. I asked about him in the Reference Library, as there was nothing on the dust cover of the book about him. The Library knew nothing about him but kindly got in touch with another Library who might have a book by him. They did. He was a Dominican monk who had been disowned by them ... and one remembers the problems of Teilhard de Chardin's writings.

I was going to cancel my booking for the Yorkshire Easter Settlement owing to my lack of sight, but was asked to do an evening reading. I explained my problem, but I was urged to come and help would be arranged. I did not know the subject of the

Conference. I learned by heart a short quotation by Frijof Capra and explained why I had chosen it. It linked up with my reading of Matthew Fox. When I arrived I found the theme of the Conference was so close to the quotation, I feared someone else would use it. Luckily they didn't. One of the speakers had just returned from a year in America, studying under Matthew Fox, who was lecturing to many people at a Catholic College that was only too pleased to have such an eminent lecturer. His 'creation spirituality' ties up so well with my quotation from Frijof Capra:

> For the earth is a living web, subtle, fragile,
> Mysteriously linked
> Air and water, tree and bird, are shot with the glory of God.

I sense that living web. I hear that Matthew Fox is now applying for membership of the Church of England (interesting that some C of E priests are applying to join the Catholic Church as they prefer the infallibility of the Pope to women priests!).

There is a strange synchronicity sometimes. A few weeks ago, one of my adopted daughters, Cao Ngoc Phuong had sent me her book *Learning True Love* in which she had briefly mentioned me and that I lived in Huddersfield. My daughter Erica read the book to me when she came home for Christmas. A Buddhist in Leeds read the book but there seemed to be no way of getting in contact with me. She asked a friend, not a Buddhist – the only person in Leeds who knows me! She came over to see me and we found we had so much common ground, it was a joy.

I realise that blindness in the spring of 1994, now happily only partial, was beginning to develop other senses in me. On two occasions my fingers found objects in drawers that people with sight had said were not there, so my fingers were better than their eyes for some things.

The series of heart attacks that began in October 1994 remind me that at 88 I need to use my time skilfully ... a little gardening, taking my dog for short walks, beginning to dispose of things I no longer need and finding the right home for them and taking stock of one's own inner life and outer life which is One.

I'm glad I was asked to write of experiences that had nourished my inner life ... it was an excuse to ramble, to remember old friends, my travels in Asia, the books and the guidance of dreams which opened doors at a crucial time. My feet are close to the ground, bringing back the old primitive dances and realising that life is One and we are part of the living web of life on this planet. When I see David Attenborough's nature films, seeing the mother crocodile gently carrying her babies in her mouth to take them to a safer place, the loving and caring is there. Too often we have projected our own fear and venom on to what we call 'wild beasts'. Few creatures, if any, are as unnecessarily cruel as human beings.

A stray cat who adopted me – his torn ear showed he had been a fighter in his day – adopted a wild kitten and cared for him. They both slept in a pussy house in an old arm chair in the garden. When the old cat died three years later, my dog took over the care of the wild cat that would sometimes come into the kitchen and snuggle up to him. I suppose I have always had sheep dogs who instinctively cared for my family when we were out walking, so I am judging 'dogs' from sheep dogs' behaviour.

I end with a quotation that is so applicable today but I found it in a private book I kept when I was fourteen or fifteen; that I cared for it then amazes me. It is from the *Tao Te Ching* written some 2500 years ago:

> The world is sacred: it cannot be improved.
> If you tamper with it you will ruin it.
> If you treat it like an object you will ruin it.
> When man interferes with the Tao
> The sky becomes filthy, the equilibrium crumbles,
> Creatures become extinct.

'The planet is fragile, handle with prayer' is on the Quaker reusable envelope wrapper that I use.

I owe much to Buddhism. It relieved me of rejecting the God in the sky, taught me that much of our distress is due to our own attitudes and how to deal with this; that suffering and discontent were to be accepted as it is the world we live in, but to accept it creatively and learn from its experience – as I certainly have tried to do these last three years and before that! I accept that I must try to follow Buddha's teaching and put it into practice. I must bring these ramblings to a close and leave others to decide how 'spiritual' they are. They are nourishment to my inner life and I'm close to earth. I feel my journey is continuing in strange unexpected ways. There is a Chinese saying to the effect that he who knows is well if he doesn't know he knows. I presume that means that he knows something but he must not close the door, but be open to increasing understanding which is the infinite quest.

I dreamt the Buddha and a few followers came to my large garden in a village. I was busy making tea to welcome them. When they left, my square overgrown boggy garden had been drained, but there was plenty of work left for me to do. I'm pondering on how this can be translated into appropriate action.

I'm grateful to what appeared to be disasters at the time, but in fact were turning points and led to the discarding of an old skin. I'm grateful for my dreams over many years that have guided me and led me into fresh awareness and experience of people, places and spiritual understanding. I've forgotten the writer on the development of religious awareness in children who said that all experience in depth is religious. My dreams mostly helped when I was weighing up different courses of action – when my daughter was born and not expected to live – when my eyes and heart gave cause for concern it was my job to face the situation as best I could – with help already given. No dependence or addiction to dreams permitted.

I'm grateful to the many books, the opportunities to meet people of an inner quality – that of the Holy Spirit – of so many faiths and cultures that I have shared on my travels. If we meet again in an afterlife – I think there is enough evidence that some people reincarnate – possibly highly developed souls who remember previous lives ... but this is not within my experience and so is an open question ... but if there is I'm sure five dogs that we've had a very close relationship with, will come running to be enfolded in my arms ... and perhaps my husband – an atheist – but a man caring for the poor and dispossessed – will come toddling along later. He never discovered that there was 'that of God' within him. I don't suppose much of these pages could be classed as spiritual, just a journey into greater awareness.